Cook To Your Heart's Content

Cook To Your Heart's Content On A Low-Fat, Low-Salt Diet

Revised Edition

W. Jann Brown, M.D.
Daniel Liebowitz, M.D.
Marlene Olness, R.D.

VNR VAN NOSTRAND REINHOLD COMPANY
New York Cincinnati Toronto London Melbourne

Copyright (c) 1976 by Litton Educational Publishing, Inc.
Library of Congress Catalog Card Number 75-45090
ISBN 0-442-24812-1

Published in 1976 by Van Nostrand Reinhold Company
A division of Litton Educational Publishing, Inc.
450 West 33rd Street, New York, NY 10001

Van Nostrand Reinhold Limited
1410 Birchmount Road, Scarborough, Ontario M1P 2E7, Canada

Van Nostrand Reinhold Australia Pty. Limited
17 Queen Street, Mitcham, Victoria 3132, Australia

Van Nostrand Reinhold Company Limited
Molly Millars Lane, Wokingham, Berkshire, England

16 15 14 13 12 11 10 9 8 7 6 5 4 3 2 1

Library of Congress Cataloging in Publication Data

Brown, William Jann, 1919–
    Cook to your heart's content on a low-fat, low-salt
diet.

    Previous ed. by D. Liebowitz, W. J. Brown, and
M. Olness.
    Bibliography: p.
    Includes index.
    1. Low-fat diet. 2. Salt-free diet. I. Liebo-
witz, Daniel, 1921–   joint author. II. Olness,
Marlene, joint author. III. Liebowitz, Daniel,
1921–   Cook to your Heart's content on a low-fat.
low-salt diet. IV. Title.
RM237.7.L53 1976   641.5'63   75-45090

ISBN 0-442-24812-1

FOREWORD

A high concentration of cholesterol and "triglycerides" in the blood plasma can be enhanced by the intake of large amounts of saturated fats and sugar respectively. Since there seems to be a relationship of blood lipids to the development of narrowing of the channels in arteries (atherosclerosis), and, since the narrowing of these channels by fatty deposits contributes to the development of heart disease and strokes, any attempt to lower the fat content in foods in the American diet is a potential contribution to the control of these diseases.

This book offers practical and easy-to-prepare recipes which are low in saturated fats. It also provides low sodium modifications of these recipes for patients whose salt intake, as well as fat intake, has been restricted by their physician. The diets are either low in saturated fats or they are low in both fat and sodium, depending upon whether or not the patient is being treated for atherosclerosis or high blood pressure or some other medical condition that requires restriction of fat alone or both fat and salt.

The book is designed to enable a patient's physician or dietitian a choice of diets of three different caloric values. These sample diets are offered for a full two-week period.

These two-week menu guides, therefore, offer great versatility and can be varied even more by substituting recipes from other sections of the book. Thus, the patient with heart disease or high blood pressure can look forward to a varied, tasty menu.

Many commercial food manufacturers have now recognized the need for providing adequate substitutes for saturated fats, sodium, and sugar in the American diet. Almost every grocery store now has a section where such items may be purchased. The authors list many of these in the appendix. Wine is used liberally as a flavoring for low-fat recipes as well as the low-sodium modifications. It is especially an aid to palatability when salt cannot be used.

The number of calories and sodium in a serving is listed for each recipe. This makes it simple to substitute one foodstuff for another.

As the world grows smaller and new methods of refrigeration and rapid transportation continue to expand, foods and seasonings now considered exotic or costly will appear more frequently in the daily menus of the average family.

The authors have made good use of certain fruits and vegetables as well as spices to enhance the flavor and quality of their international recipes. The two physicians and the dietitian have compiled an outstanding culinary guide for patients with diets of low-fat and low-sodium content.

John J. Sampson, M.D.
Clinical Professor of Medicine
The University of California
San Francisco Medical Center
Past President American Heart Association

PREFACE

Many of these recipes have been adapted from those found in the files of various chefs, friends, kibitzers, famous restaurants—and not-so-famous ones—from all over the world. They were chosen because they were adaptable to the calorie, fat, and sodium (salt) requirements of our low-fat and low-fat-low-sodium diets, as well as for their excellence.

We are indebted to many people and authors of other books on cooking and diets for the stimulating experience of becoming acquainted with their own methods of providing good fare for people who watch their fat and salt intake. It would be impossible to give a complete list of all the sources from which these recipes have been derived, but appropriate supplemental reading material is listed in the bibliography.

Our thanks and appreciation is extended to Mrs. F. B. Hart for her invaluable help during the early phases of the book. We also extend our thanks to Mrs. Doris Senger and the San Mateo Heart Association for providing dietetic counseling for some of the recipes.

W. J. B.
D. L.
M. O.

Contents

Food For Thought

You may well ask, why publish another diet cookbook when so many are already on the market? The answer lies in these pages. In the past few years research has pointed to the role of diet in the aggravation of heart disease and strokes. The appalling rate of deaths in this country from vascular disease has led doctors, dietitians, research workers, alarmed citizens and even the Federal Government to not only ask why, but to do something about it. The authors of this book intend to do something about it by giving you a practical common sense way of preparing foods so as to minimize the effects of bad eating habits on your body, and thus help diminish your chance of having a stroke or heart attack. But these chapters on healthful tasty food preparation are only designed to be read and their diet guides and recipes used under the guidance of your physician and dietitian.

We have learned through years of research that diet is not enough. The Bible pictures the patriarchs as lean, sinewy, vigorous men, eating the simple foods of the desert while leading their people to win a new land. Although pictured as old, with long flowing white beards, these men, according to the scriptures, were physically fit and morally strong. Active and energetic men despite their venerable years, they were, we are told, able to march 40 to 50 miles in a day.

For those of us who take all this "with a grain of salt", just picture the businessman of today, caught up in the whirlwind of a highly competitive society. He sits behind his desk during working hours, or in his car, or on a bus or train during rush hours. When he arrives home, the first thing he does after perfunctorily kissing his wife and patting the children on the head, is to relax with a couple of martinis, for he has "had it". After a few sips of this potent beverage, he lights his twentieth or thirtieth cigarette of the day, and having by now digested the cheeseburger and milk shake which he gulped down in twenty minutes or less at the lunch counter, he is hungry again and ready for dinner. His wife knows that he likes "man food"; the steak and potato topper with sour cream followed by rich pie and ice cream for dessert. It is now time for television and another dozen cigarettes before bed. The process of feeding begins all over again a bare eight hours later when he sits down to his usual breakfast of bacon, eggs, toast, jam, and a couple of glasses of "wholesome" enriched whole milk.

Our affluent middle-class modern man has consumed between 2,500 and 3,000 calories in 24 hours, 50 percent or more of which may be fat of animal origin. He has smoked one or two packs of cigarettes in the same 24 hour period and is now re-charged and ready to throw himself back into the fracas of our technological society. He has walked a total of 15 minutes in the 24 hours; this has been his only physical exercise. On Sunday he moans at the thought of having to go out and mow the lawn. After completing this strenuous and unaccustomed chore, his whole body aches from the effort. He wipes the sweat from his brow and proceeds to plop himself into a comfortable arm chair and turns on the ball game—of course, he relaxes with a bag of potato chips and a couple of beers.

Is it any wonder that after living this way for 30 or 40 years our modern man is one of the ever-increasing multitude doomed to die of a *heart attack* or a *stroke* before the Biblical age of three score and ten?

What is a heart attack? A heart attack, or coronary thrombosis, occurs when blood flow through a blood vessel, called a coronary artery, is suddenly cut off from a portion of the heart. This can occur in several ways but the most common one is when a blood clot blocks the blood vessel's opening, thus preventing the flow of life-giving blood through the artery to the heart muscle itself. The blood clot is frequently formed on the inside wall of the blood vessel because the blood vessel wall has become narrowed by an accumulation of fatty deposits just like rust inside a pipe. This process is called hardening of the arteries or atherosclerosis. It can occur in other blood vessels in the body, but here we are only concerned with the heart and the coronary arteries which carry blood to the heart.

In the past few years, scientific investigators in the field of hardening of the arteries have been shocked to find that the United States is leading the world in deaths from heart disease. Statistics can be misleading, however, and more studies were undertaken to find out "why us?" The investigators then began collecting statistics from other countries concerning things that might have some bearing on this problem. They collected data on the amount and types of fat produced and consumed; statistics on the quantity of cattle, pork, and poultry sold, on the tonnage of fish caught and eaten, on the number bicycles purchased each year, on the number of automobiles per capita in different countries, on the accessibility of public transportation to schools, shopping centers, and dwellings. These different statistics may seem meaningless to you, but from the hodgepodge of accumulated facts certain patterns emerged. The more cattle and pigs, butter, milk, cream and eggs, the more automobiles and super-highways, and the fewer fish, bicycles and footpaths in the country, the more deaths occurred from strokes and heart disease . . . WHY?

THE ROLE OF FAT IN THE DIET

During the past half century, as the hardy pioneer has been replaced by the tense office worker and our nation has prospered in wealth, we have encountered a paradox in our daily living. Creature comforts such as the automobile have increased and fewer people get the exercise they need. In addition, expensive fat-laden foods such as steaks can be bought by the majority of our affluent compatriots. As a result of this, thousands are gorging themselves on these high-fat foods and feeding them to their children. The amount of fat in our diet has steadily increased over the last 50 years to provide 40 to 50 percent of the daily caloric intake. What is worse, the majority of this is derived from eggs, butter, milk, cream, meat, and solid shortenings. Such fats are called saturated fats (that is, their chemical structure is saturated with hydrogen). These fats are usually of a solid consistency at room temperature.

Many physicians are now of the opinion that by lowering the total fat intake to a level of 25 to 35 percent of the daily caloric intake, and, in addition, substituting *unsaturated* fats for much of the *saturated* fat, the narrowing of our arteries by fatty deposits can be retarded.

Unsaturated fats (also called polyunsaturated) are mostly derived from vegetables, vegetable oils such as corn oil and safflower oil, fish, certain nuts, and from other sources. These fats have much less hydrogen and are liquified at room temperature. They are frequently in the form of oils, but some new margarines also contain them.

These more healthful *unsaturated* oils and margarines should be used instead of so much butter or solid shortenings such as coconut oil, meat drippings, and chicken fat which are high in saturated fats. A note of caution, here. Certain sweet and sour cream substitutes and some whipped cream and ice cream "diet specials" contain undesirable saturated fats such as coconut oil and may be no better or worse than regular cream. The same thing applies to a number of margarines and cooking fats on the market although some manufacturers have changed their product's composition in order to provide more unsaturated fat content. *Read the label* and, if in

doubt, check with your physician, dietitian, or local Heart Association. Some new products (unsaturated fat substitutes) are listed in the appendix.

A Word About Cholesterol

The word "cholesterol" has been bandied about for the past two decades, ever since doctors became aware of the possible relation between diet and heart disease. Saturated fats and cholesterol, a fatty substance, are often found together in certain meats, sea foods and dairy products. About half of our cholesterol is manufactured by the body. The other half comes from food. It has been recommended that ingested cholesterol be limited to about 300 mgs daily in individuals with elevated blood cholesterol. This can be accomplished by eating fewer cholesterol-containing foods.

Certain organ meats such as "brains" are high in cholesterol. Liver, especially calves liver, contains cholesterol but the total amount of fat is low so that some may be eaten on a fat restricted diet. Fortunately, it is not present in significant amounts in foods like nuts, fruit, vegetables, fish, and cereals. Shellfish should not be eaten in amounts greater than indicated in the recipes, as they, too, contain some cholesterol. Cholesterol can be measured by a simple blood test. It is, however, only one of a number of fatty substances which can, if eaten in excess, contribute to premature hardening of the arteries.

"Triglycerides" are another type of fat or lipid in the bloodstream which can now be measured by a simple blood test. Triglycerides are sometimes elevated when the cholesterol is not, and their concentration in the blood plasma can be increased by eating large amounts of starch, sugar, and other sweets. A high triglyceride level and low cholesterol level is relatively uncommon, as triglycerides usually rise with the blood cholesterol. There is recent evidence that triglycerides as well as cholesterol participate in depositing fatty substances on the inside of arteries.

Those with mainly high blood triglycerides may need to restrict sugar and sugar-containing foods, such as certain raw and canned fruits. Excessive intake of starchy food should be limited and in such cases your physician may wish to prescribe a special diet including sugar substitutes. If, on the other hand, you have elevated blood cholesterol, your doctor may have you substitute foods high in unsaturated fat for those high in saturated fats and cholesterol. Finally, many persons with elevated cholesterol and/or triglycerides are overweight. Reducing excessive weight should go hand in hand with alterations of these constituents in the diet.

It is not within the scope of this book to discuss

diet for children or teenagers. Their dietary requirements differ to a degree from those of the sedentary middle-aged adult. Nevertheless, a word of caution could be written concerning the high fat and sugar intake among our youngsters.

THE ROLE OF SALT IN THE DIET

If you have been told that you have high blood pressure (hypertension) or certain types of heart disease or kidney disease where sodium (salt)* retention is a problem your doctor may wish you to follow a diet that is low in sodium as well as fat.

High blood pressure or hypertension is due to a variety of causes but a narrowing or spasm of the blood vessels providing blood to the kidneys is one cause. Experiments on animals and man have repeatedly demonstrated that those animals or humans whose diet is limited in salt respond by lowering their blood pressure. Too high a blood pressure can cause a rupture of blood vessels in the brain causing a cerebral hemorrhage or stroke. The investigators also found that in persons with a sustained high blood pressure the process of hardening of the arteries or atherosclerosis is accelerated. The inside lining of the arteries becomes coated with fat, becomes rigid and narrowed. The flow of blood is retarded, clots form and can go either to the heart causing a coronary thrombosis or to the brain causing another type of stroke called a cerebral thrombosis.

Therefore, you can see that someone with high blood pressure needs to restrict not only the sodium in his diet but also the fat. Sodium is found in everything, but is most concentrated in certain foods which are excluded from or limited in these recipes, such as celery, spinach, bacon, ham and most lunch meats, potato chips, commercial pickles, baking soda, ordinary canned soups, and many other canned foods.

Therefore, if your doctor has discovered that you have high blood pressure, it is important for you to limit not only the amount and type of fat in the diet, but also the amount of sodium. Fortunately, Americans are ingenious people. Many food-processing companies have marketed prepared foods not only low in fat but with a low-sodium content. The brand names of many of these will be found in the appendix. Be sure you read the label on new products and be sure you know how many *milligrams* of

---

* Although the terms "Low Salt" and "Low Sodium" are often used interchangeably, the term "Low Sodium" will be used in this book since the culprit is the chemical "sodium" found in salt.

sodium you are allowed each day. Don't forget to read the fine print on the label. If in doubt, don't buy the product. We mentioned *milligrams* of sodium. The term milligram (mg.) is a unit of weight equivalent to one thousandth of a gram and is a convenient way of measuring sodium. Remember, *sodium chloride* is *salt* and anything with salt in it means that it contains sodium.

As new products appear on your grocer's shelves, we urge you to examine them carefully and "Read the Labels" or check with your doctor or dietitian before trying any of them. One such product contains 550 mgs of sodium and 733 mgs of potassium per ½ teaspoon. If you are on a sodium restricted diet this product, if used too liberally, may provide more sodium than you are allowed in your daily menu and you may be better off with salt substitutes which contain virtually no sodium but consist of potassium chloride or other potassium salts. (See appendix.)

Monosodium glutamate is used in moderate amounts in some of our recipes. It contains quite a bit of sodium. A few people cannot tolerate monosodium glutamate and should omit it.

In some parts of the country, the water is naturally high in sodium, so that another source of sodium can be ingested without realizing it from the water you drink. Another hidden source of sodium comes from water softeners. Beware, and use only bottled water of known sodium content if you must rely on a water softener for other uses because of hard water in your area.

In addition, sodium may be present in some frozen foods, particularly in frozen fish fillets, which are frequently washed in brine before freezing. Meats have a moderate sodium content for the most part, but processed meats such as corned beef, which is corned with salt, are high in sodium. Even luncheon meats fall in this category. Many of the foods high in sodium, such as the dairy products, are also high in saturated fats. Remember too, that egg whites contain a fair amount of sodium, just as egg yolks contain a fair amount of saturated fat.

Cheer up! This does not mean that you can't eat eggs; one egg used in a cake that serves ten, is not going to provide you with much sodium or fat. Thus, amounts are important. Get to thinking in terms of how much an average portion contains. Moreover, egg substitutes have begun to appear on the market. Some of these are relatively low in saturated and high in unsaturated fats. They may be used as egg substitutes in cooking. If you are on a sodium restricted diet, check their sodium content before using.

Sodium restriction is not good for everyone with

heart disease. In certain cases it may even be harmful. So let your doctor decide what kind of a diet is best for you.

GENERAL DIETARY CONSIDERATIONS

If you have digestive problems such as ulcer, milk or wheat intolerance or colitis, consult your doctor for modifications of these recipes and possible vitamin supplements. The same applies if you have diabetes or kidney disease. A high fiber diet (bran, cereal grains, raw fruits and vegetables) has recently been recommended by some physicians. It is believed that cholesterol synthesis in the intestine is diminished by the increased bulk in this diet. Such a diet may be harmful in certain disorders of the stomach and bowel. Your physician needs to see you at regular intervals to evaluate your dietary needs.

EXERCISE

Remember the statistics! When there were more bicycles and footpaths and fewer cars and superhighways, people were forced to walk or ride bicycles to their destinations. Perhaps they wished they could be like us and drive shiny new cars on endless concrete ribbons, but the very act of walking or bicycling gave them their daily exercise. This helped dissipate extra calories, burn fat and take tension-producing thoughts away from the mind. Thus, daily moderate exercise, even in the form of walking two to three miles a day, or bicycling for an hour or two, is another essential ingredient in keeping the body in a biologically healthy state.

TENSION

Nervous tension such as we encounter in our complicated, high paced, contemporary life also aggravates the development of heart attacks and high blood pressure. Regular moderate exercise, as mentioned, is great for helping dissipate our worries. A philosophical yet optimistic attitude towards life's problems is also most important in controlling the effects of everyday anxieties on the nervous system. Mind-relaxing techniques such as Transcendental Meditation "T. M.", non-goal oriented hobbies, and, in some instances, psychotherapy for the tense driving personality are very helpful. Such an approach to life coupled with regular exercise and a prudent diet may help decrease both the accumulation of fat in blood vessels and the tendency to high blood pressure.

MEDICATION

Your doctor may have prescribed certain medicines for lowering your blood cholesterol or triglycerides or both. Neglecting your diet may decrease the beneficial effects of such medication. High blood pressure pills, such as diuretics, work by helping your body get rid of sodium. Sometimes they may cause your body to also lose potassium. If this should happen, your physician will either prescribe a potassium supplement or ask you to eat foods which are naturally high in potassium. (See "Foods High in Potassium" in the appendix.)

FAMILY HISTORY AND DIET

There are a number of recent studies to point the finger to a hereditary cause of both heart attacks and high blood pressure. Many people with a family predisposition to heart disease and high blood pressure can help aggravate these conditions by eating high animal fat and salt diets and by taking on weight.

IS SMOKING HARMFUL?

Smoking cigarettes is not only a harbinger of lung cancer, but the carbon monoxide from the cigarette fumes gets into the blood stream, replacing some of the oxygen. Without oxygen, body tissues die. Heavy smokers, that is those who smoke over one package daily, have a higher incidence of heart attacks!

OUR CURRENT THINKING IS:

High saturated fats and
   cholesterol diet
Cigarette smoking
Tension
Little exercise
Family tendency to high
   blood pressure
High sodium intake

} Hardening of the arteries   High blood pressure } Heart Attack   Stroke

Recommendations and Hints on Food Selection and Preparation

HOW TO SELECT FOODS

Your physician will decide which one of the diets in this book is best for you. He and your dietitian both know that the guide to good nutrition lies in a balance between different types of foods. Thus, you will need a minimum daily requirement, even on a reducing diet of a thousand calories, of vital minerals, vitamins, proteins, carbohydrate (starch) and fat. While reducing the fat in your diet, we do not eliminate all fat but we reduce it to a healthful level and substitute as much unsaturated fat for saturated fat as possible.

For those whose caloric allowance is generous, such as in the 2,000 calorie diet, we have listed the amounts of each type of food to be consumed each day. These amounts are of course modified in diets with fewer calories but the concept of a balance between different types of foods remains.

For example, such a daily balanced intake includes:

1. 2 or more cups of skim milk or equivalent, unsalted for those with sodium restriction.

2. 5 to 8 ounces of cooked lean meats, poultry or fish. Use more fish and poultry than red meats. Dry beans and nuts, (unsalted for those on a low-sodium diet), may be used instead of meats. The quality of protein in nuts, such as walnuts, filberts, cashews, hickory nuts and peanuts is considered by some to be as good as that in meats. They are also high in unsaturated oils. ½ cup of beans or nuts equals 5 oz. of meat.

3. 4 or more servings of fruits and vegetables (a serving is ½ cup). Yellow vegetables like carrots are a good source of Vitamin A. Citrus fruits are a good source of Vitamin C.

4. 4 or more servings of breads or cereals. A serving is equivalent to 1 slice of bread (low-sodium for those whose sodium is restricted) or ½ cup of cooked cereal or ½ cup cooked noodles, spaghetti, macaroni, or rice.

5. 1½ to 2 ounces of fat, mainly unsaturated in the form of vegetable oils or margarine made with vegetable oils. One tablespoon of vegetable oil contains about ½ of an ounce of fat mostly unsaturated. One tablespoon of margarine contains about ⅜ of an ounce of fat mostly unsaturated. (use low-sodium varieties for those on a low-sodium diet).

6. Among the minerals, calcium is important. This is why we urge the consumption or use in cooking of the equivalent of two cups of skim milk or buttermilk a day, or the equivalent in low-fat cottage cheese (low sodium varieties for those on a low-sodium diet). Other sources of calcium which may be used instead of milk, if consumed in large enough amounts and if permitted in your diet, are spinach, kale, fennel, swiss chard, and artichokes. Home made soups, if cooked with meat bones for a long time, provide calcium. Be sure to remove the fat first by cooling the soup and skimming off the hardened fat. (Check the sodium content of some of these high calcium vegetables if your diet is sodium restricted.)

1 cup skim milk = approx. 298 mg. calcium
1 cup kale raw = approx. 400 mg. calcium
   (with stems)
1 cup fennel raw = approx. 230 mg. calcium
1 cup cooked edible
   portion artichoke = approx. 120 mg. calcium
1 cup cooked
     spinach = approx. 166 mg. calcium
1 cup cooked swiss
     chard = approx. 120 mg. calcium

7. Your doctor will advise you on what other minerals and vitamins you need.

The portions in some of our recipes vary a bit from the average to conform to caloric and sodium allowances in the diets.

HOW FREE CAN I BE WITH DAIRY FOODS?

For patients on a low-fat diet, two glasses of skim milk or buttermilk may be used each day, as already mentioned. If more milk is wanted for cooking or drinking, be sure it is the skim or low-fat variety. As many as two whole eggs may be eaten each week. If not on a low sodium diet, you may wish to try your hand at an omelet of 4 egg whites (high in sodium) and half an egg yolk with a dollop of unsaturated fat cream substitute, a dash of cayenne pepper and a whiff of oregano. Ummmmmm! Use unsaturated margarine instead of butter and use tasty cream substitutes listed in the Appendix. Use very little cheese other than low-fat cottage cheese, as most others contain too much saturated fat. Some recipes use a little, but only for flavoring.

If you are on the low-sodium modification, use low-sodium skim milk and other low-sodium dairy substitutes as listed in the Appendix.

BREAD AND CEREALS

Enriched or whole-grain breads and cereals contain valuable sources of the B vitamins. Try to eat some at each meal to help establish good eating habits. Use the low-sodium-varieties listed in the Appendix if on the low-sodium modification.

VEGETABLES AND FRUIT

Fresh fruits, particularly citrus, provide the vitamin C necessary for your diet. If using canned fruits, use those which are artificially sweetened or unsweetened and thus lower in calories. Green and yellow vegetables are good sources of vitamins and minerals. Eat at least two servings of these daily.

Fruits and vegetables are generally low in sodium and contain little or no fat.

Unless fortified with vitamin C after cooking, fruits and vegetables will be deficient in this vitamin, which is destroyed by heat.

HOW MUCH BEEF, LAMB, POULTRY, EACH DAY?

Certain meats such as beef, lamb, and pork contain much microscopic or invisible fat between their muscle fibers. When this fat is visible it appears as white or yellow marbling throughout the meat. In general, it can be stated that the cheaper grades of meat contain less fat than the more expensive grades. Broiling removes some of the fat, as it melts and drops away in the process.

Since red meats contain both fat and sodium, the amounts you can eat are limited in both the low-fat and low-sodium diets. Chicken, turkey, and fish are preferable as they are lower in fat. Among the fish, fresh water fish have less sodium (trout, pike) and are best for those whose sodium is restricted.

The white meat of chicken and turkey contains less sodium and slightly less fat than the dark. Cornish game hen is similar to chicken but duck and goose are too high in fat to be included. Pheasant—if you can get it has relatively little fat. The same applies to venison. But we can't assume that all our readers are avid sportsmen.

Portions of protein containing foods with equivalent amounts of fat:

1/3 ounce sirloin steak, beef or lamb roast
equals,

2/3 ounce veal chop or roast
equals

2 ounces lean chicken or turkey
equals

5 ounces haddock, sole, cod, etc.

You can see that if your diet is to be low in total and saturated fats, you should consume servings of low-fat varieties of fish four to five times a week, poultry four or five times a week, the leaner cuts of beef, veal or lamb not more than three or four times weekly.

Here are a few pointers to use in defatting all meats which will greatly reduce their total fat content:

1. All visible fat must be completely trimmed. The skin of poultry should be removed before cooking.

2. Try to use a low temperature of about 350° when roasting meats. The lower the temperature, the more chance of melting off fat. The higher the temperature, the more chance of a searing effect which seals some fat into the meat.

3. Purchase one of those grills equipped with little metal legs. Such a grill, which stands an inch or so above the counter surface, should be placed in the bottom of your roasting pan like a regular roasting rack. Place your roast on the grill. The meat is now an inch or so above pan bottom. This permits the unwanted animal fat drippings to escape to the bottom of the pan. They should then be discarded. If any basting should be done, use vegetable oil, margarine, wine, or vegetable puree.

4. Try to develop the habit of removing all visible fat at the table. This will be of special value to you when eating out where steps to lower the fat content before cooking may not have been taken.

LIVER

Chicken, beef and veal livers are low in fat, relatively speaking, but what fat they do contain is mostly cholesterol. The recipe using chicken livers found in this book is still relatively low in total fat. If not eaten frequently and on a day when other dishes low in animal fats are used, this dish will be within the provisions of your diet.

A WORD ABOUT PORK PRODUCTS AND LUNCH MEATS

Most portions of the pig are high in animal fat and are not generally suitable for inclusion in this book. However, we have included a few recipes calling for small amounts of *lean* pork containing no more saturated fat then found in lean beef.

A small piece of Italian sausage is used for flavoring in one of the recipes. The amount is so small it does not appreciably add to the fat content per serving but it is high in sodium and, therefore, is not used in the low-sodium modification.

Avoid lunch meats—delicatessen cold cuts—such as liverwurst, salami, bologna, head cheese, copa, prosciutto, or sausages of various types, as they are high in animal fat.

If you shop in a delicatessen, choose lean roast beef, smoked turkey, or lean corned beef (not the cheap type made from brisket of beef which is a fatty cut).

In general, the delicatessen foods are also out for those on a sodium-restricted diet since these meats are loaded with salt as well as fat.

REMEMBER

On the days that you eat meat with a higher saturated fat content, particular attention should be paid to the rest of the food eaten that day to make sure that you do not ingest more than your daily fat allowance.

SUGAR AND SWEETS

Keep in mind that sweets only add calories. Many physicians feel that when taken in excessive amounts, they may contribute to the process of hardening of the arteries by increasing the *serum triglycerides*.

You may still satisfy your sweet tooth by using artificial sweeteners. Saccharin is the oldest of these products, but unfortunately produces an unpleasant bitter after-taste for some people when used in cooking.* Artificial sweeteners should be used according to the directions that come with them. The amount of sugar substitute equivalent to a teaspoon of sugar

---

* Certain people may be allergic to saccharin. If in doubt, consult your physician, especially if on other medications.

is listed on most commercially available bottles or packets of sugar substitutes. For those on a low-sodium diet, avoid sugar substitutes made with sodium. Many of the commercially available products are listed in the Appendix.

Occasionally sugar is needed for correct texture or as a syrup producer in recipes. This effect cannot be produced with artificial sweeteners; however, a mixture of the two can be used sometimes and keeps the calories down. Many people believe that honey is better than sugar. Although it contains small amounts of minerals and vitamins absent in refined sugar, its sugar content is virtually the same. Substituting honey for sugar will not help cut calories if used in equivalent amounts.

Why not get reacquainted with the real taste of fresh fruit, keeping in mind that large amounts of fruit sugar may be detrimental in patients with high blood triglycerides? The tart, yet sweet taste of fresh grapefruit and strawberries is a real luxury denied many before the advent of refrigerated transport. Taste things again!

HOW TO CUT DOWN ON THE AMOUNT OF OIL WHEN SAUTÉING (Frying).

Even though you are using an unsaturated oil or margarine to grease a frying pan, muffin tin, loaf pan, cookie sheet, or pie pan, you will still want to grease the pan *lightly* as the fat in the oil or margarine is absorbed into the food you are preparing and you have to keep the total amount of fat in your diet low. Why not use a Teflon (R) coated pan? This material is a nonstick, flurocarbon, and can be obtained as a coating on frying pans and other baking pans. Some of the better quality pans have a heavier coating of Teflon (R) and generally last longer and cook more evenly. Although these Teflon (R) coated pans do not require greasing at all, some people still prefer to rub them very lightly with an unsaturated margarine or oil. Directions for cleaning usually come with these pans. Follow them. Never put a Teflon (R) coated pan directly on high heat. When frying, use medium heat. When baking, use 450° F. as your maximum oven temperature.

MARINATING

Marinating enhances the flavor of many meats and vegetables. If you are not careful, you can waste a great deal of oil and vinegar by attempting to cover the food with the marinade. This is not necessary. It is only necessary to coat the food with the marinade and turn it in the bowl from time to time.

Another way is to use a plastic bag. Place the food to be marinated and the marinade in a plastic bag large enough to completely enclose the food. Squeeze out all but the amount of marinade coating the food by compressing the bag evenly until the excess marinade has been forced out. Tie the top of the bag and place in a bowl in the refrigerator.

TIPS ON EATING OUT FOR THE FAT-CONTROLLED DIET

GENERAL: Order ala-carte. Avoid combination dishes and foods made beforehand. Give specific instructions regarding method of preparation. Do not eat pastries, fatty meats, fried foods, casseroles and creamed foods, whole-milk products, butter, cheese, gravy, cream soups, potato chips, cheeseburgers, or cheese cake. You will, of course, be able to have fruits, gelatin, and vegetables. Use only salad dressing made with lemon, vinegar, and oil. Example: Avoid Roquefort or blue-cheese dressing. Use oil and vinegar with a touch of garlic or lemon instead.

APPETIZERS: Clear soups, tomato juice, fruit cup, seafood cocktail, raw vegetables such as carrots, radishes, celery, and cucumbers.

MAIN DISH: Baked or broiled fish, lean meat, poultry without skin, fish or seafood salad (with dressing served separately), low-fat cottage cheese, eggs (when allowed).

VEGETABLES: All vegetables prepared *without* butter, or cream sauce. Lemon juice, bouillon (high in sodium except low sodium variety) or herbs add taste to vegetables.

STARCHES: Baked or boiled without dressing, plain rice, macaroni, spaghetti with tomato sauce fortified with beef extract.

BREADS: Hard rolls, ryecrisp, plain tortillas, English muffins, bread (especially whole wheat or rye).

DESSERTS: Fruit, sherbet, gelatin, unfrosted angel food cake. Combinations add greatly.

BEVERAGES: Coffee or tea *without* cream (use dairy substitute), low-calorie carbonated beverages, fruit juices, non-fat milk.

BREAKFAST CEREAL: All cereals, served with skim milk.

TIPS ON EATING OUT FOR THE LOW-SODIUM, FAT-CONTROLLED DIET

Select a restaurant where foods are prepared to order. Explain carefully that salt should be omitted in their preparation. This also includes cooked vegetables. Carry your own salt substitute and ask for lemon wedges to flavor your food. Check with restaurants ahead of time as some do carry low-sodium products. If you get into the habit of eating in the same restaurant time and time again, get to know the Chef and let him know you and some of the recipes in this book. He will usually be only too glad to prepare your favorite dish if he knows that you are coming. Avoid regular breads and milk unless you are on the 1000 milligram sodium diet. If in doubt, take a box of matzohs or low-sodium bread with you. Don't be ashamed or embarrassed. Your body is at stake! More and more people are doing it today!

Don't be afraid to take your own dinner to your neighbor's house when invited out. Better yet, eat it beforehand as it may be too much to ask his wife to prepare your diet for you. As Confucious might say "Don't strain a friendship if it isn't really a close one".

AFTER THOUGHTS

Black coffee or tea contain virtually no calories or sodium and, if permitted by your physician, may be imbibed within reason. Ask him if you should have regular or de-caffeinated coffee.

Alcohol contains calories (see "Alcoholic Beverage" chart). It is therefore used in limited amounts in cooking. It goes without saying that your physician will advise you as to how much, if any, of the pure stuff you may have.

Regular sweets like candy have been omitted from the menu guides and recipes as they contain too much animal (saturated) fat, sugar, and in some cases salt for those who are sodium restricted. The amount of sugar in our recipes is strictly limited but you can satisfy your sweet tooth by eating the low calorie sweets listed in the appendix.

There is great psychological value in presenting foods on a restricted diet as attractively as possible. Tasteful arrangement and preparation of food prevents the feeling of being cheated of one of life's great pleasures—eating.

Long famed as gastronomic leaders of the western world, the French have finally produced a chef, Michel Guerard, who, inspired by Chinese and Japanese cuisine, prepares dishes low in saturated fat while retaining the zest and flavor of "haute cuisine". Low fat sauces are made with vegetables pureed by using a blender or low fat cheeses such as ricotta, farmer's, yogurt and low fat cream cheese.

Herbs placed in the bottom of tightly covered dutch ovens permeate the meat, vegetables, poultry or fish to give them an exquisite flavor.

NOTE: This cookbook is not for Diabetics. However, some of the recipes can be adapted for use by diabetics under a physician's direction.

Seasonings
An encyclopedia of spices

Spice up your life on a low-salt or low-fat, low-salt diet by reading this short encyclopedia of spices used in food preparation. You will not only learn how spices enhance food flavor but also something about the history of spices.

Spices are especially helpful when the diet has had salt removed from it. The idea of eating bland, tasteless food, is enough to discourage anyone, but a few simple taste tricks with spices will set you straight.

Your new sodium or/and fat restricted diet will not only be a health treat but a taste treat as well!

SEASONING FOR LOW-FAT AND LOW-SODIUM, LOW-FAT DIETS

Now's the time to be adventurous and try some of the herbs, spices, and seasonings which you may not have used before. Go lightly—a little goes a long way. Enhance the good flavor, don't overwhelm it! Here are suggestions for a start.

ALLSPICE: A seed derived from the myrtle tree, which is sold both whole and ground. The spice may be added to lean ground meat, scattered over the surface of roast veal or lamb, put into tomato sauces, and used in beef meat stews, especially those cooked with Burgundy. It is good with fruit, such as whole spiced peaches or pears, to be used as a garnish for roast turkey or chicken. Try some whole mushrooms, simmered for about a minute in water and lemon juice, then covered with hot vinegar, a little oil, lemon juice, and whole allspice.

ANISE: These seeds are taken from an annual plant and are commonly used to flavor candy and liqueurs (Anisette). A less common use, but a really great one, is in certain types of Scandinavian breads, cakes, and cookies. Anise is also excellent in the court bouillon used for cooking sea food, (See recipe section) and a tiny bit may be used in bouillabaisse (a fine Mediterranian fish stew).

ALMOND EXTRACT: Adds interest to nose and tongue. Wonderful in puddings, fruits, and cake.

BASIL: The green leaves of this beautiful low-growing plant have a wonderful odor and impart much of the flavor interest to Italian food when added to tomato sauce and canned Italian-style tomatoes. An excellent and unusual vinegar for your salads may be easily made by adding 1½ tablespoons of dried basil to a pint of boiling wine vinegar. Let stand for two days and strain before using.

BAY LEAF: This leaf may be found in a number of geographic locales and each has some slight difference in smell and taste. The variety from California, when fresh from the tree, is sharply pungent when crushed and inhaled and causes the nose to actually pain. All the bays need to be used sparingly and one leaf is enough in a good stew, in a marinade for mushrooms, or cooked with beets, or added to cold cooked vegetables marinated with lemon juice.

CARAWAY SEEDS: These elongated dark brown seeds are known to everyone as the seeds in rye bread. The Dutch are responsible for the major supply of this spice. It is extensively used by the Germans and in many dishes from Scandinavia. It is especially good sprinkled over hot green beans with a squeeze of fresh lemon, or use it instead of celery seed in cole slaw dressed with light safflower oil and white wine vinegar.

CARDAMON: These are small black pungent seeds found inside a whitish pod that resembles a small nut. The seeds are used to flavor black demi-tasse. In Indian restaurants and homes they are often served following a meal; the taste of the seed refreshes the mouth after curry. The Scandinavians use the seeds in special cakes and buns. Some people like to chew the seeds after dinner coffee.

CELERY SEED: Take it easy with this powerful little seed, or all you will taste is celery. It is excellent sprinkled very lightly on raw vegetable salads, such as cole slaw, or used with fresh green cabbage and onions sautéed with a teaspoon of corn oil; try it in court bouillon, when simmering lobster or shrimp. It is also used in tomato sauces and tomato juice concoctions made up for hangovers. It has a high sodium content, but you only use a tiny amount.

CHERVIL: This is an excellent delicate green leaf related to parsley. It is easily grown in a pot in your kitchen window or just outside the door. Chopped fresh, it adds wonderful taste to green salad and a scrambled egg. Whip the egg with a teaspoon or so of low fat or low fat low-sodium milk or water and then scramble; sprinkle with the chopped fresh herb. Mix some with low-fat yogurt and chopped cucumber—Fabulous!

CHILI: It is difficult to describe this spice derived from ground peppers, usually from Mexico, but also from India. It is often mixed with cumin, garlic, oregano, and coriander to make chili con carne, which you may eat if you are careful with the leaness of the chopped meat. Some curries have chili powder added to them. It is indispensable with Mexican dishes.

CHIVES: The slimmest stalk in the onion family, it is often sold growing in cans or pots in the market. If kept watered, it will grow in the kitchen or outside in the ground. When you need some of these tiny green tubes, cut them gently with scissors, and the plant will continue to prosper. Sprinkle on salad with oil and vinegar or lemon juice dressing. Use in marinades for boiled artichokes, dust on the surface of puréed potato soup, or with a squeeze of lime on a piece of broiled fish.

CINNAMON: Who hasn't smelled this odor wafting up from bubbling apple sauce? It comes from the strips of bark taken from small saplings of the trees which grow in Southern India, Ceylon, China, and Vietnam. Sticks of the bark are put into hot alcoholic punch, excellent on cold days, mixed with pickled fruit, and used to flavor demi-tasse of coffee. This is good also in pickled vegetables such as beets. Ground cinnamon is used in baked goods. A dash mixed with boiled, artificially sweetened, pumpkin, squash, sweet potatoes, or puréed carrots is excellent.

CLOVES: These are the dried flower buds of the clove tree. The locale where they grow is as exotic as their odor and taste. They come from Zanzibar, Panama, and points west. Two of these dark brown buds may be added to hot rum drinks or placed in the juice used to heat or poach fresh fruit. Stick a few cloves in a whole onion used to flavor court bouillon or use a few when simmering shrimp or lobster. They give a spicy contrast when added to stewed apricot sauce made to pour hot over a piece of baked chicken breast. Put one in boiled or Harvard beets

CORIANDER: This seed has a tantalizing odor and is for some strange reason not too well known, but it is very good and especially useful to add variety to well-known foods. Try experimenting with a little of it in a few things to develop its usefulness in your diet. Sneak some into washed sauerkraut (not for those on a low-salt diet) or in a stew, and have the family members wonder what is strange but tasty about your old dish.

CUMIN: Seeds are used both whole and ground. When you try to duplicate someone's chili con carne and can't find the right taste, chances are you have forgotten the cumin, which is used in many other Mexican dishes too. It has been used on matzos and in German sauerkraut. Sprinkle a little cumin in a scrambled egg for that true Mexican taste.

CURRY: This seasoning is made of a combination of spices, including turmeric, ginger, pepper, mace, coriander, cumin, cardamon, and others, depending upon the locality in which it is used and the individual housewife in India who grinds and mixes her own curry powder for various dishes. Unless you have access to an Indian grocery or a friend who prepares it, you would do better to stick to one of the standard commercial mixes. It tastes better when it is cooked for some time. Sauté a large chopped onion and two chopped apples, in a tablespoon of corn oil and cook until the vegetables are limp and clear; then add the curry powder and simmer for awhile. Slip in a few shrimp, or a piece of cooked chicken breast along with a little chicken stock and a bit of flour. Serve the curry with a few unsalted peanuts, a teaspoon of mango chutney (not for salt restricted diets), a few raisins and chopped green pepper, sweet red pepper, or cucumber. Spoon the curry over a few tablespoons of rice and serve a green salad with lemon dressing.

DILL: This comes as seeds and dried weed. It is another member of the parsley family and is really best when purchased at the greens counter or cut from a small patch growing in the backyard. Chopped fresh dill, sprinkled over broiled trout, bass, or perch, with a squirt of fresh lemon juice is simply great and gives a Scandinavian slant to a meal. Add some to a salad mixed with a little oil and lemon juice and use it to season marinated mushrooms or simmered shrimp. Everybody knows of its use with pickles and it is good chopped and mixed with coleslaw. The dried weed can be used in the same way. The acid of lemon juice heightens the taste of dried dill.

FENNEL: This seed has a sweet anise-like taste and is used extensively in Italian foods, especially fish and stews containing fish. Less well known is the fresh plant called Italian celery, or finnochio; sometimes with affection it is referred to as "finoch." The stem is a bulbous type of sweet celery and the leaves are a feathery bright green and may be chopped and mixed in green salad; or a stalk with leaves may be put into the court bouillon used to simmer seafood, or in bouillabaisse. The leaves and stalk lend a beautiful garnishing touch to many dishes. This is of great importance in any diet because many dieters feel they are somehow being punished; however, eye appeal is a great "out" to moderate restriction.

FINES HERBES: The French have a penchant for interesting herbal combinations. This is a great one, which is generally composed of parsley, thyme, chervil, or chives. Other herbs may be included such as basil, tarragon, fresh savory, and a bit of bay. Sprinkle over a small game hen about halfway through baking or mix with a little lemon juice and a speck of oil and pour over hot asparagus or brocolli. This is always good in dressing made with vinegar and an unsaturated oil along with a tiny sliver of garlic.

GARLIC: The most pungent member of the onion family. It was once worn in a bag around the neck to ward off various diseases. However, it is much better to put a clove of garlic in a bottle of wine vinegar or to rub the wooden salad bowl with it before putting in the crisp greens, sliced peeled cucumber, and a fresh, coarsely chopped tomato, or an artichoke heart. A tasty clove of garlic lends real character to fried Chinese dishes. A word of caution: Use fresh garlic—*avoid garlic salt* because all herb salts contain *masses of salt (sodium)*. Besides which the real character is in the fresh bulb. (Avoid breathing in your sweetheart's face —nibble his or her ear instead!!)

GINGER: This is generally sold as a dried ground root of a beautiful leaved plant, easily grown in warm areas from the Caribbean to Asia. It is really better, however, to get a segment of the fresh root from any store that sells Oriental goods. A thin slice of fresh ginger is indescribably different from the ground dried product. The slice may be used in Chinese, Japanese, and Polynesian dishes. A fresh root can be kept for a long time in the refrigerator by placing it peeled in a covered jar of white vinegar. The slices can be gently simmered with a small amount of sugar substitute, tinted pink, and served as a relish with broiled fish or chicken.

JUNIPER BERRIES: These come from Europe but the common local varieties may also be used. They are excellent for flavoring gin (if you make your own). Juniper berries are also used to great advantage in game dishes such as venison, quail, or wild duck.

MACE AND NUTMEG: Mace is an outer membrane that covers the nutmeg. The two spices are sold separately and it is interesting to learn to distinguish the taste of the two substances. Mace, may enhance the natural flavor of baked apples, steamed carrot slices, hot oatmeal, or pancakes. It is added to many stewed fruits and compotes and sprinkled on fish and meat. Experiment with the intensity of flavor you like best. Nutmeg is the inner kernel of the fruit from the nutmeg tree and is generally used similarly to mace; however, its taste is somewhat different. Mix a bit with creamed spinach or in white sauce made with unsaturated oil and seasoned with a little chopped onion or shallot.

MARJORAM: A type of mint found in many parts of the world, including California. It is ordinarily bought as a dried herb, but it is easy to grow in a pot on a shelf or in the yard. Its taste and smell are potent and may overwhelm; use it gently. With sage, it makes up a mixture used in poultry stuffing. Use it with simmered squash and mushrooms, meat loaf, and veal. The fresh herb is also used in a bouquet garni (a group of herbs such as parsley, bay leaf, thyme, and marjoram tied in a bundle) and put into soup.

MINT: This aromatic plant can be grown easily in any yard near a faucet and should be used to decorate food as well as an ingredient. For instance, chopped and mixed with low-fat yogurt, it is a fine side dish for shish kebab, broiled veal chops, or with curry dishes. A sprig of green mint in an iced drink such as tea or lemonade makes a real summer-day refresher. Mix several types of peeled melon with fresh mint leaves and a little white wine.

MUSTARD: This weed is a prominent pest in Southern California, but the seed is very useful. Great quantities are used as a seasoning and large quantities of prepared mustard are spread on the hot dog. The prepared mustard has a good deal of added sodium chloride, hence it is more desirable to make your own mustard or use the low-soldium variety*. Prepare the Chinese or English style by taking the dried, ground seed and mixing it into a paste with water, beer, or white wine. Be careful with this potent material however, because too much, in the words of Belafonte, brings "a tear to me eye." The seeds are often used whole or slightly cracked in simmering shrimp, or sprinkled over green or white coleslaw. It is equally delicious scattered over a pan of wilted cabbage and

---

* See list of products in appendix.

sautéed onion. Add a bit of the dried mustard to oil and vinegar to sharpen the dressing.

OREGANO: This easily grown member of the mint group is sometimes a member of the Fines Herbes seasonings. It is really great, freshly chopped and mixed with sliced ripe tomatoes dressed with a few teaspoons of unsaturated oil and lemon dressing. Chill the tomatoes, then serve with a piece of broiled meat or chicken. The dried herb is commonly used in tomato sauce for pasta and on zucchini.

PAPRIKA: The attractive red color, with no hot taste, makes paprika especially useful to sprinkle over foods for eye appeal. However, it also has a distinctive flavor and much of it is used in Hungarian and Spanish cookery. In this country it is used in French dressing and imparts a red color to the dressing. It is very useful to shake over broiled chicken to enhance the browning. Paprika may be mixed with lean ground meat, to which it adds a piquant and exotic flavor.

PARSLEY: This curly-leafed plant is used as a garnish on platters of cold and hot foods. Try some coarsely chopped and mixed with other greens such as spinach, chives, and water cress; add a little fat-free sour cream to make a great dip for spiced or marinated shrimp. A handful of the finely chopped herb gives a real fillip to spaghetti sauce. Parsley, coarsely pulled apart and mixed with salad greens, gives interesting color and texture contrast as well as good taste and vitamins.

PEPPER: The seeds, picked from their vine at variable degrees of ripeness and then dried, make both black and white pepper. This spice is so commonly used that little needs to be added to its description.

POPPY SEEDS: These are tiny beautiful blue-gray seeds used to fill certain types of breads and strudel. Try the seeds mixed in a fruit salad or tossed with hot fine noodles and served with a nicely browned brook trout and plenty of lemon wedges—beautiful!

ROSEMARY: A powerful herb which releases a refreshing and stimulating scent in the garden when brushed or otherwise disturbed. It must be used with some care because it may be overpowering. It is magnificent with lamb marinated with red wine and then skewered and broiled with squares of green peppers and whole mushrooms.

SAFFRON: This condiment is very expensive. However, its distinctive flavor is worth the price. It is also a wonderful coloring agent. The actual native material containing the saffron is the stigma of crocus plants, painstakingly collected and dried. Mix a little ground saffron with chicken stock or hot water to use in making saffron rice or to put into fish stews such as bouil-

labaisse. The Iranians make a good rice pudding that also contains a little saffron.

SAGE: A leaf commonly used to season poultry and meat loaf. It is good with other broiled meats, especially pork.

SAVORY: This plant is easily grown in gardens and comes in two distinct types designated winter and summer savory. The latter variety is an ingredient of poultry seasoning. Use it alone and in combination with finely chopped parsley to sprinkle over hot green beans, fresh garden peas, and lentils cooked as a side-dish vegetable.

SESAME: These seeds are extensively used in the Orient and Middle East, toasted and sprinkled over spinach and on wafers or certain crackers and breads. An unusual oil (highly unsaturated) is made from the crushed seeds. The oil is a gourmet item in Chinese cooking and may actually be used to flavor other oils with a special nut-like taste. In Lebanon, Greece, and Egypt, the seeds are beaten into a type of paste called tahini. This may be purchased in cans. Thin the tahini with lemon juice then whirl it in the blender with a bit of crushed garlic and cooked garbanzo beans. What a fabulous dip for matzos or raw cauliflour!

TARRAGON: Another herb easily grown in the garden in warm climates or in a pot in the kitchen in colder regions. It has an interesting licorice-like taste which enhances fish and sauces. Place a piece inside a roast chicken or mix with a scrambled egg.

THYME: A garden herb about 12 inches high and easy to grow. Sprigs are included in the old-fashioned "pot herb" now called bouquet garni (thyme, leek, red pepper, parsley, oftentimes bay leaf). The herb is a valuable seasoning for soups and stuffings, and it is especially good chopped and sprinkled over steamed okra or used in gumbo soup.

VANILLA: This voluptuous fragrance comes from the long, dark, bean-like fruits of a tropical orchid. Generally it is marketed as a 10 per-cent alcoholic extract of the bean. It is an indispensible flavoring in cakes or puddings, or it may be added to a thin, artificially sweetened sauce for a baked Rome Beauty Apple.

VINEGARS: These are basically solutions of acetic acid of various strengths (2-5%). The acid is derived from a number of sources, such as fermented wine or fruit juice. Cider vinegar, of course, comes from apples, this constitutes the major source of such material in the United States. There is more taste in this than in the white vinegars, but colored vinegar sometimes adds an unpleasant appearance to food, so colorless or white is used. Herb vinegars are composed of basic wine vinegars or white vinegar from fruit fermentation and added sprigs of tarragon, basil, thyme, garlic, or dill.

TWO-WEEK MENU GUIDES

A glance at the following two-week menu guides will show that there is little reason for you to restrict yourself in the variety of foods you eat. For your convenience, we have organized your meals for 14 consecutive days: first for the *controlled-fat diet* and then for the *controlled-fat, low-sodium diet.* Under each of these categories we have offered diets of three different caloric values.

The first *controlled-fat diet* guide provides approximately 1,000 calories a day. This is good for reducing—under doctor's orders, of course. The second provides approximately 1,500 calories a day which is fine for some sedentary workers. The third provides 2,000 calories a day for people who are more active physically.

For individuals who have been put on a combination controlled-fat, low-sodium diet, another set of three menu guides are offered providing the same schedule of calories (in some cases minor changes have been made) but in addition permitting only 500 milligrams of sodium per day. It should be mentioned here that because low-sodium skim milk does not make a very palatable beverage, you may drink 2 cups of regular skim milk per day when on a 500 milligram sodium diet.

These menu guides offer a specific plan for good eating. A dot (●) preceding a menu item indicates this entry will be found in the recipe section. If you are on a low-sodium diet, remember to use only the low-sodium modifications which follow the main recipe. For the most part, patients who really need to be restricted in sodium cannot usually take in more than 500 milligrams a day. However, in the event your physician or dietitian allows you to increase the sodium in your diet, instructions on how to adapt this increase to 1000 milligrams per day are outlined on the last page of this section.

After you select a diet, it is important that you follow it closely. Limit yourself to the portion indicated in the applicable recipe. You may substitute other recipes in the book for those in your 14-day menu guide, but be sure to substitute recipes of equal caloric value, or if you are using a low-sodium diet, make sure you are exchanging recipes of an equivalent sodium content by referring to the list of ingredients in the Appendix. The diets are also planned with a daily balanced intake of types of food as well as amounts, so if you make a substitution be sure it is for the same kind of food. For example, in the case of a meat dish, another recipe may be substituted, provided that the same amount of protein is present in the substitute. If in doubt, check with your dietitian.

It is the hope of those who spent many long hours compiling these menus that this section will succeed in allowing you to enjoy the best possible eating while following your physician's orders.

THE MENU

	MONDAY	TUESDAY	WEDNESDAY

WEEK NO. 1
 	
BREAKFAST
	½ Cup Orange Juice
	¾ Cup Cornflakes
	1 Cup Skim Milk
		Fresh Grapefruit Half
		1 Poached Egg on 1 Slice
		  Whole Wheat Toast
		1 Cup Skim Milk
			½ Cup Tomato Juice
			• 1 Basic Pancake with
			  Low-Calorie Maple Syrup
			1 Cup Skim Milk

LUNCH	¾ Cup Low-Fat Cottage Cheese
	  and Cold Vegetable Plate (1
	  Cup Assortment of Asparagus,
	  Beets, Carrots, Cauliflower,
	  Etc.)
	1 Melba Toast with ½ Pat
	  Unsaturated Margarine
	• 1 Orange Refrigerator Cookie
	1 Cup Skim Milk
		• Tuna Casserole with Toasted
		  Almond Sauce
		4-6 Celery Sticks
		Sliced Banana Half
		1 Cup Skim Milk
			1 Cup Beef Consommé
			2 oz. Breast of Turkey on 1 Slice
			  Russian Rye with Lettuce
			  (open face)
			12 Fresh Grapes or ½ Apple
			1 Cup Skim Milk

DINNER	• Tomato Beef Stroganoff
	½ Cup Brussels Sprouts
	½ Head Butter Lettuce with
	  Lemon or Vinegar
	2 Fresh Apricots
	1 Cup Skim Milk
		Broiled Chicken Breast
		½ Cup Swiss Chard with
		  Lemon Wedge
		• Cucumber in Yogurt
		½ Cup Diced Fresh Fruit
			• Fish Dugléré
			5 Cherry Tomatoes
			2 Broccoli Spears
			• Molded Fruit Gelatin (See
			  Gelatin Desserts)

WEEK NO. 2
 	
BREAKFAST
	½ Cup Fresh Grapefruit Sections
	1 Soft Boiled Egg
	• 1 Buttermilk Scone
	½ Pat Unsaturated Margarine
		¾ Cup Cold Cereal with ½ Cup
		  Fresh Berries
		1 Cup Skim Milk
		1 Slice Toasted Raisin Bread
		½ Pat Unsaturated Margarine
			½ Cup Orange Juice
			1 Slice Toasted Whole Wheat
			  Bread
			1 Pat Unsaturated Margarine
			1 Teaspoon Low-Calorie Jelly
			1 Cup Skim Milk

LUNCH	2 Ounces Cold Sliced Beef on
	  Pumpernickel (1 Slice) with
	  Lettuce and 1 Teaspoon
	  Unsaturated Mayonnaise
	• Oriental Orange
	1 Cup Skim Milk
		• Shrimp Louis Salad with
		• 1 Tablespoon Louis Dressing
		1 Rye Krisp Cracker, or
		  Equivalent Dry Toast
		• Minted Fruit Cup
		1 Cup Skim Milk
			• Consommé Madrilene
			2 Ounces Sliced Turkey on ½
			  Toasted English Muffin
			• Glorified Rice
			1 Cup Skim Milk

DINNER	• Barbecued Fish
	½ Cup French Cut Green Beans
	Hearts of Romaine with Lemon
	¼ Chilled Cantaloupe
		1 Cup Beef Broth with Sliced
		  Mushrooms
		• Chicken Breast Farcies (Stuffed)
		4-6 Asparagus Spears
		½ Cup Fresh Pineapple Wedges
		  with a Teaspoon
		  of Creme de Menthe
			• Broiled Pike with Lemon
			  (See Broiled Fish)
			½ Cup Stewed Tomatoes
			• Crisp Coleslaw

CALORIES 1000 (Unrestricted Sodium)

THURSDAY	FRIDAY	SATURDAY	SUNDAY

4 Fresh Orange Slices
½ Cup Oatmeal
1 Cup Skim Milk
	Sliced Fresh Peach Half
	1 Soft Boiled Egg
	½ Slice Dry Toast
	1 Cup Skim Milk
		¾ Cup Stewed Artificially
		   Sweetened Rhubarb
		1 Toasted English Muffin
		Low-Calorie Orange Marmalade
			½ Cup Orange Juice
			1 Blueberry Pancake with
			   Low-Calorie Maple Syrup
			1 Cup Skim Milk

Shrimp Remoulade
1 French Roll
½ Pat Unsaturated Margarine
Strawberry Bavarian
1 Cup Skim Milk
	½ Cup Turkey Salad and 5
	   Asparagus Spears on Lettuce
	1 Cornmeal Muffin
	½ Pat Unsaturated Margarine
	1 Fresh Pear
		Crab or Chicken Gumbo
		1 Seasoned Rye Krisp, or
		   Equivalent Dry Toast
		4-6 Carrot Sticks
		Baked Apple
		1 Cup Skim Milk
			Fish Dugléré
			½ Cup Zucchini
			Perfection Salad
			1 Cup Fresh Strawberries

3 oz. Roast Leg O' Lamb
Artichoke with 1 Teaspoon
   Unsaturated Mayonnaise
Chocolate Pudding with
   Whipped Topping
	Skewered Scallops
	Lettuce Wedge with Vinegar
	½ Cup Artificially Sweetened
	   Canned Fruit
		Linguini with Clam Sauce
		Braised Belgian Endive
		1 Slice French Bread
		½ Pat Unsaturated Margarine
		⅓ Cup Low-Calorie Gelatin
		   with ½ Cup Added Fresh
		   Fruit
			3 Ounces Broiled Ground Round
			   Pattie on Hamburger Bun with
			   1 Teaspoon Catsup & Mustard
			Pineapple Tapioca
			1 Cup Skim Milk

½ Cup Tomato Juice
2 Slices French Toast
Low Calorie Maple Syrup
	¼ Fresh Canteloupe
	1 Blueberry Pancake with
	   Low-Calorie Syrup
	1 Cup Skim Milk
		½ Cup Orange Juice
		1 Poached Egg on
		   1 Slice of Toast
		1 Cup Skim Milk
			½ Cup Diced Fresh Fruit Cup
			½ Cup Oatmeal
			½ Toasted English Muffin
			½ Pat Unsaturated Margarine
			1 Cup Skim Milk

Chicken Salad Supreme
1 Small Hot Roll
½ Pat Unsaturated Margarine
3 Tomato Slices on Lettuce
Poached Pear Half
1 Cup Skim Milk
	Broiled Filet of Sole with
	   Lemon (See Broiled Fish)
	Green Beans in Tomato Sauce
	½ Cup Fresh Fruit with
	   2 Tablespoons Aloha Dip
		Peanut Butter and Low Calorie
		   Jelly Sandwich
		   (2 Slices of Bread)
		1 Fresh Pear
		1 Cup Skim Milk
			1 Cup Cold Beef Consommé
			Chicken with Mushrooms
			Baked Carrots Julienne
			Fluffy Orange Mold

Veal Meat Balls
½ Cup Fluffy Rice
Hearts of Romaine with
   Tarragon Vinegar
12 Fresh Grapes or ½ Apple
Chilled Fresh Apple
	Bouillabaisse
	Mixed Green Salad with
	1 Tablespoon Vinegar
	   and Oil Dressing
	⅓ Cup Low-Calorie Gelatin
	   (See Gelatin Desserts)
	   with Whipped Topping
		Broiled Flank Steak
		½ Cup Brussels Sprouts
		Tomato in Herb Vinegar
		⅓ Cup Whipped Low-Calorie
		   Gelatin
			Maryland Crab Cake with
			   Lemon Wedge
			2 Broccoli Spears
			½ Cup Artificially Sweetened
			   Canned Fruit

THE MENU

	MONDAY	TUESDAY	WEDNESDAY
WEEK NO. 1 **BREAKFAST**	½ Cup Orange Juice ¾ Cup Dry Cereal 1 Cup Skim Milk 1 Slice Raisin Toast 1 Pat Unsaturated Margarine	Half Fresh Grapefruit 1 Soft Cooked Egg • 1 Cornmeal Muffin 1 Pat Unsaturated Margarine 1 Cup Skim Milk	½ Cup Tomato Juice • 1 Basic Pancake (Wrap Pancake Like a Crepe Around ¼ Cup Stewed Fruit) Low-Calorie Maple Syrup 1 Cup Skim Milk
LUNCH	¾ Cup Low Fat Cottage Cheese and Cold Vegetable Plate (1 Cup Assortment of Asparagus, Beets, Carrots, Cauliflower, etc.) 2 Rye Melba ½ Pat Unsaturated Margarine • 1 Orange Refrigerator Cookie 1 Cup Skim Milk (Stir in Some Low Calorie Chocolate Syrup)	• Tuna Casserole with Toasted Almond Sauce 4-5 Celery Sticks • 1 Broiled Banana 1 Cup Skim Milk (Stir in Some Coffee with Sugar Substitute)	Consommé with a Few Cross-Sections of Scallion or Chives 3 oz. Breast of Turkey on 2 Slices Russian Rye—½ Pat Unsaturated Margarine 5 Cherry Tomatoes 12 Fresh Grapes or ½ Apple 1 Cup Skim Milk (or Tea or Coffee with Artificial Sweetener)
DINNER	• Tomato Beef Stroganoff ½ Cup Brussels Sprouts • Butter Lettuce with 1 Tablespoon Vinegar and Oil Dressing 2 Hot Baking Powder Biscuits 1 Pat Unsaturated Margarine 2 Canned or Fresh Apricots	• Chicken Piquant ½ Cup Baby Beets Hearts of Romaine with • 1 Tablespoon Vinegar and Oil Dressing ½ Cup Fresh Fruit Cup with a Teaspoon of Liqueur	• Fish Dugléré and Lemon ½ Cup Broccoli with Pimento Bits or Almond Slivers • 1 Corn on the Cob • Gelatin Fruit Salad (See Gelatin Desserts) • Baked Apple Dessert with Lemon Sauce
WEEK NO. 2 **BREAKFAST**	½ Cup Fresh Grapefruit Sections 1 Soft Boiled or Poached Egg • 2 Buttermilk Scones 1 Pat Unsaturated Margarine 1 Cup Skim Milk	¾ Cup Dry Cereal with ½ Cup Fresh Berries 1 Slice Toasted French Bread 1 Pat Unsaturated Margarine and Honey (1 Teaspoon) 1 Cup Skim Milk	• Spicy Fruit Compote • 1 Buttermilk Biscuit 1 Pat Unsaturated Margarine Low Calorie Jelly 1 Cup Skim Milk (Add Some Low Calorie Chocolate Syrup)
LUNCH	• Vegetable Soup 3 oz. Cold Sliced Beef on 2 Slices Pumpernickel ½ Pat Unsaturated Margarine • Oriental Orange 1 Cup Skim Milk	• Shrimp Louis Salad with 2 Tablespoons Louis Dressing 2 Rye Crisp Crackers, or Equivalent Dry Toast • Minted Fruit Cup 1 Cup Skim Milk	• Consommé Madrilene 3 oz. Sliced Turkey on Hard Roll with Lettuce • Glorified Rice 1 Cup Skim Milk
DINNER	• Barbecued Fish 1 Small Baked Potato ½ Cup French Cut Green Beans Hearts of Romaine with • 2 Tablespoons Vinegar and Oil Dressing 1 Cup Melon Balls	1 Cup Beef Broth with Sliced Mushrooms • Chicken Cumberland ½ Cup Steamed Rice with a Bit of Saffron 4–5 Asparagus Spears 1 Sliced Tomato on Lettuce ½ Cup Fresh Pineapple Wedges with a Teaspoon Creme de Menthe	• Borsch • Broiled Pike (See Broiled Fish) ½ Cup Peas and Green Onions • Cool Cucumber Mold • Apple Crisp and Whipped Topping

CALORIES 1500 (Unrestricted Sodium)

THURSDAY	FRIDAY	SATURDAY	SUNDAY
4 Orange Slices ½ Cup Oatmeal—Add a Few Raisins or Currants When Cooking 1 Cup Skim Milk 1 Slice Wheat Toast 1 Pat Unsaturated Margarine 1 Teaspoon *regular* Strawberry Jam	1 Sliced Fresh Peach ½ Cup Dry Cereal 1 Cup Skim Milk, Coffee or Tea 1 Slice Cinnamon Toast	Rhubarb Compote 1 Fried Egg 1 Toasted English Muffin Low-Calorie Orange Marmalade 1 Cup Skim Milk	½ Cup Orange Juice or ½ Fresh Grapefruit 2 Blueberry Pancakes with Low Calorie Syrup 1 Cup Skim Milk
Watercress Soup Shrimp Remoulade 1 Sour French Roll 1 Pat Unsaturated Margarine Strawberry Bavarian 1 Cup Skim Milk	Turkey Salad on 5 Asparagus Tips 1 Cornmeal Muffin 1 Pat Unsaturated Margarine 1 Fresh Pear 1 Cup Skim Milk	Crab or Chicken Gumbo Peanut Butter (non-homogenized) and Jelly Sandwich on 2 Slices Whole Wheat Bread 6 Carrot Sticks or Raw Cauliflower Baked Apple 1 Cup Skim Milk	Fish Dugléré Parsley Potato with ½ Pat Unsaturated Margarine ½ Cup Swiss Chard with Lemon Perfection Salad Angel Food Cake with Whipped Topping and ¼ Cup Fresh Strawberries
Roast Leg O' Lamb (Make a Sauce with Chopped Mint Leaves in a Little Stock) 1 Small Baked Potato 1 Pat Unsaturated Margarine 3 Tomato Slices on Butter Lettuce Chocolate Pudding with Whipped Topping Black Coffee	Shrimp Kebab on ½ Cup Fluffy Rice Summer Squash with Dill ¼ Head Lettuce Wedge with 2 Tablespoons Vinegar and Oil Dressing Cherry Crisp	Linguini with Clam Sauce Tossed Green Salad with 2 Tablespoons Vinegar and Oil Dressing 1 Slice Sour Dough French Bread 1 Pat Unsaturated Margarine ⅓ Cup Low Calorie Gelatin with Added Fresh Fruit (See Gelatin Desserts)	3 oz. Broiled Ground Round on Hamburger Bun with 1 Teaspoon Catsup or Mustard Wilted Endive Salad Pineapple Tapioca 1 Cup Skim Milk
½ Cup Tomato Juice 1 Slice French Toast with Low Calorie Jam 1 Cup Skim Milk	Melon Wedge (¼ Melon) 2 Blueberry Pancakes with Low Calorie Maple Syrup 1 Pat Unsaturated Margarine 1 Cup Skim Milk	½ Cup Orange Juice 1 Poached Egg on Toast 1 Cup Skim Milk	½ Cup Fresh Fruit Cup 2 Slices of French Toast 1 Pat Unsaturated Margarine Low Calorie Maple Syrup 1 Cup Skim Milk
French Onion Soup Creamed Chipped Beef over 1 Slice Toast Tossed Green Salad with 1 Tablespoon Vinegar and Oil Dressing Poached Pear Half 1 Cup Skim Milk	Broiled Filet of Sole (See Broiled Fish) ½ Cup Baby Lima Beans Stuffed Baked Tomato ½ Cup Fresh Fruit with 2 Tablespoons Aloha Dip 1 Cup Skim Milk	Turkey Salad with 4–5 Asparagus Spears 1 Rye Crisp, or Equivalent Dry Toast 1 Fresh Pear 1 Cup Skim Milk	1 Cup Cold Consommé Chicken with Mushrooms ½ Cup Fluffy Rice Baked Carrots Julienne Fluffy Orange Mold
Beef Oriental on ½ Cup Fluffy Rice Hearts of Romaine with Vinegar and Oil Dressing ½ Cup Mandarin Oranges in 1 Teaspoon Curacao	Bouillabaise Tossed Green Salad with 2 Tablespoons Vinegar and Oil Dressing 2 Bread Sticks 1 Pat Unsaturated Margarine ⅓ Cup Low Calorie Gelatine with Whipped Topping	Apple Stuffed Veal Roll ½ Cup Brussels Sprouts Tomato in Herb Vinegar Fresh Peach Pie	Maryland Crab Cake with Lemon Wedge ½ Cup Broccoli Cucumber in Yogurt Baked Apple 1 Cup Skim Milk

THE MENU

	MONDAY	TUESDAY	WEDNESDAY
WEEK NO. 1 **BREAKFAST**	½ Cup Orange Juice ¾ Cup Dry Cereal Sweetened with 1 Teaspoon Honey 1 Cup Skim Milk 2 Slices Raisin Toast 1 Pat Unsaturated Margarine	• Half Broiled Grapefruit 1 Soft Cooked Egg • 2 Cornmeal Muffins 2 Pats Unsaturated Margarine 1 Cup Skim Milk	½ Cup Tomato Juice • 2 Basic Pancakes 2 Pats Unsaturated Margarine 1 Tablespoon Maple Syrup (Regular) 1 Cup Skim Milk
LUNCH	¾ Cup Low Fat Cottage Cheese and Cold Vegetable Plate (1 Cup Assortment of Asparagus, Beets, Carrots, Cauliflower, Etc) 2 Melba Toasts 1 Pat Unsaturated Margarine • 2 Slices Date Raisin Nut Loaf 1 Cup Skim Milk	• Tuna Casserole with Toasted Almond Sauce 4-6 Celery Sticks • Broiled Banana 1 Cup Skim Milk	1 Cup Canned Beef Consommé 3 oz. Breast of Turkey on 2 Slices Russian Rye with Lettuce and 1 Teaspoon Unsaturated Mayonnaise 5 Cherry Tomatoes 12 Fresh Grapes or ½ Apple 1 Cup Skim Milk
DINNER	• Tomato Beef Stroganoff ½ Cup Parsleyed Noodles ½ Cup Brussels Sprouts Butter Lettuce with • 2 Tablespoons Oil and Vinegar Dressing 2 Hot Baking Powder Biscuits 2 Pats Unsaturated Margarine 2 Chilled Apricots • 2 Orange Refrigerator Cookies	• Chicken Piquant 1 Small Baked Potato with 1 Teaspoon Unsaturated Margarine ½ Cup Baby Beets Hearts of Romaine with • 2 Tablespoons Vinegar and Oil Dressing ½ Cup Fresh Fruit Cup with 1 Teaspoon Cointreau	• Poached Fish with Lemon Wedge ½ Cup Broccoli with a Sprinkle of Almonds • 1 Corn on the Cob • Gelatin Fruit Salad (See Gelatin Desserts) 1 Baking Powder Biscuit 1 Pat Unsaturated Margarine • Baked Apple Dessert with Lemon Sauce
WEEK NO. 2 **BREAKFAST**	½ Cup Canned Grapefruit Sections 1 Soft Boiled Egg • 2 Hot Buttermilk Scones 2 Pats Unsaturated Margarine 1 Cup Skim Milk	¾ Cup Dry Cereal with ¼ Cup Fresh Berries (or Frozen without Sugar) 1 Teaspoon Sugar 1 Cup Skim Milk 1 Slice Toasted French Bread 1 Pat Unsaturated Margarine 1 Teaspoon Honey	• Spicy Fruit Compote • 2 Hot Buttermilk Biscuits 2 Pats Unsaturated Margarine 1 Tablespoon Apple Jelly 1 Cup Skim Milk
LUNCH	• Cream of Mushroom Soup 3 oz. Cold Sliced Beef on 2 Slices Pumpernickel with Lettuce and 1 Teaspoon Unsaturated Mayonnaise • Oriental Orange 1 Cup Skim Milk	• Shrimp Louis Salad Plate with • 2 Tablespoons Louis Dressing 2 Rye Krisps, or Equivalent Dry Toast 1 Pat Unsaturated Margarine • Minted Fruit Cup • 1 Slice Cranberry Nut Loaf 1 Cup Skim Milk	• Consommé Madrilene 3 oz. Sliced Turkey on Hard Roll with Lettuce and 1 Teaspoon Unsaturated Mayonnaise • Glorified Rice 1 Cup Skim Milk
DINNER	• Barbecued Fish Baked Potato with 1 Tablespoon Imitation Sour Cream ½ Cup French Cut Green Beans Hearts of Romaine with • 2 Tablespoons Vinegar and Oil Dressing • 1 Cornmeal Muffin 1 Pat Unsaturated Margarine • Melon au Liqueurs	1 Cup Beef Broth with Sliced Mushrooms • Chicken Cumberland • Pilaff 4-5 Asparagus Spears with Mock Hollandaise Sauce ½ Cup Fresh or Canned Unsweetened Pineapple Wedges with 1 Teaspoon of Creme de Menthe	• Borsch • Broiled Pike (See Broiled Fish) • Sweet Potatoes with Orange ½ Cup Green Peas and Green Onions • Cool Cucumber Mold • Apple Crisp with Whipped Topping

CALORIES 2000 (Unrestricted Sodium)

THURSDAY	FRIDAY	SATURDAY	SUNDAY
4 Fresh Orange Slices ½ Cup Oatmeal with a few Raisins 1 Teaspoon Sugar 1 Cup Skim Milk 1 Slice Whole Wheat Toast 1 Pat Unsaturated Margarine 1 Teaspoon Strawberry Jam	• Rhubarb Compote 1 Fried Egg 1 Toasted English Muffin 1 Pat Unsaturated Margarine 1 Tablespoon Orange Marmalade 1 Cup Skim Milk	Sliced Fresh Peach or ½ Grapefruit ¾ Cup Dry Cereal 1 Teaspoon Sugar 1 Cup Skim Milk • 2 Slices Cinnamon Toast	½ Cup Orange Juice • 2 Blueberry Pancakes 1 Pat Unsaturated Margarine 1 Tablespoon Maple Syrup 1 Cup Skim Milk
• Watercress Soup • Shrimp Remoulade 1 Sour Dough French Roll 1 Pat Unsaturated Margarine • Strawberry Sherbet 1 Cup Skim Milk	• Crab or Chicken Gumbo • Peanut Butter and Jelly Sandwich on Whole Wheat Bread (2 Slices) 4-6 Carrot Sticks • Pommes Chateaubriand (Poached Apple) 1 Cup Skim Milk	• ¾ Cup Turkey Salad and 5 Asparagus Spears on Lettuce • 2 Cornmeal Muffins 2 Pats Unsaturated Margarine • Poached Pear Half 1 Cup Skim Milk	• Fish Dugléré Parsleyed Potato with 1 Pat Unsaturated Margarine ½ Cup Swiss Chard with Lemon • Molded Apple Salad • Angel Food Cake with Whipped Topping and ¼ Cup Fresh Strawberries
• 4 Ounces Roast Leg O'Lamb with 1 Tablespoon Mint Jelly ½ Cup Whipped Potatoes 1 Tablespoon Unsaturated Mayonnaise on Artichoke 3 Tomato Slices on Lettuce • 1 Homebaked Yeast Roll 1 Pat Unsaturated Margarine • Chocolate Pudding with Whipped Topping 1 Cup Skim Milk	• Baked Manicotti Assorted Tossed Greens with • 2 Tablespoons Vinegar and Oil Dressing 1 Slice Sour Dough French Bread 1 Pat Unsaturated Margarine • Gelatin Fruit Dessert (See Gelatin Dessert) Topped with 1 Tablespoon Cream Substitute	• Shrimp Kebab on ½ Cup Fluffy Rice • Summer Squash with Dill Lettuce Wedge with • 2 Tablespoons Vinegar and Oil Dressing • 1 Homebaked Parkerhouse Roll 1 Pat Unsaturated Margarine • Cherry Crisp with Whipped Topping	• Vegetable Soup 4 oz. Broiled Ground Round on Hamburger Bun with Catsup and Mustard • Broiled Onion Rings • Wilted Endive Salad • Orange Sherbet 1 Cup Skim Milk
½ Cup Tomato Juice • 2 Slices French Toast with 1 Tablespoon Regular Maple Syrup 1 Cup Skim Milk	• ½ Cup Fresh Diced Fruit Cup 1 Scrambled Egg • 2 Cornmeal Muffins 2 Pats Unsaturated Margarine 1 Cup Skim Milk	• Poached Peach • Nut Muffin 1 Pat Unsaturated Margarine 1 Cup Skim Milk	Fresh Canteloupe (¼ Melon) • 2 Blueberry Pancakes 1 Pat Unsaturated Margarine 1 Tablespoon Regular Berry Syrup 1 Cup Skim Milk
• French Onion Soup • Stuffed Green Peppers Tossed Green Salad with • 2 Tablespoons Vinegar and Oil Dressing • Poached Pear Half 1 Cup Skim Milk	• Broiled Filet of Sole (See Broiled Fish) with Tartar Sauce ½ Cup Baby Lima Beans • Stuffed Baked Tomato • 1 Whole Wheat Muffin 1 Pat Unsaturated Margarine ½ Cup Fresh Fruit with • 2 Tablespoons Aloha Dip 1 Cup Skim Milk	• Turkey Salad with 4-5 Asparagus Spears and 4-5 Beet Slices • Artichoke Vinaigrette 1 Rye Krisp 1 Pat Unsaturated Margarine ½ Cup Artificially Sweetened Royal Anne Cherries • Spiced Applesauce Cupcake 1 Cup Skim Milk	1 Cup Consommé with 1 Rye Krisp • Chicken Breast with Apricots • Confetti Rice • Creamed Spinach • Meringue Shell with Lemon Sherbet
• Beef Oriental Over ½ Cup Rice Hearts of Romaine with • 2 Tablespoons Tarragon Vinegar and Oil Dressing ½ Cup Mandarin Oranges in 1 Teaspoon Curacao 1 Cup Skim Milk	• Bouillabaise Tossed Green Salad with • 2 Tablespoons Vinegar and Oil Dressing 2 Bread Sticks 1 Pat Unsaturated Margarine • Gelatin Dessert with Whipped Topping	• Apple Stuffed Veal Roll 1 Small Baked Potato with 1 Pat Unsaturated Margarine ½ Cup Brussel Sprouts • Tomato in Herb Vinegar • Fresh Peach Pie	• Maryland Crab Cake with Lemon Wedge ½ Cup Broccoli with 1 Teaspoon Unsaturated Mayonnaise • Tomato Aspic with ½ Sliced Cucumber 1 Slice Sour Dough French Bread 1 Pat Unsaturated Margarine • Gingered Pears 1 Cup Skim Milk

THE MENU

	MONDAY	TUESDAY	WEDNESDAY

WEEK NO. 1
 	
BREAKFAST
	½ Cup Orange Juice
	¾ Cup Puffed Wheat
	1 Cup Skim Milk
		Fresh Grapefruit Half
		1 Poached Egg on 1 Slice
		    Low Sodium Toast
		1 Cup Skim Milk
			½ Cup Unsalted Tomato Juice
			• 1 Basic Pancake with
			    Low-Calorie Maple Syrup
			1 Cup Skim Milk

LUNCH	• Cold Plate: Seafood Mold with
	    Walnuts and 3 Cold Asparagus
	    Spears
	1 Low Sodium Melba Toast
	½ Pat Low Sodium
	    Unsaturated Margarine
	• 1 Orange Refrigerator Cookie
	1 Cup Skim Milk
		• Tuna Casserole with Toasted
		    Almond Sauce
		• Coleslaw
		Sliced Banana Half
		1 Cup Skim Milk
			1 Cup Low Sodium Consommé
			2 oz. Breast of Turkey on 1
			    Slice Low-Sodium Bread with
			    Lettuce (open face)
			12 Fresh Grapes or ½ Apple
			1 Cup Skim Milk

DINNER	• Tomato Beef Stroganoff
	½ Cup Brussels Sprouts
	Butter Lettuce with Lemon or
	    Vinegar
	2 Fresh or Artificially
	    Sweetened Apricots
		Broiled Chicken Breast
		½ Cup Fresh Green Peas
		• Cucumber in Yogurt
		• ½ Cup Minted Fruit Cup
			• Poached Fish (See Fish
			    Dugléré)
			5 Cherry Tomatoes
			2 Broccoli Spears
			• Fruit Gelatin (See
			    Gelatin Dessert)

WEEK NO. 2
 	
BREAKFAST
	½ Cup Fresh Grapefruit
	    Sections
	1 Soft Boiled Egg
	• 1 Buttermilk Scone
	½ Pat Low Sodium
	    Unsaturated Margarine
		¾ Cup Puffed Rice
		½ Cup Fresh Berries
		1 Cup Skim Milk
		1 Slice Low Sodium Toast
		½ Pat Low Sodium
		    Unsaturated Margarine
			½ Cup Orange Juice
			1 Slice Toasted Low-Sodium
			    Whole Wheat Bread
			1 Pat Low-Sodium
			    Unsaturated Margarine
			1 Teaspoon Low Calorie Jelly
			1 Cup Skim Milk

LUNCH	2 oz. Cold Sliced Beef on 1
	    Slice of Low Sodium
	    Toast with Lettuce and 1
	    Teaspoon Low Sodium
	    Unsaturated Mayonnaise
	• Oriental Orange
	1 Cup Skim Milk
		• Shrimp Louis Salad Plate with
		• 2 Tablespoons Louis Dressing
		1 Slice Low Sodium Melba
		    Toast
		• Minted Fruit Cup
		1 Cup Skim Milk
			• Consommé Madrilene
			2 oz. Sliced Turkey on 1 Slice
			    Low-Sodium Bread
			• Glorified Rice
			1 Cup Skim Milk

DINNER	• Barbecued Fish
	½ Cup Cooked Fresh Green
	    Beans
	Hearts of Romaine with
	    Lemon
	Chilled Cantaloupe (¼ Melon)
	1 Cup Skim Milk
		1 Cup Low Sodium Beef
		    Bouillon with Mushrooms
		• Chicken Breast Farcies (Stuffed)
		4-6 Asparagus Spears
		½ Cup Fresh Pineapple
		    Wedges with a Teaspoon of
		    Creme de Menthe
			• Broiled Pike with Lemon
			½ Cup Stewed Tomatoes
			    (unsalted)
			• Crisp Coleslaw
			Chilled Fresh Apple

MILLIGRAMS SODIUM 500   CALORIES 1000

THURSDAY	FRIDAY	SATURDAY	SUNDAY

4 Fresh Orange Slices
½ Cup Oatmeal
1 Cup Skim Milk
	Sliced Fresh Peach Half
	1 Soft Boiled Egg
	½ Slice Dry Low Sodium
	   Toast
	1 Cup Skim Milk
		¾ Cup Stewed Rhubarb
		   Artificially Sweetened
		1 Slice Low Sodium White Toast
		½ Pat Low Sodium
		   Unsaturated Margarine
		1 Teaspoon Low Calorie
		   Orange Marmalade
		1 Cup Skim Milk
			½ Cup Orange Juice
			• 1 Apple Pancake
			   Low-Calorie Maple Syrup
			1 Cup Skim Milk

• Shrimp Remoulade
• 1 Home Baked Yeast Roll
½ Pat Low Sodium
   Unsaturated Margarine
• Strawberry Bavarian
1 Cup Skim Milk
	• Turkey Salad Plate with 2
	   Tomato Slices and 2 Cooked
	   Cauliflowerettes
	1 Fresh Pear
	1 Cup Skim Milk
		• Crab or Chicken Gumbo
		1 Low Sodium Melba Toast
		4-6 Carrot Sticks
		• Baked Apple
		1 Cup Skim Milk
			• Fish Duglére
			½ Cup Baked Carrots Julienne
			• Perfection Salad
			1 Cup Fresh Strawberries

• 3 Ounces Roast Leg O'Lamb
Artichoke with 1 Teaspoon
   Low Sodium Unsaturated
   Mayonnaise
3 Tomato Slices on Lettuce
• Chocolate Pudding with
   Whipped Topping
	• Veal Marengo
	• Summer Squash with Dill
	Lettuce Wedge with Vinegar
	½ Cup Artificially Sweetened
	   Canned Fruit
		• Linguini with Clam Sauce
		• Braised Belgian Endive
		1 Slice Low Sodium Bread
		½ Pat Low Sodium
		   Unsaturated Margarine
		⅓ Cup Low-Calorie Gelatin
		   with ½ Cup Added Fruit
		   (See Gelatin Desserts)
			3 oz. Broiled Ground Round
			   Patty on
			2 Slices Low Sodium Bread
			   with 1 Teaspoon Low Sodium
			   Catsup and Low Sodium
			   Mustard
			• Pineapple Tapioca
			1 Cup Skim Milk

½ Cup Unsalted Tomato Juice
½ Cup Oatmeal
1 Slice Low-Sodium Toast
½ Pat Low-Sodium
   Unsaturated Margarine
	Fresh Cantaloupe (¼ Melon)
	• 1 Blueberry Pancake with
	   Low Calorie Syrup
	1 Cup Skim Milk
		½ Cup Orange Juice
		1 Poached Egg on 1
		   Slice Low-Sodium Toast
		1 Cup Skim Milk
			½ Cup Fresh Fruit Cup
			1 Slice Low-Sodium
			   Cinnamon Toast
			1 Cup Skim Milk

• Chicken Salad Supreme
• 1 Baking Powder Biscuit
½ Pat Unsaturated Margarine
2 Tomato Slices on Lettuce
• Poached Pear Half
1 Cup Skim Milk
	• Broiled Filet of Sole with
	   Lemon
	• Green Beans in Tomato Sauce
	• ½ Cup Fresh Fruit with
	   2 Tablespoons Aloha Dip
		• Unsalted Peanut Butter and Low
		   Calorie Jelly Sandwich on
		   2 Slices of Low-Sodium Bread
		1 Fresh Pear
		1 Cup Skim Milk
			1 Cup Cold Low-Sodium Beef
			   Bouillon with Lemon
			• Baked Chicken
			• Baked Carrots
			• Fluffy Orange Mold

• Shish Kebab
½ Cup Fluffy Rice
Hearts of Romaine with
   Vinegar or Lemon Juice
• Kale, Dutch Style
½ Cup Artificially Sweetened
   Fruit Cocktail
1 Cup Skim Milk
	• Bouillabaise
	Tossed Green Salad with
	• 1 Tablespoon Vinegar and
	   Oil Dressing (Low Sodium)
	⅓ Cup Low Calorie Gelatin
	   with Whipped Topping
		• Broiled Flank Steak
		½ Cup Brussels Sprouts
		• Tomato in Herb Vinegar
		⅓ Cup Whipped Low
		   Calorie Gelatin
			• 1 Maryland Tuna Cake
			   with Lemon Wedge
			2 Broccoli Spears
			½ Cup Artificially Sweetened
			   Canned Fruit
			1 Cup Skim Milk

THE MENU

		MONDAY	TUESDAY	WEDNESDAY

WEEK NO. 1
 	
BREAKFAST
		½ Cup Orange Juice
		¾ Cup Puffed Wheat
		1 Cup Skim Milk
		1 Slice Low-Sodium Toast
		1 Pat Unsaturated Margarine
			Fresh Grapefruit half
			1 Soft Cooked Egg
			1 Slice Low-Sodium Toast
			1 Pat Low-Sodium
			  Unsaturated Margarine
			1 Cup Skim Milk
				½ Cup Prune Juice
				1 Plain Pancake
				  Low Calorie Maple Syrup (or
				  Wrap Pancake Like a Crepe
				  Around Some Stewed Fruit)
				1 Cup Skim Milk

LUNCH		Seafood Mold with Walnuts and
		3 Cold Asparagus Spears
		2 Low-Sodium Melba Toast
		Chilled Cantaloupe (¼ Melon)
		1 Cup Skim Milk (add 1
		  Tablespoon Low Calorie
		  Chocolate Syrup)
			Tuna Casserole with Toasted
			  Almond Sauce
			Coleslaw
			Broiled Banana
			1 Cup Skim Milk—Stir in Some
			  Coffee and Sugar Substitute
				Stuffed Green Pepper with
				  Tomato Sauce
				Macédoine of Fruit
				1 Cup Skim Milk

DINNER		Tomato Beef Stroganoff
		½ Cup Brussels Sprouts
		Butter Lettuce with
		2 Tablespoons Vinegar
		  and Oil Dressing
		2 Hot Baking Powder Biscuits
		1 Pat Low-Sodium Unsaturated
		  Margarine
		2 Canned or Fresh Apricots
			Chicken Piquant
			1 Small Baked Potato
			½ Cup Fresh Green Peas
			Hearts of Romaine with 1
			  Tablespoon Creamed
			  Low-Sodium Herb Dressing
			Minted Fruit Cup
				Poached Fish
				½ Cup Broccoli
				1 Corn on the Cob
				Molded Tomato Aspic
				Baked Apple Dessert with
				  Lemon Sauce

WEEK NO. 2
 	
BREAKFAST
		½ Cup Fresh Grapefruit
		  Sections
		1 Soft Boiled Egg
		2 Buttermilk Scones
		1 Pat Low-Sodium
		  Unsaturated Margarine
		1 Cup Skim Milk
			¾ Cup Puffed Rice with ½
			  Cup Fresh Strawberries
			1 Cup Skim Milk
			1 Slice Low-Sodium Toast
			1 Pat Low-Sodium
			  Unsaturated Margarine
				Spicy Fruit Compote
				1 Buttermilk Biscuit
				1 Pat Low-Sodium
				  Unsaturated Margarine
				Low Calorie Jelly
				1 Cup Skim Milk (Add Some
				  Low Calorie Chocolate Syrup

LUNCH		Low-Sodium Minestrone
		3 Oz. Cold Sliced Beef with
		Potato Salad on Lettuce
		Oriental Orange
		1 Cup Skim Milk
			Lamb Stew
			1 Low-Sodium Melba Toast
			1 Pat Low-Sodium
			  Unsaturated Margarine
			1 Slice Date Raisin Nut Loaf
			1 Cup Skim Milk
				Consommé Madrilene
				3 Oz. Sliced Turkey on 1 Slice
				  Low-Sodium Whole Wheat
				  Bread with Lettuce and 1
				  Teaspoon Low-Sodium
				  Unsaturated Mayonnaise
				Chilled Peach Half (Artificially
				  Sweetened)
				1 Cup Skim Milk

DINNER		Barbecued Fish
		Boiled Potato with Seasoned
		  Sauce
		½ Cup French Cut Green
		  Beans
		Hearts of Romaine with
		2 Tablespoons Low Sodium
		  Vinegar and Oil Dressing
		12 Fresh Grapes or ½ Apple
			1 Cup Low-Sodium Beef Broth
			  with Sliced Mushrooms
			Chicken Cumberland
			½ Cup Steamed Rice with a bit
			  of Saffron
			4-5 Asparagus Spears
			½ Cup Fresh Pineapple
			  Wedges with a Teaspoon of
			  Creme de Menthe
				Broiled Pike (See Broiled Fish)
				½ Cup Fresh Green Peas with
				  Green Onions
				Cucumber in Yogurt
				Apple Crisp with Whipped
				  Topping

THURSDAY	FRIDAY	SATURDAY	SUNDAY
½ Cup Orange Slices ½ Cup Cream of Wheat 1 Cup Skim Milk 1 Slice Low-Sodium Wheat Toast 1 Pat Low-Sodium Unsaturated Margarine 1 Teaspoon Strawberry Jam (Regular)	1 Sliced Fresh Peach 1 Shredded Wheat Biscuit 1 Cup Skim Milk 1 Slice Cinnamon Toast	Rhubarb Compote 1 Fried Egg 1 Slice Low-Sodium Toast Low Calorie Orange Marmalade 1 Cup Skim Milk	½ Cup Orange Juice 2 Blueberry Pancakes 1 Cup Skim Milk Low Calorie Maple Syrup
1 Cup Low-Sodium Beef Broth 3 Oz. Sliced Breast of Chicken on 2 Slices Low-Sodium Bread 5 Cherry Tomatoes Glorified Rice 1 Cup Skim Milk	Chicken Salad Supreme 1 Corn Meal Muffin 1 Pat Low-Sodium Unsaturated Margarine 1 Fresh Pear 1 Cup Skim Milk	Chicken Gumbo Unsalted Peanut Butter and Regular Jelly Sandwich on 2 Slices Low Sodium Bread 4-6 Carrot Sticks Baked Apple 1 Cup Skim Milk	Fish Duglére 1 Small Parsley Potato and 1 Pat Low-Sodium Unsaturated Margarine ½ Cup Baked Carrots Julienne Perfection Salad Rhubarb Compote with Sugar and ¼ Cup Fresh Strawberries
French Onion Soup 3 Oz. Roast Leg o' Lamb ½ Cup Mashed Potatoes Mixed Vegetable Sauté, Italian Style Pineapple Tapioca with Whipped Topping	Veal Marengo ½ Cup Fluffy Steamed Rice ½ Cup Mixed Peas and Carrots Lettuce Wedge with 2 Tablespoons Low Sodium Vinegar and Oil Dressing Cherry Crisp	Spaghettini in Marinara Sauce Tossed Green Salad with 2 Tablespoons Vinegar Oil and Dressing 1 Slice Sour Dough French Bread 1 Pat Low-Sodium Unsaturated Margarine ⅓ Cup Low-Calorie Whipped Gelatin with ½ Cup added Fruit	Chili Con Carne 2 Unsalted Crackers Molded Apple Salad Cantaloupe (¼ Melon) 1 Cup Skim Milk
½ Cup Unsalted Tomato Juice ½ Cup Oatmeal with 1 Tablespoon Raisins 1 Cup Skim Milk 1 Slice Low-Sodium Toast 1 Pat Low-Sodium Unsaturated Margarine	1 Cup Melon Balls 2 Basic Pancakes Low Calorie Maple Syrup 1 Pat Low-Sodium Unsaturated Margarine 1 Cup Skim Milk	½ Cup Orange Juice 1 Poached Egg on 1 Slice Low-Sodium Toast 1 Cup Skim Milk	½ Cup Diced Fresh Fruit Cup 2 Slices French Toast 1 Pat Low-Sodium Unsaturated Margarine Low Calorie Maple Syrup 1 Cup Skim Milk
French Onion Soup Tuna Salad Sandwich on 2 slices Sour Dough French Bread Poached Pear Half 1 Cup Skim Milk	Broiled Filet of Sole (See Broiled Fish) with Tartar Sauce ½ Cup Whole Kernel Corn Stuffed Baked Tomato ½ Cup Fresh Fruit with 2 Tablespoons Aloha Dip 1 Cup Skim Milk	Cold Plate: Turkey Salad with 3 Asparagus Spears 1 Slice Low-Sodium Toast 2 Chilled Crimson Plums 1 Cup Skim Milk	1 Cup Low-Sodium Beef Broth Chicken with Mushrooms ½ Cup Fluffy Rice Corn and Tomato Casserole Strawberry Bavarian
Chicken with Walnuts on ½ Cup Fluffy Rice ½ Cup Green Beans Hearts of Romaine with 2 Tbsp. Tarragon Vinegar and Oil Dressing ½ Cup Mandarin Oranges in 1 Teaspoon Curacao	Low-Sodium Minestrone Hearts of Lettuce with 2 Tablespoons Vinegar and Oil Dressing 1 Low-Sodium Melba Toast 1 Pat Low-Sodium Unsaturated Margarine No Bake Pumpkin Pie with Whipped Topping	Apple Stuffed Veal Roll ½ Cup Brussels Sprouts Tomato in Herb Vinegar Fresh Peach Pie	Split Pea Soup, Canadian 2 Unsalted Crackers 1 Pat Low-Sodium Unsaturated Margarine 1 Cup Assorted Fresh Fruit Salad with 1 Tablespoon French Dressing 1 Slice Cranberry Nut Loaf 1 Cup Skim Milk

THE MENU

	MONDAY	TUESDAY	WEDNESDAY
WEEK NO. 1 **BREAKFAST**	½ Cup Orange Juice ¾ Cup Puffed Wheat Sweetened with 1 Tablespoon Honey 1 Cup Skim Milk 2 Slices Low-Sodium Toast 1 Pat Low-Sodium Unsaturated Margarine	Half Broiled Grapefruit 1 Soft Boiled Egg 2 Cornmeal Muffins 2 Pats Low-Sodium Unsaturated Margarine 1 Cup Skim Milk	½ Cup Unsalted Tomato Juice 2 Basic Pancakes 1 Pat Low-Sodium Unsaturated Margarine 1 Tablespoon Regular Maple Syrup 1 Cup Skim Milk
LUNCH	Cold Plate: Seafood Mold with Walnuts 3 Cold Asparagus Spears 2 Low-Sodium Melba Crackers 1 Pat Low-Sodium Unsaturated Margarine 2 Slices Date Raisin Nut Loaf 1 Cup Skim Milk	Tuna Casserole with Toasted Almond Sauce Coleslaw Broiled Banana 1 Cup Skim Milk	1 Cup Low-Sodium Beef Bouillon 3 Oz. Breast of Turkey on 2 Slices Low-Sodium Bread with Lettuce and 1 Teaspoon Low-Sodium Unsaturated Margarine 5 Cherry Tomatoes 12 Fresh Grapes or ½ Apple 1 Cup Skim Milk
DINNER	Tomato Beef Stroganoff ½ Cup Parsleyed Noodles ½ Cup Brussels Sprouts Butter Lettuce with 1 Tablespoon Oil and Vinegar Dressing 2 Hot Baking Powder Biscuits 2 Pats Low-Sodium Unsaturated Margarine 2 Chilled Apricots 2 Orange Refrigerator Cookies	Chicken Piquant 1 Small Baked Potato with 1 Pat Low-Sodium Unsaturated Margarine ½ Cup Fresh Green Peas Hearts of Romaine with 2 Tablespoons Low-Sodium Vinegar and Oil Dressing ½ Cup Fresh Fruit Cup with 1 Teaspoon Cointreau	Poached Fish with Lemon Wedge ½ Cup Broccoli with a Sprinkle of Almonds 1 Corn on the Cob Molded Fruit Salad (See Gelatin Desserts) 1 Baking Powder Biscuit 1 Pat Low-Sodium Unsaturated Margarine Baked Apple Dessert with Lemon Sauce
WEEK NO. 2 **BREAKFAST**	½ Cup Regular Canned Grapefruit Sections 1 Soft Boiled Egg 2 Hot Buttermilk Scones 2 Pats Low-Sodium Unsaturated Margarine 1 Cup Skim Milk	¾ Cup Puffed Rice with ½ Cup Fresh Berries 1 Teaspoon Sugar 1 Cup Skim Milk 1 Slice Low-Sodium Toast 1 Pat Low-Sodium Unsaturated Margarine 1 Teaspoon Honey	Spicy Fruit Compote 2 Hot Baking Powder Biscuits 2 Pats Low-Sodium Unsaturated Margarine 1 Teaspoon regular Apple Jelly 1 Cup Skim Milk
LUNCH	Cream of Mushroom Soup 3 oz. Cold Sliced Beef on 2 Slices Low-Sodium Bread with Lettuce and 1 Teaspoon Low-Sodium Unsaturated Margarine Oriental Oranges 1 Cup Skim Milk	Shrimp Louis Salad Plate with 2 Tablespoons Louis Dressing 2 Low-Sodium Melba Toast 1 Pat Low-Sodium Unsaturated Margarine ½ Cup Minted Fruit Cup 1 Slice Cranberry Nut Loaf 1 Cup Skim Milk	Consommé Madrilene 3 oz. Sliced Turkey on 2 slices Low-Sodium bread with Lettuce and 1 Teaspoon Low-Sodium Unsaturated Mayonnaise Glorified Rice 1 Cup Skim Milk
DINNER	Barbecued Fish 1 Small Baked Potato with 2 Pats Low-Sodium Unsaturated Margarine ½ Cup Fresh Green Beans Hearts of Romaine with 2 Tablespoons Vinegar and Oil Dressing 1 Cornmeal Muffin 1 Pat Unsaturated Margarine Melon au Liqueurs	1 Cup Low-Sodium Beef Bouillon with Sliced Mushrooms Chicken Cumberland Pilaff 3-4 Asparagus Spears with Mock Hollandaise Sauce ½ Cup Fresh Pineapple Wedges with 1 Teaspoon of Creme de Menthe	Borsch Broiled Pike with Lemon Wedge Sweet Potatoes with Orange ½ Cup Fresh Green Peas and Green Onions Cool Cucumber Mold Apple Crisp with Whipped Topping

THURSDAY	FRIDAY	SATURDAY	SUNDAY
4 Fresh Orange Slices ½ Cup Oatmeal (with a few Raisins) 1 Teaspoon Sugar 1 Cup Skim Milk 1 Slice Low-Sodium Whole Wheat Toast 1 Tablespoon Low-Sodium Unsaturated Margarine 1 Teaspoon Strawberry Jam	Rhubarb Compote 1 Fried Egg 2 Slices Low-Sodium Toast 1 Pat Low-Sodium Unsaturated Margarine 1 Tablespoon Regular Orange Marmalade 1 Cup Skim Milk	1 Sliced Fresh Peach 1 Shredded Wheat Biscuit 1 Teaspoon Sugar 1 Cup Skim Milk 2 Slices Low-Sodium Cinnamon Toast	½ Cup Orange Juice 2 Apple Pancakes 1 Pat Low-Sodium Unsaturated Margarine 1 Tablespoon Regular Maple Syrup 1 Cup Skim Milk
Watercress Soup Shrimp Remoulade 1 Home Baked Yeast Dinner Roll 1 Pat Low-Sodium Unsaturated Margarine Strawberry Sherbet 1 Cup Skim Milk	Chicken Gumbo Unsalted Peanut Butter and Regular Jelly on 2 Slices Low-Sodium Whole Wheat Bread 6 Carrot Sticks Pommes Chateaubriand (Poached Apple) 1 Cup Skim Milk	Turkey Salad Plate with 2 Tomato Slices and ½ Cup Cooked Cauliflower 2 Corn Meal Muffins 1 Pat Low-Sodium Unsaturated Margarine Poached Pear Half 1 Cup Skim Milk	Fish Dugléré 1 Parsleyed Potato with 1 Pat Low-Sodium Unsaturated Margarine ½ Cup Baked Carrots Julienne Perfection Salad Angel Food Cake with Whipped Topping and ½ Cup Fresh Strawberries
4 Ounces Roast Leg o' Lamb with 1 Tablespoon Mint Jelly ½ Cup Mashed Potatoes Artichoke with 1 Tablespoon Low-Sodium Unsaturated Mayonnaise 3 Tomato Slices on Lettuce 1 Slice Low-Sodium Whole Wheat Bread 1 Pat Low-Sodium Unsaturated Margarine Chocolate Pudding with Whipped Topping	Baked Manicotti Assorted Tossed Greens with 2 Tablespoons Vinegar and Oil Dressing 1 Slice Low-Sodium White Bread 1 Pat Low-Sodium Unsaturated Margarine Gelatin Dessert with Fruit Topped with 1 Tablespoon Cream Substitute	Shrimp Kebab on ½ Cup Fluffy Low-Sodium Rice Summer Squash with Dill Lettuce Wedge with 1 Tablespoon Low-Sodium Vinegar and Oil Dressing 1 Home Baked Yeast Roll 1 Pat Low-Sodium Unsaturated Margarine Cherry Crisp with Whipped Topping	Vegetable Soup 4 Ounces Broiled Ground Round Pattie on Homemade Low-Sodium Hamburger Bun (or 2 slices Low-Sodium Bread) 1 Teaspoon Low-Sodium Catsup and Mustard Broiled Onion Rings Endive Salad Orange Sherbet 1 Cup Skim Milk
½ Cup Unsalted Tomato Juice 2 Slices Low-Sodium French Toast with 1 Tablespoon Regular Maple Syrup 1 Cup Skim Milk	½ Cup Fresh Diced Fruit 1 Soft Boiled Egg 2 Cornmeal Muffins 2 Pats Low-Sodium Unsaturated Margarine 1 Cup Skim Milk	1 Poached Peach 2 Slices French Toast with Low Calorie Syrup 1 Cup Skim Milk	Fresh Cantaloupe (¼ Melon) 2 Blueberry Pancakes 1 Pat Low-Sodium Unsaturated Margarine 1 Tablespoon Regular Berry Syrup 1 Cup Skim Milk
French Onion Soup Stuffed Green Pepper Tossed Greens with 2 Tablespoons Vinegar and Oil Dressing Poached Pear Half 1 Cup Skim Milk	Broiled Filet of Sole with 1 Tablespoon Tartar Sauce ½ Cup Baby Lima Beans Stuffed Baked Tomato 1 Whole Wheat Muffin 1 Pat Low-Sodium Unsaturated Margarine ½ Cup Fresh Fruit with 2 Tablespoons Aloha Dip 1 Cup Skim Milk	Cold Plate: Turkey Salad with 3 Asparagus Spears and Artichoke Vinaigrette 2 Low-Sodium Melba Crackers 1 Pat Low-Sodium Unsaturated Margarine 12 Fresh Grapes or ½ Cup Fruit Spiced Applesauce Cupcake 1 Cup Skim Milk	1 Cup Low-Sodium Cold Consommé Chicken Breast with Apricots ½ Cup Confetti Rice Kale, Dutch Style Meringue Shell with Lemon Sherbet
Beef Oriental over ½ Cup Low-Sodium Rice Hearts of Romaine with 2 Tablespoons Vinegar and Oil Dressing ½ Cup Mandarin Oranges in 1 Teaspoon Curacao	Bouillabaise Tossed Green Salad with 2 Tablespoons Vinegar and Oil Dressing 2 Low-Sodium Melba Toast 1 Pat Low-Sodium Unsaturated Margarine ⅓ Cup Low Calorie Low-Sodium Flavored Gelatin with 2 Tablespoons Cream Substitute	Apple Stuffed Veal Roll 1 Small Baked Potato 1 Pat Low-Sodium Unsaturated Margarine ½ Cup Brussels Sprouts Tomato in Herb Vinegar 1 Piece Peach Pie	Maryland Tuna Cake with Lemon Wedge ½ Cup Broccoli with 1 Teaspoon Low-Sodium Unsaturated Mayonnaise Low-Sodium Tomato Aspic ½ Cucumber, Sliced 1 Slice Low-Sodium Bread 1 Pat Low-Sodium Unsaturated Margarine Gingered Pears 1 Cup Skim Milk

ADAPTING THE MENU GUIDES TO 1000 MILLIGRAMS OF SODIUM

The amount of sodium to be included in a sodium-restricted diet must be decided by the physician. Therefore, if his directions say to use more than 500 milligrams of sodium each day, the 14 day menu guide and recipes can be readily adapted to a 1000 milligram sodium diet by following a few basic rules.

1. Use regular skim milk instead of the low sodium variety in cooking.

2. Regular unsaturated margarines can be used instead of sticking to the low sodium varieties.

3. Low sodium breads can be replaced with regular white or dark bread.

4. Continue to follow the "low sodium modification" of the recipes, keeping in mind that the milk, margarine and bread ingredients can be regular instead of low sodium types.

5. Look at the difference in the sodium content of the items just mentioned. Check the appendix for the sodium content of other foods you may question.

ITEM	AMOUNT	MILLIGRAMS OF SODIUM
Regular bread	1 slice	118
Low sodium bread	1 slice	7
Regular skim milk	1 cup	128
Low sodium skim milk	1 cup	12
Regular unsaturated margarine	1 teaspoon	49
Low sodium unsaturated margarine	1 teaspoon	trace

If you are on the weight reducing *1000 calorie* controlled-fat, low-sodium diet, these minor changes will not quite bring the sodium content up to the 1000 milligram level due to the limited amount of total food. Therefore, you will be able to add a few other ingredients back into the recipes—*celery, shrimp,* and *regular canned vegetables* where these items were used in the original recipes which were not low in sodium. But be sure to continue using other low sodium items as listed.

In diets of greater *caloric* value, check with your dietitian before substituting any of the regular controlled fat recipes for the low sodium modifications.

THE RECIPES

If your Doctor puts you on a low-fat or low-sodium diet (or a combination of both) don't despair, there is plenty of good eating in these pages.

Note:

These recipes make liberal use of specialty foods such as "unsaturated margarine", "imitation sour cream", "sugar substitutes," etc. For your convenience, a box check ☑ indicates the item is listed in the Appendix.

As a means of alerting individuals adhering to a low-sodium diet, low-sodium modification headings are printed in color.

ANTIPASTO

Antipasto is the Italian version of hors d'oeuvres which is, of course, French for these gastronomical tidbits which whet the appetite and stir the imagination.

A prelude to the heartier portions of the meal, antipasto includes a variety of international dishes, mostly small and colorful, with varied tastes and seasonings.

As a matter of fact, in Middle Eastern countries like Lebanon, the antipasto or hors d'oeuvres, called *masos,* can include over 40 different dishes—then comes the yogurt soup, roast whole lamb, and other accoutrements of the banquet.

Gentle reader, turn the pages to a healthful, zestful antipasto.

Spiced Mushrooms

    1 pound small fresh mushrooms
    2 cloves garlic, mashed or minced
    ¼ cup lemon juice
    6 whole black peppers
    ½ teaspoon salt
    1 small bay leaf
    1 small hot red pepper
      Pinch of marjoram
    1 cup white wine vinegar
    1 cup unsaturated oil ☑
    1 can (about 1½ cups) chicken bouillon
      Sprigs of parsley

Mushrooms are a wonderful food and have been used for centuries in Europe and Asia to enhance the flavor and texture of foods. We offer you mushrooms as an antipasto. These spiced mushrooms are great at a cocktail party. They also go well with meat, vegetable dishes, and salads. Select mushrooms that are firm and free of bruises. Wash quiekly in cold water and pat dry with paper towels; cut off dry end of stem. Quarter mushrooms if they are larger than button-size.

In a 3-quart saucepan, place the garlic, lemon juice, pepper, salt, bay leaf, red pepper, marjoram, wine vinegar, unsaturated oil, and chicken bouillon. Simmer for 45 minutes, then strain. Return marinade to pan with the mushrooms, and cover and simmer for 10 minutes. Pour into a bowl to cool, then cover and refrigerate at least 4 hours before serving. To serve, remove mushrooms from marinade and arrange attractively on a plate with sprigs of parsley. Don't forget the toothpicks! Serves 6.

You may keep the excess marinade in the refrigerator and use it to marinate fish or chicken. It will keep for several weeks.

CALORIES per serving: 41

LOW-SODIUM MODIFICATION. Omit salt and use low-sodium chicken bouillon ☑. Add a few drops of low-sodium flavoring, such as Tabasco ☑.

MG. SODIUM per serving: 11

Carrot Nibblers

    1 pound carrots (6 medium sized)
    1 tablespoon finely chopped onion
    1 clove garlic, peeled
    2 tablespoons unsaturated oil ☑
    ¼ cup vinegar
    1 teaspoon salt
    ½ teaspoon monosodium glutamate
    ½ teaspoon dry mustard
    ¼ teaspoon sugar or substitute ☑
    1 sprig parsley

Peel carrots; cut into lengthwise slices 3 inches long and ½ inch wide. Sauté onion and whole garlic in oil until limp. Stir in vinegar, salt, monosodium glutamate, mustard, and sugar. Add carrots and cover and simmer for 5 minutes. Carrots should be crisp tender. Remove garlic. Transfer carrots and marinade to a shallow dish; cover and refrigerate until needed. To serve, remove carrots from marinade and arrange on a serving dish; sprinkle over chopped parsley. Serve cold along with cherry tomatoes, crisp celery, and bunches of green grapes. Serves 6.

CALORIES per serving: 60

LOW-SODIUM MODIFICATION: Omit salt and monosodium glutamate. Season with a salt substitute ☑ and lemon juice to taste.

MG. SODIUM per serving: 14

Aloha Dip

 1 cup imitation sour cream ☑ or low-fat yogurt ☑
 ½ cup drained dietetic crushed pineapple ☑
 ¼ cup finely chopped pecans
 1 tablespoon maraschino cherry juice
 ⅛ teaspoon powdered ginger or ½ teaspoon chopped fresh ginger
    Assorted fresh fruit

Stir together the imitation sour cream, crushed pineapple, pecans, cherry juice, and ginger. Spoon into a serving bowl and chill. To serve, place the bowl on a chop plate and surround with fresh fruit such as whole strawberries, large grapes, pineapple spears, and slices of fresh peach. Use the fruit as dippers, or you can provide toothpicks to pick up the fruit for dunking. Makes 1¾ cups.

CALORIES per ounce (2 tablespoons): 30

VARIATIONS: Make this recipe as directed and then freeze for a delicious and refreshing dessert.

LOW-SODIUM MODIFICATION: Use low-fat yogurt ☑.

MG. SODIUM per ounce (using low-fat yogurt): 9

Clam Dip

 1 cup dry cottage cheese ☑
 1 teaspoon prepared horseradish
 ½ teaspoon each salt, monosodium glutamate, and paprika
 2 teaspoons lemon juice
 ½ cup skim milk
 1 can (7 oz.) minced clams, drained

Blend the cottage cheese, horseradish, salt, monosodium glutamate, paprika, lemon juice, and milk in a blender or electric mixer. When mixture is creamy, stir in clams. Turn into a serving bowl and dust the top with additional paprika. For dippers you might use radishes, sliced cucumbers, thinly sliced kohlrabe, sliced raw zucchini, cherry tomatoes, and cauliflower. Makes 2½ cups.

CALORIES per ounce (2 tablespoons): 12

LOW-SODIUM MODIFICATION: Omit monosodium glutamate; use low-sodium cottage cheese ☑ and salt substitute ☑ Replace clams with fresh fish fillet that has been poached and flaked. Avoid horseradish packed in salt and use low-sodium skim milk ☑.

MG. SODIUM per ounce: 8½

Kidney Bean Dip

 1 can (1 lb.) kidney beans, well drained
 ⅓ cup catsup
 ⅓ cup finely chopped onion
    Dash of Tabasco

Mash beans with fork. Stir in catsup, onion and Tabasco. Let stand for a few hours to allow flavors to blend. Serves 6.

CALORIES per serving: 56

VARIATIONS: Chopped onion may be replaced with chopped green pepper or chopped nuts.

LOW-SODIUM MODIFICATION: Boil your own beans from the dried variety. Substitute low-sodium chili sauce ☑ or catsup ☑ and cayenne pepper.

MG. SODIUM per serving: 5

Sesame Sherry Log

1 cup sesame seeds
4 tablespoons unsaturated margarine ☑
½ cup dry cottage cheese ☑
¼ teaspoon nutmeg
¼ teaspoon salt
1 tablespoon Sherry
1 tablespoon water
5 tablespoons prepared instant mashed potatoes or left-over mashed potatoes

Toast sesame seeds by sprinkling on baking sheet. Place in a moderate oven (350°), stirring occasionally, until lightly browned. Soften margarine with mixer, then add the cottage cheese, nutmeg, salt, Sherry, water, and mashed potatoes; blend well. Spread sesame seeds on a piece of waxed paper to cover an area 12 inches by 4 inches. Spoon cheese mixture thickly over the center length of sesame seeds. Roll cheese log by picking up and lifting the sides of waxed paper, allowing seeds to come in contact with the cheese. Continue until cheese is in a log shape and completely covered with seeds. Carefully lift onto a serving tray and chill for several hours. To serve, provide a knife and let each person cut his own slice. Serve with rye crackers or thinly sliced toast. Serves 8.

CALORIES per serving: 75

LOW-SODIUM MODIFICATION: Use low-sodium, unsaturated margarine ☑, low-sodium cottage cheese ☑, salt substitute ☑, and a squeeze of lemon juice. Use only fresh mashed potatoes. Serve with low-sodium crackers ☑

MG. SODIUM per serving: 6

Chive Spread

1 cup dry cottage cheese ☑
¼ cup buttermilk
1 tablespoon chopped chives
1½ teaspoons finely chopped parsley
Slice of pimiento

Mix cottage cheese and buttermilk in blender. Stir in chives and parsley. Spread on crackers or breads. Top with slice of pimiento. Serves 12.

CALORIES per cracker with spread: 35

LOW-SODIUM MODIFICATION: Use low-sodium cottage cheese ☑ and low-sodium skim milk ☑ instead of buttermilk. Vary the taste by adding chopped fresh dill, Mexican or Chinese parsley or dried coriander, or sprinkle top with poppy seeds.

MG. SODIUM per salt-free cracker ☑ with spread: 5

Cucumber in Yogurt

1 medium sized cucumber
½ cup low-fat yogurt ☑
1 tablespoon lemon juice
Pinch of salt
2 sprigs fresh mint, finely chopped, or ½ teaspoon crumbled dried mint

Wash and peel cucumber (skin is generally coated with a wax or oil), split lengthwise, scrape out seeds, and thinly slice crosswise. Allow to stand for 15 minutes, then pat dry with paper towels. Mix cucumber with yogurt, lemon juice, salt, and mint. Chill before serving. Serve on a plate and provide toothpicks for spearing the cucumber. Garnish with slices of red or black radish or chopped parsley. Serves 4.

CALORIES per serving: 25

LOW-SODIUM MODIFICATION: Omit salt and use salt substitute ☑

MG. SODIUM per serving: 22

Vegetables a la Grecque

1½ pounds of assorted vegetables
   Slightly salted water
3 tablespoons unsaturated oil ☑
3 tablespoons lemon juice
   Various seasonings

Select vegetables such as broccoli spears, asparagus, celery root, parsnips, carrots, and beets. Cook each vegetable separately in slightly salted water until crisp tender. Drain, and place each vegetable in a separate container. Mix the oil and lemon juice and divide into six bowls. Season each marinade according to different vegetables: for instance, garlic, capers, and lemon are good with broccoli and asparagus; curry powder with carrots and parsnips; dill with beets; and lemon with celery root. Spoon each marinade on the appropriate vegetable, then chill for 24 hours. To serve, drain off marinade and arrange vegetables on a serving plate. Serves 4.

CALORIES per ½ cup serving: 50

LOW-SODIUM MODIFICATION: Cook the vegetables in water seasoned with lemon juice and omit salt. Experiment with the variety of seasonings available such as low-sodium gourmet seasoning ☑. Stick with broccoli, asparagus, and parsnips—these have a low sodium content. Avoid capers; they are usually packed with salt.

MG. SODIUM per ½ cup serving: 6-10

Humus

(Arabic Garbanzo Paté)

1 can (1 lb.) garbanzos
   Salt and white pepper to taste
1 tablespoon Tahini ☑ (sesame paste) or sesame oil
2 tablespoon lemon juice
1 clove garlic, mashed or minced
   Pomegranate seeds

Drain the garbanzos but save the liquid. Mash the garbanzos slightly, then blend in a blender with a little of the canned liquid or push through a sieve. Season with salt and pepper, Tahini, lemon juice, and garlic. Spoon humus into a mound on a plate and sprinkle with a few pomegranate seeds. Serve with flat Arabic bread or matzohs ☑. Serves 12.

CALORIES per serving: 55

VARIATIONS: Season with a little coriander and sprinkle with toasted sesame seeds. Serve with chopped fresh mint or chopped parsley. No calorie change.

LOW-SODIUM MODIFICATION: Do not use canned garbanzos, but cook your own. Cover dried garbanzos with water, boil briskly 2 minutes, then cover and let stand 1 hour. Add more water if necessary to cover garbanzos and simmer for 2 hours or until tender. Use peanut oil or sesame oil instead of Tahini. Omit the salt and season with salt substitute ☑, lemon juice and/or mint.

MG. SODIUM per serving: 3

Eggplant Spread

1 medium sized eggplant
3 tablespoons Tahini ☑ (sesame paste)
   Lemon juice and salt to taste
2 tablespoons unsaturated oil ☑
1 tablespoon chopped parsley

Roast unpeeled eggplant under the broiler, turning frequently. When fork tender, peel off skin immediately and mash eggplant. Season with Tahini, lemon juice, and salt, and mix well. Spoon eggplant into a mound on a shallow serving dish. Drizzle oil over the top and sprinkle with parsley. Serves 6 to 8.

CALORIES per recipe: 500

LOW-SODIUM MODIFICATION: When mixing eggplant, stir in a crushed clove of garlic. Use salt substitute ☑; however, this spread still has too much sodium for strict diets!

MG. SODIUM per serving: 200

Braised Belgian Endive

2 heads Belgian endive
½ onion, sliced
1 carrot, sliced
1 to 2 cups chicken consommé or water
Juice of ½ lemon
1 sprig parsley
2 teaspoons chopped capers
1 teaspoon chopped parsley
1 teaspoon chopped chives or green onion tops
4 tablespoons French dressing

Split endive lengthwise and wash; arrange in a shallow oven-proof dish. Cover with onion and carrot and pour over consommé or water; add lemon juice and parsley. Cover dish with aluminum foil and punch a small hole in the center of the foil. Bake in a moderately hot oven (375°) for about 40 minutes or until endive is tender. Be sure not to overcook! Drain any remaining stock. Sprinkle endive with capers, parsley, and chives or green onion tops and spoon the French dressing over all. Chill for at least 2 hours. Drain endive and serve one-half head per person on a small plate with a bit of the garnish and a sprig of parsley. Serves 4.

CALORIES per serving: 108

VARIATIONS: Simmer celery or fennel instead and treat similarly. In place of French dressing, use unsaturated mayonnaise ☑ mixed with a little lemon juice and sharp mustard. Sprinkle with chopped hard cooked egg white. No calorie change.

LOW-SODIUM MODIFICATION: Cook the vegetables in low-sodium consomme ☑ seasoned with salt substitute ☑ or lemon juice. Avoid capers that are loaded with salt; use low-sodium mustard ☑ and low-sodium French dressing ☑. Celery should be avoided. Use low-sodium unsaturated mayonnaise in the variation.

MG. SODIUM per serving: 24

Shrimp Cocktail

3 medium sized raw shrimp per cocktail
Water
1 lemon slice
1 bay leaf
¼ teaspoon salt
Dash pepper
Small leaves of romaine lettuce
1 tablespoon cocktail sauce per cocktail

Place unshelled shrimp in a pan with cold water to cover, lemon, bay leaf, salt, and pepper. Bring water to a boil, then reduce heat and simmer 3 to 5 minutes. Too much cooking ruins shrimp so don't cook them to a frazzle. When shrimp are cool enough to handle, remove shells and cut out sand vein running along the back. The latter isn't really necessary, but the shrimp look more appetizing. For each serving, tuck a leaf of romaine in a sherbet glass or fancy cup, arrange three shrimp on each leaf, and top with a tablespoon of cocktail sauce.

CALORIES per cocktail: 45

VARIATIONS: Instead of cocktail sauce, spoon a little low-calorie French dressing ☑ over the shrimp or use unsaturated mayonnaise ☑. Vary the taste of the French dressing by adding chopped fresh herbs if you have them growing in a garden or pot. Especially good are fresh dill or fresh or dried tarragon. Try flaked poached fish as a substitute for shrimp or use crab meat. No calorie change.

LOW-SODIUM MODIFICATION: Avoid salt in cooking water and use a salt substitute ☑; use low sodium mayonnaise ☑ and low-sodium cocktail (chili) sauce ☑. Avoid crab meat as it has a high level of sodium.

MG. SODIUM per serving: 40

Ceviche

2 medium sized fresh fish fillets, about 5 oz. each
1 green pepper, seeded and chopped
1 red onion, finely chopped
    Salt to taste
    Freshly ground black pepper
¾ cup lemon juice or lime juice
2 tablespoons chopped Mexican or Chinese parsley
    Romaine or Boston lettuce leaves and sliced lime
        for garnish
1 teaspoon chopped sweet red pepper or pimiento

Wash fillets (snapper, sole, halibut, or fresh tuna) in cold water and pat dry with paper towels. Cut fish into narrow strips about ¼ inch wide and 1 inch long. Place fish in a shallow bowl with the green pepper, onion, salt, and pepper; pour lemon or lime juice over the fish. Cover bowl and chill in refrigerator for two days, occasionally basting the fish with the marinade. The fish will become white and opaque as it slowly "cooks" in the citric acid of the lemon or lime juice. To serve, drain fish and arrange in chilled cups or glasses lined with lettuce leaves. Sprinkle the chopped parsley and red pepper over the fish and garnish with slices of lime. Eat on rounds of toast thinly spread with unsaturated margarine ☑. Serves 6.

CALORIES per cracker and fish: 30

LOW-SODIUM MODIFICATION: Delete salt; use salt substitute ☑.

MG. SODIUM per cracker and fish: 6½

Eggplant Caviar

1 eggplant
1 onion, finely chopped
1 clove garlic, mashed or minced
1 tomato
1 teaspoon sugar
2 teaspoons lemon juice
2 tablespoons unsaturated oil ☑
    Salt and pepper to taste

Boil the whole eggplant in water until tender or roast the unpeeled eggplant under the broiler, turning frequently, until tender. Peel off skin immediately and chop eggplant. Mix with the onion and garlic. Peel the tomato and squeeze out most of the seeds and juice; chop the pulp and add to eggplant along with the sugar, lemon juice, oil, and salt and pepper. Mix well; chill for 2 hours before serving. Serve as a spread on thinly sliced toast and sprinkle with a bit of very finely chopped parsley, oregano, or basil. Serves 6 to 8.

CALORIES with 1 slice toast and 2 tablespoons spread: 82

VARIATIONS: Add chopped raw mushrooms or a little finely chopped celery. *Do not fry* the eggplant! It soaks up fat like mad. No calorie change.

LOW-SODIUM MODIFICATION: Delete salt and add more herbs, lemon juice, or sugar. Do not add celery in the variations.

MG. SODIUM per serving with 2 tablespoons spread and 1 slice salt free toast: 8

To Emphasize the Dippy Theme

Serve antipasto and dips with the following crackers, breads, or raw vegetables:

CRACKERS AND BREADS: Rye Krisp, melba rye or wheat rounds, matzohs, sesame seed crackers, toasted rye, whole wheat, cracked wheat or white bread rounds, miniature baking powder biscuits (see recipe page ☑).

LOW-SODIUM MODIFICATION: Salt-free matzohs (low-salt variety), miniature baking powder biscuits, toasted unsalted bread rounds, or unsalted melba toast ☑.

VEGETABLES: Raw carrots, raw cauliflower, cherry tomatoes, peeled cucumber strips, raw zucchini strips, radishes, scallions, ripe olives (not for low-sodium diets).

LOW-SODIUM MODIFICATION: Most fresh vegetables are low in salt and you need not worry about the above except for the olives, which are processed by packing in salt.

SOUPS AND CHOWDERS

Soups are "heart warming" on a cold winter's day. Some are refreshing when served cold in the heat of summer. Others can be used as a main course, like the traditional fish chowder or minestrone.

Gazpacho

1 medium sized onion, cut in quarters
1 clove garlic
1 cup beef stock or 1 bouillon cube dissolved in 1 cup hot water
3 tablespoons unsaturated oil ☑
2 tablespoons chopped parsley
2 tablespoons cider vinegar
⅛ teaspoon paprika
   Garnishes
1 onion, finely chopped
1 green pepper, seeded and chopped
2 tomatoes, chopped
1 cucumber, peeled and chopped

Place the quartered onion, peeled garlic, beef stock, oil, parsley, vinegar, and paprika in a blender and blend until smooth; chill. Serve this soup with separate side dishes of the onion, green pepper, tomato, and cucumber so each person can add these according to his liking. Serves 4.

By the way, we have found that beef tea ☑ makes an excellent beef stock substitute. Furthermore, this delicious, vitamin-packed stock is virtually fat free.

CALORIES per serving: 112

LOW-SODIUM MODIFICATION: Use low-sodium beef bouillon cubes ☑ and salt substitute ☑ to taste.

MG. SODIUM per serving: 9

Borsch

2 quarts beef broth
2 raw beets, peeled and grated
1 large onion, chopped
2 tablespoons sliced celery
   Sugar substitute ☑ equal to 2 tablespoons sugar
   Juice of ½ lemon
½ teaspoon salt
3 small cloves garlic
6 small potatoes
6 tablespoons imitation sour cream ☑

In a large saucepan, bring the beef broth to a gentle simmer. Add the beets, onion, celery, sugar substitute, lemon juice, salt, and garlic which has been skewered on a toothpick so you can remove it later. Simmer over low heat for 1 hour. Strain broth, if desired, or remove garlic and serve soup as it is. While the soup is cooking, boil the potatoes, then peel. Place a hot potato in each serving bowl and ladle over the soup. Top each serving with a spoonful of imitation sour cream. Serves 6.

CALORIES per serving: 175

VARIATIONS: Serve Borsch icy cold over hot, peeled, boiled potatoes. Add 1 tablespoon imitation sour cream ☑ to each bowl. No calorie or sodium change.

LOW-SODIUM MODIFICATION: Use low-sodium beef bouillon cubes ☑ to make 2 quarts beef broth. Omit celery and salt.

MG. SODIUM per serving: 70

Spinach Soup

3 tablespoons unsaturated oil ☑
1 large onion, finely chopped
2 cloves garlic, mashed or minced
¾ pound (2 medium sized) potatoes, peeled and thinly sliced
Salt and freshly ground black pepper
1½ cups water
¼ teaspoon powdered saffron
1½ pounds fresh spinach
1 tablespoon chopped parsley
¼ teaspoon each thyme and fennel
1 bay leaf
Piece of lemon peel
1 egg per person (Remember, this is one of your eggs for the week!)
1 slice bread, cut in 4 triangles
1 teaspoon unsaturated margarine ☑

Heat oil in a frying pan. Sauté onion and garlic until limp and clear. Add potatoes and fry 1 minute; transfer to an oven-proof baking dish. Sprinkle over salt and pepper to taste. Heat water and stir in saffron to dissolve; pour over potato mixture.

Cook spinach in a small amount of boiling water just until tender, about 5 minutes. Turn into a sieve or colander and press out all of liquid with a spoon. Chop spinach, then add to the potato mixture along with the parsley, thyme, fennel, bay leaf, and lemon peel. Stir until lightly mixed; cover and bake in a moderate oven (350°) for 1 hour.

Serve as a main course in deep soup bowls. Just before serving, poach 1 egg per person and place on each serving of spinach. Toast bread triangles; spread with margarine, and use as a garnish on this hearty soup. Serves 4.

CALORIES per serving: 188

LOW-SODIUM MODIFICATION: Use salt substitute ☑ in place of salt and low-sodium unsaturated margarine ☑.

MG. SODIUM per serving: 52

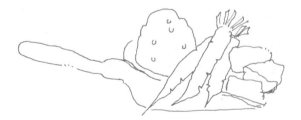

Cream of Mushroom Soup

¼ pound fresh mushrooms
2 tablespoons unsaturated margarine ☑
2 tablespoons chopped onion
2 tablespoons flour
1 cup chicken broth
1 cup skim milk
½ cup imitation sour cream ☑
½ teaspoon salt
¼ teaspoon pepper

Wash mushrooms and thinly slice. Melt margarine in a saucepan; sauté mushrooms and onion for 5 minutes. Blend in flour until smooth. Add chicken broth and milk, and stirring, cook until slightly thickened. Cool slightly; blend in imitation sour cream. Season with salt and pepper. Heat gently and serve immediately. Serves 4.

CALORIES per serving: 190

LOW-SODIUM MODIFICATION: Use low-sodium, unsaturated margarine ☑, low-sodium skim milk and low-sodium chicken bouillon cubes ☑. Use salt substitute ☑.

MG. SODIUM per serving: 34

Vegetable Soup

3 to 4 pound beef knuckle bone
2 quarts water
1 small onion, chopped
1 teaspoon salt
¼ cup pearl barley
1 can (1 lb.) tomatoes
2 cups cut green beans
2 stalks celery, sliced
1 large potato, diced
5 carrots, sliced
2 cups coarsely chopped cabbage
Bouquet garni (1 bay leaf, 1 sprig of thyme, 2 sprigs of parsley, 1 sprig of rosemary, and a few celery leaves)

Trim fat, if there is any, from the knuckle bone. Place the bone in a large heavy kettle with the water, onion, and salt; simmer for 2 hours. Add the barley, tomatoes, green beans, celery, potato, carrots, cabbage, and *bouquet garni* and continue cooking for 1 hour. Remove bone before serving. Serves 10.

CALORIES per serving: 65

LOW-SODIUM MODIFICATION: Use salt substitute ☑ or ¼ teaspoon lemon juice. Delete celery; use only 3 carrots. Use low-sodium canned tomatoes ☑.

MG. SODIUM per serving: 17

Consommé Madrilene

2 cups chicken broth
2 cups beef broth
1 can (1 lb.) solid pack tomatoes
1 medium sized carrot, finely sliced
1 stalk celery, sliced
1 small onion, sliced
1 teaspoon sugar
1 teaspoon salt
3 whole cloves

Combine all the ingredients and simmer, covered, for 1 hour. Strain before serving. Serves 6.

CALORIES per serving: 25

VARIATIONS: You may also serve this soup cold. Soften 1½ tablespoons unflavored gelatin in ½ cup cold water; add to hot soup and stir until dissolved. Chill soup; stir with a fork before serving, and garnish with chopped parsley or lemon slices.

CALORIES per serving: 40

LOW-SODIUM MODIFICATION: Use low-sodium chicken and beef bouillon cubes ☑, salt substitute ☑, and omit celery. Use low-sodium canned tomatoes ☑.

MG. SODIUM per serving for Consommé and variation: 21

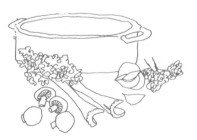

Crab or Chicken Gumbo

1 medium sized onion, chopped
1 clove garlic, mashed or minced
3 tablespoons unsaturated oil ☑
1 green pepper, seeded and chopped
4 cups beef or chicken broth
1 can (1 lb.) solid pack tomatoes
2 cups fresh corn or 1 can (1 lb.) whole kernel corn
2 cups sliced okra or 1 can (1 lb.) okra
1 cup flaked crab meat or 1 cup diced cooked chicken
2 teaspoons filé powder moistened with a little water, optional

In a large kettle sauté onion and garlic in the oil until limp. Add the green pepper and sauté lightly for 5 minutes. Add the broth, tomatoes, and corn and simmer for 30 minutes. Add the okra and crab meat or diced chicken and cook for 10 minutes or until okra is tender. Blend in filé powder before serving. Serves 8.

CALORIES per serving: 146

LOW-SODIUM MODIFICATION: Use low-sodium, unsaturated margarine ☑, low-sodium canned tomatoes ☑, and low-sodium beef bouillon cubes ☑. For the corn, use low-sodium canned corn ☑ and whirl it in the blender. Use diced chicken—not crab.

MG. SODIUM per serving: 17

Chinese Vegetable Soup

8 cups (2 quarts) chicken consommé
½ teaspoon monosodium glutamate
salt and pepper to taste
1 cup canned tomatoes
1 cup sliced onions, mushrooms, water cress, or bok choy (Chinese cabbage)
½ cup diced tofu (soybean cake)

Heat chicken broth in a large kettle (If you have made the stock yourself, chill it first and remove the fat from the top.) Correct the seasoning with monosodium glutamate, salt, and pepper to taste. Squeeze the seeds from the tomatoes and coarsely chop; add to soup along with the onions, mushrooms, water cress, or bok choy. Simmer briefly for 5 minutes or until vegetables are crisp tender. A few minutes before serving, add the tofu and heat through. Serve in deep bowls so you can pick up the bowl with both hands and drink the soup. Serves 10.

CALORIES per serving: 36

LOW-SODIUM MODIFICATION: Use low-sodium chicken bouillon ☑. Delete salt and monosodium glutamate; use a salt substitute ☑. You may also add a little low-sodium flavoring ☑ or Tabasco ☑. Use low-sodium canned tomatoes ☑.

MG. SODIUM per serving: 12

Fish Chowder, New England Style

1½ pounds firm white fish (snapper, halibut, cod)
2 cups water
1 teaspoon monosodium glutamate
  Salt and pepper
2 tablespoons unsaturated margarine ☑
2 onions, thinly sliced
2 medium-sized potatoes, peeled and cut in ½-inch cubes
4 cups (1 quart) skim milk
1 tablespoon chopped parsley
  Pinch of thyme (optional)
  Paprika

Simmer fish (fresh if you've been fishing) in the water seasoned with monosodium glutamate, salt, and pepper for 10 to 15 minutes or until fish flakes with a fork. Remove fish, and when cool enough to handle, take out the skin and bones and flake the meat. Reserve stock.

Melt margarine in the kettle and add the onions and potatoes. Sauté slowly until onions are transparent and potatoes are tender. Add the flaked fish, reserved stock, and skim milk to the onion mixture. (You may add some non fat dried milk solids to the skim milk first to increase the protein content and enrich the tast.) Stir in parsley and salt and pepper to taste. Some appreciate a pinch of thyme, others do not. Heat slowly without boiling and serve with a dusting of paprika. Serves 8.

CALORIES per serving: 188

LOW-SODIUM MODIFICATION: Do not use frozen fish as it contains too much sodium. Omit salt

and monosodium glutamate; use salt substitute ☑ and a bit of cayenne. Use low-sodium, unsaturated margarine ☑ and low-sodium skim milk ☑.

MG. SODIUM per serving: 66

Minestrone

⅔ cup dried lima beans
⅔ cup dried kidney beans
  Water
2 small hot red peppers, crumbled
1 bay leaf
3 stalks celery, sliced
1 cup chopped onion
2 cloves garlic, mashed or minced
2 tablespoons unsaturated oil ☑
½ eggplant
1 leek
1 carrot
1 large zucchini
¼ small head cabbage
3 sprigs parsley
2 bunches spinach
1 can (1 lb.) solid pack tomatoes
1 teaspoon basil
½ teaspoon dried leaf thyme
1 tablespoon sugar
½ cup elbow macaroni
2 tablespoons grated Parmesan or Romano cheese

Place beans in separate pans and cover each with 4 cups of water. Soak overnight or boil briskly 2 minutes, then cover, and let stand 1 hour. Cook beans separately until tender. Mash lima beans with the liquid to make a thick purée. Drain cooked kidney beans and add to lima beans along with the red peppers, bay leaf, and celery.

In a frying pan sauté the onion and garlic in unsaturated oil until clear; add to soup. Peel the eggplant and dice. Chop the leek, carrot, zucchini, cabbage, parsley, and spinach. Coarsely chop tomatoes. Add all the vegetables to the soup kettle; season with basil and thyme. Stir to mix, cover, and simmer for 1 hour or until the vegetables are tender. Add the macaroni the last 20 minutes of cooking. Soup should be thick, but add water if necessary to keep it from sticking to the pan. Sprinkle grated cheese over the soup before serving. Serve with crusty Italian or French bread and a glass of Chianti—"Umm"! It is even better reheated the next day. Serves 8.

CALORIES per serving: 248

   2 cups dried kidney beans
   2 quarts water
   2 hot red peppers, crumbled
   1 cup chopped onion
   1 clove garlic, mashed or minced
   4 tablespoons chopped parsley
   2 teaspoons unsaturated oil ☑
   1 cup cubed potatoes
   1 carrot, chopped
   2 cups peeled fresh tomatoes
   1 cup chopped zucchini
   1 leek, sliced
   2 tablespoons vinegar
   1 teaspoon each marjoram and thyme
     Pinch of dry mustard
   1 tablespoon sugar

Place beans in a large pan and cover with water. Soak overnight or boil briskly 2 minutes, then cover, and let stand 1 hour. Add the hot peppers and cook beans until tender. Take out the 2 cups of the beans and mash; return to pan and stir in. Sauté onion, garlic, and parsley in unsaturated oil until limp. Add to soup along with the remaining ingredients. Cover and simmer slowly until vegetables are tender. Add more water if soup seems too thick. Serves 8.

CALORIES per serving: 229

MG. SODIUM per serving: 5

Split Pea Soup, Canadian

   1 cup yellow or green split peas
   5 cups beef stock
   1 small onion
   1 carrot
   1 bay leaf
   1 small hot red pepper
     Pinch each of thyme and marjoram
     Salt
     Freshly ground pepper
   ½ cup Chablis
   1 smoked frankfurter

Wash and pick over peas; soak overnight in cold water; drain. Place peas in a soup kettle with the stock and chopped onion. Bring to a boil, then cover and simmer until the peas break up. At this point, you may force the peas through a sieve for a pureé or leave the peas roughly intact. Finely chop the carrot and add to the soup along with the bay leaf, crumbled red pepper, thyme, marjoram, and salt and pepper to taste. Cook slowly until the carrot is tender. Some devotees add Chablis or other dry white wine at this point, but it is optional. Slice the frankfurter and add to soup as a garnish. Serves 8.

If you happen to have a nice row of fresh peas in the garden or the peas look extra good in the market, a few cooked ones make a nice garnish. Lentils may be substituted above for the split peas; add a garlic clove and a pinch of summer savory and presto—lentil soup.

CALORIES per serving: 126

   1 cup split peas
   1 carrot
   1 small onion
   1 bay leaf
     Pinch each of thyme and marjoram
   4 whole black peppers
   4 cups water
   1 pork chop (optional)
   ½ cup Sauterne (optional)

Wash and pick over peas; soak overnight in cold water; drain. Chop the carrot and onion and place in a kettle with the peas, bay leaf, thyme, marjoram, black peppers, and water. For extra flavor cut the pork chop from the bone and trim the fat; cut meat in small cubes and add to soup. Cover kettle and simmer for 1 to 1½ hours or until peas are tender. Just before serving, stir in the wine. Serves 6.

CALORIES per serving: 73

MG. SODIUM per serving: 17

With pork and wine:

CALORIES per serving: 147

MG. SODIUM per serving: 31

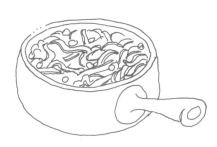

Watercress Soup

4 bunches watercress
3 stalks celery
1 large onion
2 tablespoons unsaturated margarine ☑
1 pound (3 medium sized) potatoes
8 cups (2 quarts) chicken consommé
2 tablespoons cream substitute ☑
  Monosodium glutamate or salt and white pepper
    to taste

Wash watercress; take out one-fourth bunch and reserve. Chop remaining cress, celery, and onion. Place vegetables in a kettle with unsaturated margarine; sauté until vegetables wilt. Peel and slice potatoes; add to mixture along with consommé. Simmer gently for 50 minutes; the soup will be fairly thick. Put all in a blender and whirl until fairly smooth. Return soup to kettle; stir in cream substitute. (Some like sour cream substitute ☑ instead of the sweet cream substitute.) Taste and adjust seasoning. Plunge the reserved watercress in boiling water for 2 minutes; drain well. Chop the cress finely and sprinkle it on the soup. Serves 6.

CALORIES per serving: 90

LOW-SODIUM MODIFICATION: Delete celery; use low-sodium, unsaturated margarine ☑ and low-sodium chicken bouillon ☑ or cubes. Omit monosodium glutamate and use a salt substitute ☑. This soup may be served very hot or very cold. It is excellent either way! Serve it with a piece of crusty French bread and a cold glass of Chablis for a delicious Sunday supper.

MG. SODIUM per serving: 24

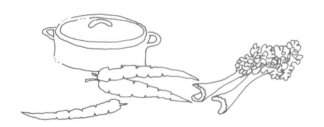

Sopa de Albondigas

(Mexican Meat Ball Soup)

4 cups (1 quart) beef broth
1 large can (No. 2½) solid pack tomatoes, sieved
1 tablespoon chili powder
1 clove garlic, mashed or minced
½ teaspoon cumin
  Pepper
1 egg
⅓ pound ground lean beef
¼ pound ground lean pork
½ teaspoon salt
  Juice of ½ lemon
2 teaspoons chopped onion
  Pinch of thyme
½ slice bread
1 tablespoon water
2 tablespoons unsaturated oil ☑
3 sprigs fresh coriander (Mexican or Chinese parsley)

In a large soup kettle place the beef broth, tomatoes, chili powder, garlic, cumin, and pepper to taste; simmer for 40 minutes. Beat egg, then mix with the beef, pork, salt, lemon juice, onion, and thyme. Moisten bread with the water, tear into small pieces, and mix lightly with the meat. Shape meat into small balls. Brown meat balls slowly in oil; drain on paper toweling. Drop meat balls into soup and simmer for 20 minutes. Finely chop the coriander and add to the soup the last 5 minutes of cooking. When you serve the soup, be sure each bowl has several meat balls in it. Pass a basket of hot steaming tortillas. Serves 6.

CALORIES per serving: 158

LOW-SODIUM MODIFICATION: In place of meat broth, use low-sodium bouillon ☑. Use salt substitute ☑ in meat balls. Use only 1 teaspoon chili powder, but add a little low-sodium gourmet seasoning ☑ to compensate. Use low-sodium canned tomatoes ☑.

MG. SODIUM per serving: 65

French Onion Soup

2 tablespoons unsaturated margarine ☑
3 tablespoons unsaturated oil ☑
5 large onions, cut in half and thinly sliced
1 tablespoon flour
8 cups beef stock
  Pepper
3 tablespoons grated Parmesan cheese
½ teaspoon oil for each slice bread

Heat unsaturated margarine and oil in a large saucepan and add the onions. Simmer very slowly and allow the onion rings to separate and become golden brown. Sprinkle flour over onions and lightly stir in. Pour about 1 cup of the stock into the mixture and blend with the flour, then pour in the remaining stock. (This stock may be made with beef concentrate or made the long slow way by cooking a mixture of beef and chicken bones. Make this stock the day before, strain, chill, and lift congealed fat from the surface. The concentrates are often heavy on salt.) Bring soup to a boil, then reduce heat and simmer for 20 to 30 minutes. Season with pepper to taste and grated cheese.

If you serve this as a main supper dish, ladle soup into individual oven-proof bowls, top with pieces of dry toasted French bread, sprinkled with oil and a little of the grated cheese. Heat under the broiler until the cheese melts. If you don't want to add extra cheese, try stirring a tablespoon of Cognac or other good brandy into each bowl of hot soup. Serves 8.

CALORIES per serving with toast and cheese: 150

LOW-SODIUM MODIFICATION: Delete salt and be sure beef concentrate is a low-sodium variety ☑; use low-sodium unsaturated margarine ☑ or use all unsaturated oil. Use salt substitute ☑ and go *very* easy on the cheese, as 1 teaspoon Parmesan cheese contains 34 milligrams sodium. Use the brandy instead of extra cheese and use salt-free melba rounds ☑ on top of the soup.

MG. SODIUM per serving: 35

Mama's Chicken Broth with Matzoh Balls

6 tablespoons egg substitute ☑ (equivalent to 2 eggs)
½ teaspoon salt
⅛ teaspoon pepper
½ teaspoon chopped parsley
1 teaspoon finely chopped onion (or ½ teaspoon onion flakes)
1 cup warm water
1 cup matzoh meal
1 tablespoon oil
6 cups chicken broth or consomme

Beat eggs with salt, pepper, and onion. Add water, parsley and oil. Mix in matzoh meal, chill mixture overnight, next day shape chilled dough into balls 1″ in diameter. Place balls in simmering salted water and cook gently for 15 minutes. Lift balls free with a slotted spoon and place two in each bowl of hot chicken broth. Garnish with a sprinkle of parsley, chopped scallions or chives. Serves 4.

CALORIES per serving: 186

LOW SODIUM MODIFICATION: Use unsalted matzoh meal ☑ and low sodium consomme ☑ or bouillon cubes ☑. Delete salt and use salt substitute.

MG. SODIUM per serving if low-sodium bouillon cubes are used: 57

SEAFOOD

These main courses consist of fish and other seafoods. Choose a succulent dish from among the many favorite, and some unusual, choices in the following pages. Captain Nemo's Fish Farm recipes were great 20,000 leagues under the sea, but we have even tastier ones here.

Fish is generally low in fat, and if fresh, not terribly high in salt. Eat fish more than once a week. Discriminate in your choice of seafoods, however, because your diet may need to be low in salt. Some seafoods have high levels of sodium. The Appendix will help you.

Oysters Casino

1½ teaspoons chopped green pepper
1½ teaspoons chopped chives or green onion
1½ teaspoons chopped pimiento
1½ teaspoons chopped parsley
¼   cup unsaturated margarine ☑
4   oysters for each serving

Mix the green pepper, chives, pimiento, and parsley with softened margarine; wrap in waxed paper and chill. Open oysters and cut oyster free from the deepest part of the shell. For each serving arrange 4 oysters on the half shell in shallow individual baking pans filled almost to the top with rock salt or clean crushed rock from a builder's supply. Push shells into the salt so they are level. Place ½ teaspoon of the margarine mixture on each oyster. Cook under the boiler until the margarine mixture bubbles. It is better to undercook than overcook oysters.

Serve the oysters with Chinese (edible pod) peas tossed with water chestnuts, a piece of crusty Italian bread, a glass of cold apple cider, champagne, Rhine wine or Sauterne, and a cup of black coffee—enough!

CALORIES per serving of recipe only: 156

LOW-SODIUM MODIFICATION: Use low-sodium, unsaturated margarine ☑.

MG. SODIUM per serving: 75

Raw Oysters

Open oysters with a sharp knife and cut oyster free from the deepest part of the shell. (Be sure none of the shells are open before you work with them as this indicates that oysters are not fresh.) Arrange oysters on the half shell on a chop plate. Slip some greens under the shells to help keep them level. Grind some fresh black pepper over the oysters. Add a squeeze of lime or lemon juice, and eat. Some like the oysters hot and add a sprinkle of cayenne or Tabasco. You won't taste any oyster this way, however. Cold dark beer and a slice of pumpernickle bread with unsaturated margarine ☑ is great with this.

CALORIES per oyster: 11

LOW-SODIUM MODIFICATION: Avoid salt. Use low-sodium flavoring ☑ and low-sodium chili sauce ☑.

MG. SODIUM per oyster: 12

Shrimp Curry

(Malibu Style)

    3 tablespoons unsaturated margarine ☑
    4 tablespoons unsaturated oil ☑
    3 large onions, chopped
    1 medium sized tart apple, peeled and chopped
    ¼ teaspoon each cinnamon and nutmeg
    2 to 3 slices fresh ginger or a pinch of powdered
        ginger
    ½ cup raisins
      Salt and pepper
    1½ teaspoons curry powder
    1 cup skim milk
      Juice of ½ lemon or lime
    2 pounds medium sized raw shrimp
    1 tablespoon chopped parsley
      Variety of condiments: chopped cucumber,
        chopped green pepper, chutney, peanuts

Heat the unsaturated margarine and 2 tablespoons of the unsaturated oil in a large heavy kettle. Cook the onions and apple slowly until the onions are tender and the apple is soft. Add the cinnamon, nutmeg, ginger, raisins, salt, pepper and curry powder to taste; mix well. Heat the skim milk and pour into the sauce along with the lemon or lime juice.

Shuck the raw shrimp and remove the sand vein. (You can use canned shrimp but they aren't as good; also they contain too much salt.) Quickly sauté the shrimp in the remaining 2 tablespoons of unsaturated oil until they turn pink. Spoon the shrimp into the curry sauce and simmer gently long enough to heat through. Don't cook too long or the shrimp will become dry and tough.

Serve the curry over steamed rice with a sprinkle of chopped parsley. Also arrange a few small dishes with the various chopped condiments to spoon over the curry. Serves 8.

CALORIES per serving including ⅓ cup cooked rice: 302

LOW-SODIUM MODIFICATION: Use low-sodium unsaturated margarine ☑ and low-sodium skim milk ☑; delete salt, and use salt substitute ☑. Use shrimp canned without salt ☑ as they are lower in sodium than the fresh. Omit chutney and use unsalted peanuts.

MG. SODIUM per serving: 34

Maryland Crab Cakes

    3 slices white bread, trimmed of crusts
    ⅓ cup melted unsaturated margarine ☑
    ⅛ teaspoon dry mustard
    ½ teaspoon salt
      Dash of paprika
    ½ teaspoon Worcestershire
    ½ teaspoon chopped parsley
    2 tablespoons skim milk
    1 pound flaked crab meat
    2 egg whites

Lay the bread in a flat pan and pour the melted margarine over the bread; let stand 1 hour. Using 2 forks, pull the bread apart into small pieces; turn into a bowl along with the mustard, salt, paprika, Worcestershire, parsley, skim milk, and crab meat. Mix lightly. Beat egg whites until stiff but not dry; carefully fold into the crab mixture. Drop by spoonfuls onto a hot frying pan or griddle brushed with unsaturated oil, and press down slightly to form patties. Sauté on both sides until lightly browned. Serves 8.

CALORIES per serving: 300

VARIATIONS: A small amount of chopped green pepper and/or parsley may be added; or season the mixture with a small minced green onion. No change in calories. Serve the crab cakes with the following salad: Line a big bowl with chilled romaine or curly endive. Fill the center with finely chopped cabbage tossed with a small apple, peeled and chopped, and a lemon and oil dressing. Sprinkle with mustard seeds or celery seeds. Ripe olives or red pimento strips sharpen the looks.

LOW-SODIUM MODIFICATION: Delete salt; use low-sodium bread ☑, low-sodium skim milk ☑, and low-sodium unsaturated margarine ☑. Substitute 1 cup low-sodium canned tuna ☑ for the crab. Add 2 tablespoons finely diced green pepper. Omit celery seeds in salad. Use ¼ teaspoon in crab cakes instead of Worcestershire sauce.

Be sure to put a few lemon quarters on a plate or in the salad bowl to encourage using the sharp acid taste of lemon as an alternative to salt.

MG. SODIUM per serving: 25

Shrimp or Lobster with Black Bean Sauce

1 pound medium sized raw shrimp or 1 pound lobster tails
1 teaspoon black beans (available in small cans in Oriental markets)
1 clove garlic
2 tablespoons unsaturated oil ☑
⅛ pound ground lean pork
1 teaspoon minced fresh ginger
2 teaspoons soy sauce
2 tablespoons Sherry or saki
1 small can water chestnuts, drained and chopped
1 teaspoon sesame oil
1 cup chicken stock
½ teaspoon monosodium glutamate
1 tablespoon cornstarch
½ cup water
2 green onions, chopped

Shuck shrimp; cut down the rounded back side and lift out the sand vein. If you use lobster tails, use a sharp knife to split in half, then cut in bite-size pieces, cutting through the meat and the shell.

Black beans are very bitter; use only the amount listed. Rinse beans in water; drain. Crush beans with the garlic; put into a hot frying pan with the 2 tablespoons oil and cook for 2 minutes. Add pork, and stirring, cook until browned and crumbly. Put the ginger, soy sauce, Sherry or saki, water chestnuts, and sesame oil into the pan and **sauté** for 1 minute. Add the shrimp or lobster; stir and cook 2 minutes, then add the chicken stock and monosodium glutamate. Cover pan and cook a few minutes until the shrimp become opaque and curl. If you use lobster, cook a littler longer until the shells turn red.

Blend the cornstarch with the cold water. Push the shrimp mixture to one side in the pan; stir the cornstarch and water into the liquid in the pan and cook until the sauce is slightly thickened. Add the green onions. Lift and turn with a large spoon or spatula so the mixture is well blended. Serve with steamed rice cooked according to package directions. Serves 6.

CALORIES per serving (does not include rice): 120

LOW-SODIUM MODIFICATION: Be sure to rinse the black beans well. Delete the soy sauce and monosodium glutamate and use low-sodium flavoring ☑ and low-sodium chicken bouillon ☑. Watch your salt intake for the day if you are on a strict low-sodium diet.

MG. SODIUM per serving: 107

Fish Stock for Bouillabaisse

4 pounds fish trimmings
1 carrot, scrubbed and coarsely chopped
1 onion, quartered
3 cloves garlic
Few celery leaves
2 to 3 sprigs parsley
1 bay leaf
⅛ teaspoon freshly ground pepper
Few fennel seeds or 2 branches fennel or a pinch of thyme
4 quarts water

To make a good *bouillabaisse* you need fish stock which is easy and inexpensive to make. For the fish trimmings you can use heads, tails, and bones left from making fillets; avoid entrails. Also avoid oily fish such as salmon or mackeral. Place the trimmings in a large kettle with the carrot, onion, garlic, celery leaves, parsley, bay leaf, pepper, fennel or thyme, and cold water. Bring to a boil, then reduce heat and simmer for 30 minutes. Strain and *voila!*—the stock is ready. You may cool and freeze the stock for later use or use immediately.

Bouillabaisse

(Fish Stew)

This may be modified slightly to make a variety of fish stews found in the Mediterranean area, such as the excellent Italian *cioppino*.

2 stalks celery, sliced
1 onion, chopped
2 leeks, chopped (use white part only)
2 large cloves garlic, mashed or minced
1 small bunch fennel, chopped, or ¼ teaspoon fennel seeds

6 tablespoons unsaturated oil ☑
1 cup dry white table wine
1 can (1 lb.) solid pack tomatoes
4 quarts fish stock (see recipe above) or chicken stock
  Pinch of saffron
  Salt and pepper
4 pounds fish steaks or fillets (bass, snapper, bluefish, or cod)
16 raw shrimp
8 clams in the shell (optional)

In a large kettle **sauté** the celery, onion, leeks, garlic, and fennel in 2 tablespoons of the unsaturated oil. Cook until the vegetables are limp; pour in the wine. Contrary to information bandied about, you don't need expensive wine for this, but it should be drinkable. Cook until the wine is reduced one half. Strain the tomatoes; reserve tomatoes and pour juice into the kettle along with the fish stock. Cover and simmer for 30 minutes or until vegetables are tender. Add a few pinches of saffron until it tastes interesting to you—too much and you'll have saffron soup. Check the other seasonings, adding a little salt and pepper if necessary. Coarsely chop the reserved tomatoes and add.

This is excellent if you use a variety of fish. A large sea eel is good too, but these are generally not available unless you catch them yourself. Cut the fish into 3-inch pieces. Peel the shrimp and remove the sand vein. **Sauté** the fish and shrimp in the remaining 4 tablespoons of oil for a few minutes; drain oil, then add to the stew. If you use clams, scrub them first and add to stew. Simmer for 10 minutes or until the fish flakes with a fork and the clam shells open.

Ladle into heated soup plates and be sure there are two shrimp and a clam in each plate along with the soup. Round out the menu with a green salad and Italian bread, followed by a crisp, cold apple and black coffee. You can't beat this for a satisfying meal. Serves 8.

CALORIES per serving: 345

LOW-SODIUM MODIFICATION: Delete salt and add 1 tablespoon lemon juice; omit celery. Use low-sodium canned tomatoes ☑. Even with the changes this recipe is quite high in sodium. Make this the main dish of the day.

MG. SODIUM per serving: 223

Gefilte Fish

3½ pounds carp
1 pound lean cod
1½ pounds pike or sucker
½ pound sole fillets
3 onions
2 eggs
15 drops liquid sugar substitute ☑
½ teaspoon onion powder
  Pinch of garlic powder and pepper
½ teaspoon salt
½ cup water
2 carrots, chopped
3 cups water

Remove bones and skin from fish. Using the medium blade of a food chopper or a hand chopper, chop the carp, cod, pike, and sole and 1 of the onions. Combine the eggs, sugar substitute, onion powder, garlic powder, pepper, salt, and ½ cup water; mix with the ground fish and onion. Blend mixture thoroughly, then shape into hamburger-like patties.

Chop the remaining 2 onions and place in a large kettle with the carrots and the 3 cups of water; bring to a boil. Gently place the fish patties in the water and simmer for 2½ to 3 hours. Remove from liquid and garnish with a slice of carrot and a sprig of parsley. Makes 18 large patties.

CALORIES per pattie: 162

LOW-SODIUM MODIFICATION: Do not use frozen fish fillets. Be sure to use pure onion and garlic powder, not salt! Better yet, use a little onion and a chopped sliver of fresh garlic and skip the powder. Use low-sodium seasoning ☑ in place of salt.

MG. SODIUM per pattie: 84

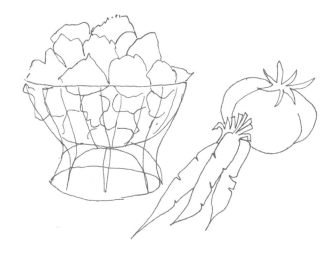

Broiled Fish

Swordfish, snapper, pike, trout or sole
Salt and pepper
Juice of ½ lemon
¼ onion, thinly sliced
2 tablespoons unsaturated margarine ☑
½ cup dry white table wine

Swordfish is usually cut in the form of a steak and snapper as fillets. Pike or trout should be split lengthwise. You'll probably have to catch the pike yourself, unless you live in a region where it is found in the market.

Place the fish skin side down (if it has skin) in an oiled baking pan. Season with salt and pepper to taste and sprinkle with the lemon juice. Arrange thin slices of onion over the fish and dot with unsaturated margarine. Place under the broiler for 2 minutes, then pour the wine (Chablis is excellent) over the dish. Basting occasionally, continue cooking until the fish flakes with a fork. Serve with a few very small boiled new potatoes sprinkled with paprika or finely chopped parsley. A generous helping of tender simmered fresh green beans or asparagus makes this a memorable meal.

If you wish to broil the fish without wine, place it on a rack, then set the rack in a pan lined with aluminum foil. With this method you need to turn the fish when the top is nicely browned; remember the second side needs much less time to cook than the first.

CALORIES per 5 ounce serving of recipe only: 227

LOW-SODIUM MODIFICATION: Use low-sodium, unsaturated margarine ☑ and more lemon juice; use salt substitute ☑. Do not use frozen fish, unless it is a frozen fresh water fish like trout.

MG. SODIUM per 5 ounce serving: 105

Barbecued Fish

1½ pounds red snapper, bass, or cod fillets or halibut steaks
3 tablespoons unsaturated oil ☑
1 teaspoon Worcestershire
¼ cup water
¼ cup catsup
1 onion, sliced
½ teaspoon salt
⅛ teaspoon pepper
1 teaspoon dry mustard
1 teaspoon lemon juice

Arrange the fish on a piece of heavy aluminum foil; trim the outer edges of foil around fish. The foil keeps the fish from sticking to the broiler pan or barbecue grill. Mix the remaining ingredients together and simmer for 5 minutes. Broil or barbecue the fish until it flakes with a fork; baste often with the barbecue sauce. Serves 6.

CALORIES per serving: 200

VARIATIONS: Try this variation if you are using a whole fish. Use a 3 pound fish or two 1½ pound fish for 6 persons. Squeeze some lemon or lime juice in the body cavity of the fish, then fill with ½ cup unsalted cashews or peanuts. Fasten the fish together with a few toothpicks. Broil or barbecue and baste with barbecue sauce. When you cook the fish, turn very carefully with two spatulas or a couple of forks. There are 350 calories and 82 milligrams sodium per serving of this fish.

Serve fish with a large mixed green salad.

Add variety to the usual greens by including dandelion, parsley, and watercress and a thinly sliced purple onion; dress with an oil and vinegar or lemon juice dressing. Toss in a few sections of grapefruit or orange for color. Serve with a glass of cold Chablis, Riesling, or Sauterne.

LOW-SODIUM MODIFICATION: Remember to use fresh fish as the frozen fish contains many extra milligrams of sodium. Delete salt in the barbecue sauce; add a dash of cayenne or a little extra lemon juice. Omit catsup and use a fresh tomato which has been chopped. Omit Worcestershire and use Tabasco ☑.

MG. SODIUM per serving: 80

Fish or Shrimp Kebabs

2 pounds firm fish fillets or steaks (cod, haddock, swordfish, halibut) or prawns
½ cup unsaturated oil ☑
½ cup lemon juice
¼ teaspoon powdered bay leaf
1 tablespoon soy sauce
12 small onions, parboiled
1 medium sized green pepper, cut in 12 pieces
Paprika

Cut fish in 1-inch cubes. If you use prawns, peel the shells and remove the sand veins. Place fish in a bowl with the unsaturated oil, lemon juice, bay leaf, and soy sauce. Stir until fish is coated with marinade. Let stand 30 minutes. Thread fish on 6 skewers, alternating with onions and green pepper. Sprinkle with paprika. Broil or barbecue the kebabs for about 10 minutes or until the fish is tender; brush frequently with the marinade and turn often. Serves 6.

Serve kebabs with rice pilaff studded with raisins and simmered green beans seasoned with a little unsaturated margarine ☑ and caraway seeds. Follow this with a slice of cold watermelon, a ripe fresh peach, or a cool crisp apple, a piece of crystallized ginger, and hot tea. Tea flavored with orange peel and spice really perks up a meal!

CALORIES per serving: 230

LOW-SODIUM MODIFICATION: Use low-sodium flavoring ☑ in place of soy sauce, serve lots of lemon or lime wedges with the fish.

MG. SODIUM per serving: 105

Fish Duglére

(Poached Fish with Tomato)

1 tablespoon unsaturated oil ☑
1 clove garlic, peeled
1 small onion, finely chopped
1 pound fish (fillet or steak of halibut, bass, cod, flounder, haddock, perch, pike, or sole)
½ teaspoon salt
⅛ teaspoon pepper
½ cup drained canned tomatoes
1 tablespoon chopped parsley
¼ cup dry white table wine
½ teaspoon lemon juice

Pour oil in a large 10-inch skillet. Thread garlic on a toothpick and place in the skillet along with the onion. Season the fish with salt and pepper and arrange over the onion. Coarsely chop the tomatoes and arrange over fish, then sprinkle with the parsley. Mix the wine and lemon juice and pour around the fish.

Cut a circle of waxed paper, greased brown paper, or aluminum foil to fit the top of the skillet; punch a small hole in the center to let out steam. Place the paper lid over the fish. Bring mixture to a boil, then continue

cooking about 10 minutes or until the fish flakes with a fork. Remove fish with a broad spatula to a heated platter. Take out the garlic and discard.

Boil down remaining sauce to 1 cup; check seasoning. Spoon sauce over the poached fish. Serves 3.

CALORIES per serving: 174

VARIATIONS: Boil down sauce to 1 cup as above. Mix in ½ cup imitation sour cream and 1 tablespoon paprika. Spoon over fish. This will add about 67 calories to each serving.

LOW-SODIUM MODIFICATION: Use only fresh fish; use salt substitute ☑ or low-sodium flavoring ☑. Use low-sodium unsaturated margarine ☑. Also, try a different fish each time. Use low-sodium canned tomatoes ☑. Do not use the variation.

MG. SODIUM per serving: 105

Fish Bonne Femme

(Fish With Mushrooms)

Prepare the recipe above for Fish Dugléré or the low-sodium modification but substitute ½ pound sliced fresh mushrooms for the tomatoes. Increase wine to ½ cup and lemon juice to 1 teaspoon. Place half of the mushrooms over the onion and the remaining half over the fish. No change in calories or sodium.

Fish Veronique

(Fish With Grapes)

Prepare Fish Dugléré or the low-sodium modification but omit the tomatoes and parsley. Increase the wine to ½ cup and lemon juice to 1 teaspoon. Add 1 cup of seedless grapes to the final sauce and heat through. Spoon sauce over fish, then place under the broiler to brown slightly. No change in calories or sodium.

Sweet and Sour Shrimp

One delight of this dish is the short preparation time required. While the rice is cooking, you can prepare the sweet and sour shrimp.

- ⅔ cup sugar
  Sugar substitute ☑ equal to ½ cup sugar
- 1 teaspoon salt
- ½ cup Madeira or Sherry
- ⅓ cup water
- 1½ tablespoons cornstarch mixed with ¼ cup cold water
- 1 pound raw shelled shrimp
- 2 tablespoons unsaturated oil ☑
- 1 sweet red pepper, cut in 1-inch squares
- 1 green pepper, cut in 1-inch squares
- 2 carrots, cut in thin diagonal slices
- 1 small can artificially sweetened pineapple chunks ☑, drained
- 2 cups hot steamed rice

To make the sweet and sour sauce, place the vinegar in a saucepan along with the sugar, sugar substitute, salt, wine, and water; heat. Slowly stir in the blended cornstarch and water. Continue stirring and cook until the sauce is clear and slightly thickened; remove pan from heat.

Clean the shrimp and remove sand vein. Sauté the shrimp in the unsaturated oil until they become opaque and turn pink. Add the shrimp to the sweet and sour sauce along with the red pepper, green pepper, and carrots. Cook gently for 5 minutes; add the pineapple and continue cooking for 2 minutes. Serve at once over hot steamed rice. Serves 4.

CALORIES per serving including rice: 250

VARIATIONS: Take a whole cleaned 2-pound fish and brush with unsaturated oil ☑. Sprinkle with white flour or water chestnut flour and slowly brown under the broiler or on a grill over low coals. When fish is browned, wrap in aluminum foil; finish cooking in a moderately hot oven (350°) for about 15 to 20 minutes. Carefully open the foil, slide the fish on oven-proof platter, and keep warm. Slice 2 carrots, 1 green pepper, 1 sweet red pepper, and 1 cup canned bamboo shoots in very thin slivers, along with a few thin slices of fresh or candied ginger. Mix with the sweet and sour sauce and simmer a few minutes, then pour over the whole fish. Sprinkle with sliced green onions. Serve with

steamed rice to 3 persons. There are 233 calories per serving.

LOW-SODIUM MODIFICATION: Try this recipe using chicken instead of shrimp to lower your sodium intake. Use salt substitute.

MG. SODIUM per serving: 86

Coquilles Saint Jacques

(Scallops in Shell with Cream Sauce)

- 1 pound scallops
- 6 medium sized mushrooms, sliced
- 2 teaspoons unsaturated margarine ☑
  Juice of ½ lemon
  Dash of salt
- 3 tablespoons chopped parsley
- 2 tablespoons chopped shallots or green onion
  Juice of 1½ lemons
- 1½ cups dry white table wine
- ½ cup fish stock or water
- 1 cup skim milk
- 1 tablespoon flour
- 1 tablespoon unsaturated margarine ☑
  White pepper
- 1 teaspoon grated Parmesan cheese

Wash scallops; cut crosswise in flat slices ⅛ to ¼ inch thick. Place the mushrooms in a large skillet with the 2 teaspoons margarine, juice of ½ lemon, and salt; cover the skillet and cook for 4 minutes. Add the scallops, parsley, shallots, juice of 1½ lemons, wine (Chablis, Rhine, Riesling, or Mountain White), and fish stock or water. Simmer uncovered for 5 minutes or until the scallops are tender. Turn the mixture into a sieve or colander and save the juices. Return the liquid to the skillet and reduce to one-third of its original volume. Pour in the milk.

Work the flour into the 1 tablespoon unsaturated margarine. The flour mixture is called *beurre manié* although in this instance the *beurre* is not quite correct since it is margarine. At any rate, add it to the hot milk mixture and stir quickly with a wire whisk or slotted spoon until the sauce is thick and smooth. Add pepper and salt, if necessary. Return the scallops and mushrooms to the sauce and mix lightly. Spoon into 4 scallop shells or individual shallow oven-proof dishes. Dust with grated cheese. Heat under the broiler until the sauce bubbles. Serves 4.

Serve with a chilled glass of Rhine wine or Chablis and a cold artichoke or chilled poached asparagus dressed with an oil and vinegar dressing or a low-calorie dressing. Serve lime sherbet with black coffee for dessert.

CALORIES per serving: 260

LOW-SODIUM MODIFICATION: Scallops are much too high in sodium; use a pound of poached and flaked white fish. Use low-sodium skim milk ☑, low-sodium unsaturated margarine ☑, and a salt substitute ☑.

MG. SODIUM per serving: 60

Tuna Casserole with Toasted Almond Sauce

    2 packages (10 oz. each) frozen asparagus
    2 cans (7 oz. each) tuna
    ½ cup sliced almonds
    ¼ cup unsaturated oil ☑
    ¼ cup flour
    ½ teaspoon salt
       Dash pepper
    2 cups skim milk
       Paprika

Cook asparagus according to package directions; drain and arrange in an oiled baking dish. Drain tuna, then arrange over the asparagus. Sauté the almonds in the unsaturated oil until lightly browned. Blend in the flour, salt, and pepper. Add the milk gradually, and stirring, cook until smooth and thick. Pour sauce over tuna; dust with paprika. Bake in a moderate oven (350°) for 30 minutes or until hot and bubbling. Serves 6.

CALORIES per serving: 348

VARIATIONS: For even fewer calories, use tuna packed in water; this will cut out about 35 calories per serving. If you are on a sodium restricted diet, be careful that the tuna is not packed in a salt brine. Use fresh asparagus when it is in season—it's better! Cook the fresh spears until just barely tender. You can vary the sauce by adding a little lemon juice and grated onion. You might also want to substitute crab meat for the tuna. Crab adds sodium however, so keep it in mind. There will be little change in calories.

LOW-SODIUM MODIFICATION: Omit the crab meat. Use salt substitute ☑, salt free tuna ☑, and low-sodium skim milk ☑.

MG. SODIUM per serving: 66

Poached Fish

    ½ pound fish for each serving (halibut, cod, or haddock)
       Water
    1 carrot, chopped
    1 onion, chopped
    2 sprigs parsley
    1 whole clove
    2 tablespoons white vinegar
       Pinch each of tarragon and thyme
    1 bay leaf
       Paprika
       Sliced lemon and parsley for garnish

Wrap each serving of fish in a small piece of cheesecloth. Lower fish into a pan of simmering water that contains the carrot, onion, parsley, clove, vinegar, tarragon, thyme, and bay leaf. Simmer gently for 10 minutes. Lift each piece out and drain; unwrap and carefully lift the fish with a spatula to a hot serving plate. Sprinkle with paprika and garnish with lemon and parsley. You can also serve this with a tartar or mustard sauce.

CALORIES per serving: 210

VARIATIONS: For a piquant flavor, substitute 1 cup of the simmering water with 1 cup of dry white table wine. Here is a nice sauce to serve over the fish: Melt 1 tablespoon unsaturated margarine and blend in 1 tablespoon flour; cook until flour is slightly browned. Add ½ cup of the stock in which you cooked the fish, and stirring, cook until smooth and thick. Stir in a little lemon juice and chopped parsley before spooning over the fish. Or try varying the seasoning in the sauce—curry powder, cayenne, or chopped chives or onion all add a great deal to such fish. Two tablespoons of the sauce will add 40 calories and 1 milligram sodium.

LOW-SODIUM MODIFICATION: Follow basic recipe.

MG. SODIUM per serving: 125

Fish in Aspic

You can make a spectacular dish with a large piece of fresh salmon. Cook the fish according to the recipe for poached fish given above; cook for 20 to 30 minutes or until the fish flakes with a fork. Drain and unwrap the salmon, lift to a serving platter, and carefully peel off the skin on the top; chill fish. Prepare a wine-flavored gelatin by softening 1 envelope (1 tablespoon) unflavored gelatin in ½ cup water; add to 1 cup hot fish stock and stir until gelatin dissolves. Stir in ½ cup dry white table wine and the juice of ½ lemon. Chill until the mixture is syrupy. Spoon a thin layer of aspic over the fish; put the fish back in the refrigerator until the aspic sets. Pour another coating of aspic carefully over the fish and return to refrigerator. Repeat a third time until the salmon is coated with clear aspic. Garnish with parsley. Serve with lots of lemon wedges.

CALORIES per 3 ounces of Chinook salmon: 190

CALORIES per 3 ounces of pink salmon: 105

LOW-SODIUM MODIFICATION: This variation should not be used with salmon. Substitute with striped bass.

MG. SODIUM per 3 ounces of bass: 65

Shrimp Remoulade

¼ cup unsaturated oil ☑
2 tablespoons wine vinegar
1 teaspoon paprika
½ teaspoon salt
Dash of Tabasco
1 tablespoon prepared horseradish
2 tablespoons prepared mustard
2 tablespoons chopped green onion
¼ cup finely chopped celery
½ pound cooked shrimp

Place the oil, vinegar, paprika, salt, Tabasco, horseradish, mustard, green onion, and celery in a bowl and stir well. Add the shrimp; toss lightly. Chill for at least 30 minutes. Serve in small lettuce cups. Serves 4 as an appetizer. The sauce is also good over sautéed fish and cold cooked lobster.

CALORIES per serving: 220

VARIATIONS: The following recipe for Remoulade Sauce is good too, but it is not for low-sodium diets! Mix together ¾ cup unsaturated mayonnaise ☑, 1 teaspoon Dijon mustard, and 1 tablespoon each chopped pickle, chopped anchovy, capers, chopped parsley, and chopped fresh tarragon. There are 276 calories per serving.

LOW-SODIUM MODIFICATION: Omit Tabasco and salt. Use cayenne and salt substitute ☑ or low-sodium flavoring ☑. Use a small amount of dry mustard in place of prepared mustard. Delete celery. Use horseradish which is not packed in salt.

MG. SODIUM per serving: 80

Fish En Papillote

For each serving of fish, have a piece of aluminum foil 12 inches by 8 inches; rub a thin film of unsaturated oil in the center of each piece. On the oiled surface lay a small cleaned fish such as trout or a fillet or slice of butterfish, red snapper, or sea bass; use ¼ pound fish per serving. Sprinkle over each piece 2 slivers of garlic, salt and monosodium glutamate to taste, a dash each of paprika and pepper, 1 celery leaf, 1 chopped mushroom, a little chopped parsley, and the juice of ½ lemon. Bring two opposite edges of foil together and fold in a drug store wrap; fold in both ends. Place all the foil packets on a baking sheet; bake in a hot oven (400°) for 15 minutes. Open one packet to see if the fish is done; it should flake easily with a fork.

Serve an envelope on each plate along with small potatoes boiled with jackets on, or, if you wish, peel the potatoes and sprinkle with chopped parsley. For a splash of color serve sliced tomatoes or this version: Cut the tops off medium sized tomatoes. Sprinkle with a little unsaturated oil, lemon juice, and chopped fresh basil or oregano. Broil until the tomatoes are heated through. Serve with a cold, sharp glass of white Rhine wine.

CALORIES per serving of fish: 200

LOW-SODIUM MODIFICATION: You know by now to delete salt and monosodium glutamate and use a salt substitute ☑; do not use frozen fish. Try one of your favorite herbs in place of the celery leaf.

MG. SODIUM per serving: 78

Skewered Scallops

16 scallops
½ cup unsaturated oil ☑
½ cup Sherry or saki
½ teaspoon grated fresh ginger
 1 clove garlic, mashed or minced
 2 tablespoon soy sauce
 4 dried Chinese black mushrooms

Wash scallops; pat dry with paper towels. Place scallops in a marinade of the oil, Sherry, ginger, garlic, and soy sauce. Let stand 2 hours; turn scallops several times while they marinate. Soak mushrooms in warm water to cover for 30 minutes; cut softened mushrooms in quarters. Thread scallops and mushrooms on small bamboo skewers, using 4 scallops and 1 mushroom for each serving. Cook under the broiler or roast over low coals until tender, about 5 to 8 minutes. Brush with marinade during cooking and turn skewers several times. Serve with rice pilaff, steamed rice, or Chinese fried rice and a sharply dressed romaine salad. Serves 4.

CALORIES per serving of recipe only: 155

LOW-SODIUM MODIFICATION: Sorry, not for you.

POULTRY

In some countries like Israel where beef is a luxury (there is not enough room to graze the cows), chicken coops are cheaper—and there is a chicken in every pot.

To keep its citizens from going "stir" crazy, chicken has been fixed in a hundred different ways in Israel, sometimes even made to resemble veal. Those breaded veal cutlets may be pressed chicken breast or turkey breaded and fried accordingly.

Here, we don't attempt to disguise chicken, instead, we enhance its flavor with delicate sauces. Since it is relatively low in fat, it lends itself well to these diets.

Skin the Bird

To reduce both saturated fat and sodium, we recommend skinning all poultry whether you are using parts or cooking the whole bird. If you plan to roast chicken, game hens, or turkey, you can ask your meat man to skin the poultry. However, it is a simple operation to do yourself. Turn the bird breast side down. Cut a slit up the back, cutting only through the skin. Pull skin away from the slit scraping your knife against it to release it from the meat. Continue pulling and scraping and bring the skin around to the breast side. Cut skin around base of the wings. You don't need to skin these, but cut off the wing tips. Release skin from the breast, then pull it back on itself and off the legs. Trim any fat which is around the openings of the bird. Follow the recipes for specific cooking directions.

Chicken Sauté and its Variations

If the limits of your fat intake are not too stringent, sautéed chicken may be your treat, but deep fried chicken is out! If you buy a whole chicken, use the breast thighs, and legs. Save the other parts for simmering with some bits of onion, celery, carrot, and the white part of a leek to make chicken stock for soup or for cooking rice.

An easier way to start nowadays is to buy the meaty parts instead of the whole chicken and season with a little salt and pepper. Pour ¼ cup unsaturated oil ☑ in a heavy skillet, and when hot and active, put in the pieces of chicken. Brown the bird quickly on both sides, but don't have the pan so hot that any burning occurs. You ought to do this in about 10 minutes. That's all there is to it, basically, but you'll want to vary the dish with seasonings, vegetables, fruits, sauces, wine, and other flavorings.

After these additions, cover the pan and continue cooking the chicken slowly for about 30 to 40 minutes. Pierce the chicken with a fork; any juice coming out should be clear, not pink. If you're cooking breasts and thighs, the breasts will be done first, so remove them and keep hot while the other parts finish. Revise your sauce and put it all together again to heat.

CALORIES per ¼ sautéed chicken: 230

MG. SODIUM per ¼ sautéed chicken seasoned with a salt substitute ☑: 80

Chicken with Mushrooms

    2 pounds chicken parts (breasts, thighs, and legs)
      Salt and pepper
    4 tablespoons unsaturated oil ☑
    8 medium sized mushrooms, sliced
    2 to 3 shallots, chopped, or 1 medium sized onion,
      chopped
    1 clove garlic, mashed or minced
    1 tablespoon chopped parsley
    1 tomato
    2 teaspoons lemon juice
    ½ cup dry white table wine

Skin chicken; season lightly with salt and pepper. Brown chicken in the hot oil. Sprinkle the mushrooms, shallots or onion, garlic, and parsley over the chicken. Peel the tomato, squeeze out the seeds, and chop the pulp; add to chicken along with the lemon juice. Simmer for 5 minutes. Pour in the wine, cover and simmer until chicken is tender (see basic recipe). Correct the seasoning; leave the lid off the last few minutes of cooking.

Serve two pieces of chicken to each person with steamed rice sprinkled with pine nuts or a few plump white raisins, and a glass of your favorite wine. Serves 4.

CALORIES per serving of recipe only: 290

LOW-SODIUM MODIFICATION: Use salt substitute ☑. Serve rice without salt—that's the way it is eaten in the Orient.

MG. SODIUM per serving: 90

Chicken Breasts with Apricots

    2 large whole chicken breasts, cut in half
      Salt and pepper to taste
    2 tablespoons unsaturated oil ☑
    1 can (1 lb.) artificially sweetened apricots ☑,
      drained
    ¼ cup brandy
    ½ cup chicken stock or bouillon

Skin chicken; season with salt and pepper. Brown chicken in oil, then reduce heat and cook slowly until tender. Remember that the white meat does not take too long to cook. Remove chicken from pan and keep warm.

Heat apricots in the pan in which you cooked the chicken. Pour brandy over apricots; heat long enough to warm (do not allow to boil), then set aflame. Stir and lift the juices over the apricots. When the brandy stops burning, add the cooked chicken and chicken stock. Simmer gently until the sauce is slightly thickened; spoon over the chicken to form a glaze. If sauce is too thin, add ½ teaspoon cornstarch in cooled juice, heat, and stir until thick. Even better is the use of canned apricot puree along with the chicken stock. Serve chicken and apricots with a crisp green salad tossed with a sharp dressing, toasted English muffins, and black coffee. Serves 4.

CALORIES per serving of recipe only: 250

LOW-SODIUM MODIFICATION: Delete salt and use a salt substitute ☑. Use low-sodium bouillon ☑. Increase lemon juice in salad.

MG. SODIUM per serving: 80

Baked Chicken

    6 meaty pieces of chicken (breasts, thighs, or
      legs)
    ½ cup Sauterne
    ½ cup bouillon or water
    2 teaspoons unsaturated margarine ☑
    2 tablespoons dehydrated onion flakes
    ¼ teaspoon monosodium glutamate
    ½ teaspoon paprika and salt to taste

Skin chicken and place in a baking pan. Pour the Sauterne and bouillon or water over chicken. Dot with margarine; sprinkle on the onion flakes along with paprika, salt, and monosodium glutamate to taste. Bake in a moderate oven (350°) for 1 hour or until tender. Turn chicken several times during baking. Serves 4.

CALORIES per serving: 200

VARIATIONS: Make a paste by chopping 1 teaspoon each of sage, garlic, parsley and rosemary and rub over chicken before cooking.

LOW-SODIUM MODIFICATION: Omit salt and monosodium glutamate; use salt substitute ☑ and low-sodium unsaturated margarine ☑. Use low-sodium bouillon ☑

MG. SODIUM per serving: 60

Chicken Piquant

2 pounds chicken parts (breasts, thighs, and legs)
1 clove garlic, mashed or minced
  Paprika, salt, and pepper to taste
¼ cup dry white table wine
2 tablespoons soy sauce
2 tablespoons unsaturated oil ☑
1 teaspoon powdered ginger
1 tablespoon brown sugar
2 dashes Angostura Bitters
1 medium sized onion, finely chopped

Skin chicken; season with garlic, paprika, salt, and pepper. Place chicken in a baking pan and let stand for 2 hours for the seasoning to be absorbed. Mix together the wine, soy sauce, oil, ginger, brown sugar, and Angostura Bitters; pour over chicken. Scatter onion over the chicken. Bake in a moderate oven (350°) for 1 hour or until chicken is tender. Baste and turn pieces several times during cooking. Serves 4.

CALORIES per serving: 250

LOW-SODIUM MODIFICATION: Omit salt and soy sauce; use salt substitute ☑ or low-sodium flavoring ☑.

MG. SODIUM per serving: 83

Chicken with Walnuts

1 large whole chicken breast
2 tablespoons unsaturated oil ☑
¼ pound mushrooms, sliced
¼ pound Chinese (edible pod) peas
1 small can bamboo shoots, cut in slivers 1 inch long
1 small can water chestnuts, thinly sliced crosswise
1 cup chicken stock
½ teaspoon monosodium glutamate
1½ tablespoon cornstarch mixed with ¼ cup cold water
¼ cup walnut halves

Skin chicken and remove meat from the bones; cut into bite-size pieces. Heat oil in a large frying pan. Quickly sauté chicken until it becomes white and opaque; do not brown. Remove chicken from pan and keep warm. Add the mushrooms to the remaining oil in the pan and sauté for 2 minutes. Put in the Chinese peas along with the bamboo shoots, water chestnuts, and sautéed chicken. Stir and fry for 2 minutes over high heat. Add chicken stock and monosodium glutamate; cover pan and steam for 2 minutes. Remove cover, pour in blended cornstarch and water, and stir and cook for 2 minutes to thicken sauce. Stir in walnut halves. Spoon over steamed rice. Serves 4.

CALORIES per serving: 220

LOW-SODIUM MODIFICATION: Delete monosodium glutamate; use salt substitute ☑ and low-sodium chicken bouillon cubes ☑. Be sure bamboo shoots and water chestnuts are packed without salt.

MG. SODIUM per serving: 50

Chicken Cumberland

3 small broiling chickens
  Salt, pepper, and monosodium glutamate
3 tablespoons lime juice
¼ cup unsaturated oil ☑
1 can (6 oz.) frozen orange juice concentrate
1 teaspoon dry mustard
⅛ teaspoon powdered ginger
¼ teaspoon Tabasco
¼ cup dry Sherry
1 cup red current jelly

Split chickens in half and skin; season with salt, pepper, and monosodium glutamate to taste. Broil chicken for 45 minutes, turning once during cooking. Mix the lime juice and oil and use this to baste chicken frequently. In a separate pan mix together the orange juice concentrate, mustard, ginger, Tabasco, Sherry and current jelly. Heat slowly until the sauce is smooth and hot. Pass the sauce so each person can spoon it over his chicken. Serves 6.

CALORIES per serving: 600

LOW-SODIUM MODIFICATION: Delete monosodium glutamate and salt; use salt substitute ☑.

MG. SODIUM per serving: 125

Chicken A La Diablo

2 broiling chickens
½ cup unsaturated oil ☑
   Oregano, salt, and pepper
12 small white onions, peeled
1½ tablespoons capers
½ cup Sauterne
½ cup pitted ripe olives

Split chickens in half and skin. Rub chickens with oil and season to taste with oregano, salt, and pepper. Arrange chicken in a baking pan; scatter the onions and capers over chicken. Bake in a moderate (350°) for 15 minutes or until chicken is brown. Pour the wine over the chicken and continue baking for 45 minutes. Baste chicken several times. Add the olives the last 10 minutes of baking. Serve with rice mixed with green peas and a salad of watercress and thinly sliced raw mushrooms tossed with oil and vinegar or lemon juice dressing. Serves 4.

CALORIES per serving: 630

LOW-SODIUM MODIFICATION: Use salt substitute ☑ or low-sodium flavoring ☑. Omit capers and olives; substitute with sliced shallots, 6 sliced mushrooms, and chopped green pepper. Add the vegetables 30 minutes before chicken has finished cooking.

MG. SODIUM per serving: 180

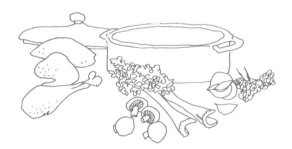

Coq Au Vin

1 (3 pound) stewing chicken
2 stalks celery, chopped
2 carrots, chopped
¼ cup chopped parsley
2 bay leaves
1 teaspoon ginger
1 teaspoon paprika
   Salt and pepper to taste
   Water
1 sweet red pepper, seeded and chopped
1 cup mushrooms, sliced
2 teaspoons unsaturated oil ☑
1 cup chicken stock or bouillon
2 cups dry white table wine
   Bouquet Garni (see below)
20 to 30 small white onions

Cut chicken in serving size pieces and skin. Place chicken in a large heavy kettle with the celery, carrots, parsley, bay leaves, ginger, paprika, salt, pepper, and enough water to cover. Simmer for 30 minutes. Sauté the red pepper and mushrooms in the oil. Drain the liquid from the chicken. (You can chill it, remove the layer of fat, and save to use for another purpose.) Add the sautéed vegetables to the chicken along with the chicken stock or bouillon, wine, and *bouquet garni* (2 sprigs of parsley, 1 bay leaf, a few celery leaves, a sprig of thyme, and a sprig of fresh rosemary or the dried herbs tied in a cheesecloth bag). Peel onions and put in with the chicken. The onions are not only good, but they may prevent you from using too much bread to soak up the delicious gravy. Cover kettle and simmer for 45 minutes. Remove *bouquet garni*. If you wish to thicken the gravy, add a little cornstarch blended with cold water. You may prepare this dish in advance as the flavor improves on standing. It freezes well too. Serves 6.

CALORIES per serving: 390

VARIATIONS: Many recipes for Coq au Vin use Burgundy instead of the white wine. This makes the gravy a deeper red-brown, and to many, it is more appetizing. A nice touch is to add 2 tablespoons of Cognac or other good brandy after you drain the chicken. Then burn the alcohol away. It will greatly enhance the taste. This adds 9 calories per serving of chicken.

LOW-SODIUM MODIFICATION: Delete salt; use salt substitute ☑. Use low-sodium chicken bouillon cubes ☑ and omit the celery.

MG. SODIUM per serving: 130

Chicken Breasts Farcies

1 cup uncooked rice
1 package onion soup mix
1 tablespoon unsaturated margarine ☑
1 teaspoon parsley
2 cups water
4 chicken breasts (2 whole breasts)
½ cup orange juice
½ cup chicken consommé, stock, or bouillon

Steam rice (wild rice if you have the wherewithal) with the onion soup mix, margarine, parsley, and water for 20 minutes or until rice is tender and all of liquid is absorbed. Skin chicken breasts and remove the meat from the bone in one piece so you have fillets. Place the fillets between sheets of waxed paper and pound with the flat side of a cleaver or mallet. Place 1 tablespoon of rice on each fillet. Roll up fillets around the rice, tucking in the ends, to form a roll; tie with string. Place chicken in a shallow baking pan. Mix the orange juice and chicken consommé and pour over the chicken. Bake in a moderately slow oven (325°) for 45 minutes, basting frequently. Remove the strings and continue baking 15 minutes. Reheat the remaining rice and serve with the chicken along with a cold boiled artichoke garnished with lemon or cold marinated green beans sprinkled with toasted sesame seeds. Serves 4.

CALORIES per chicken roll: 210

VARIATIONS: Prepare rice and use it to stuff small game hens. Skin game hens first, then stuff. Rub a little unsaturated oil over each bird and sprinkle with paprika. Place birds, breast side up, on a rack in a roasting pan. Cover with aluminum foil. Bake in a very hot oven (450°) for 10 minutes, then reduce heat to 350° and continue cooking for 45 minutes. Remove foil the last 15 minutes of cooking. Flame hens with 2 tablespoons of good brandy. There are 400 calories for each 12 ounce game hen with stuffing and 158 milligrams sodium.

LOW-SODIUM MODIFICATION: Check the onion soup mix as most contain much salt; get a low-sodium variety or cook rice with low-sodium chicken consommé ☑ and some minced onion. Do not add salt to the water when cooking rice. Use low-sodium unsaturated margarine ☑.

MG. SODIUM per chicken roll: 74

Pineapple Chicken

2 chicken breasts (1 whole breast)
¼ cup cornstarch
2 tablespoons peanut oil
1 green pepper, seeded and cut in 1-inch squares
1 medium sized onion, cut in half and thinly sliced
2 tablespoons chicken stock
½ teaspoon salt
1 teaspoon sugar
¼ teaspoon monosodium glutamate
1 teaspoon soy sauce
2 teaspoons Saki or dry Sherry
1 small can pineapple chunks, drained
1 teaspoon cornstarch
1 tablespoon water

Skin chicken; remove the meat from the bone and cut in bite-size pieces. Roll chicken in the ¼ cup cornstarch so each piece is well coated. Heat oil in a large skillet; add chicken and cook quickly until the meat is opaque and the coating firm but not brown. Add the green pepper and onion; stir and cook 3 minutes. Combine the chicken stock, salt, sugar, monosodium glutamate, soy sauce, Saki or Sherry, and pineapple; pour into the chicken mixture and heat through. Blend the 1 teaspoon cornstarch with the water, add to pan, and stirring, cook until sauce is thickened and clear. This is obviously good with rice, either fried or steamed. A nice bunch of crisp watercress with lemon oil dressing goes well with this and many cups of hot, unsweetened jasmine tea. Serves 4.

CALORIES per serving: 205

LOW-SODIUM MODIFICATION: Omit salt and monosodium glutamate. Use a salt substitute ☑ and increase sugar to taste.

MG. SODIUM per serving: 42

Deviled Turkey Breast or Legs

Small turkey parts may be sautéed like chicken. Skin turkey first, then brown slowly in a little unsaturated oil ☑. Pour in whatever liquid you like for seasoning, cover, and simmer until turkey is tender. It takes about 30 to 45 minutes longer to cook turkey parts than it does chicken. Another way to approach turkey is to cut the legs and thick slices of breast from a roast turkey. Rub a coating of Dijon mustard over the meat and let it stand 12 hours. Place the meat under the broiler and cook until it is hot, brown, and slightly crusty on all sides. You can do the same thing with uncooked skinned turkey. Season small parts with salt, cayenne, and paprika, then coat with Dijon mustard. Broil slowly to get the pieces done to a turn.

CALORIES per 5 ounce serving: 300

LOW-SODIUM MODIFICATION: Avoid salt and use a salt substitute ☑. Use low-sodium mustard ☑ or make your own by mixing a little dried English mustard with a few teaspoons of dry white table wine or water; mix to a spreading consistency.

MG. SODIUM per 5 ounce serving: 80

Note: You can now buy in the frozen food section excellent rolls of cooked turkey meat—usually white and dark meat pressed together. Turkey is low in saturated fats, but you must determine how it was cooked. If large quantities of butter and salt were used, avoid the frozen rolls.

Sweet and Sour Chicken

   1 frying chicken, about 3 pounds
   1 teaspoon unsaturated oil ☑
  ½ cup red wine vinegar
  ½ cup water
  ½ cup Madeira or Sherry
  ¼ cup sugar
     Sugar substitute ☑ equal to ½ cup sugar
1½ tablespoons cornstarch mixed with ¼ cup cold water
   1 sweet red pepper, cut in strips
   1 green pepper, cut in strips
   1 small can artificially sweetened pineapple chunks ☑, drained

Skin the chicken and cut in quarters. Brush chicken with oil, place in a roasting pan, and cover loosely with foil. Bake in a moderate oven (350°) for 1 hour. Remove foil the last 15 minutes. While chicken is cooking, heat the vinegar, water, wine, sugar, and sugar substitute in a saucepan; add the blended cornstarch and water, and stirring, cook until sauce is thickened and clear. Pour the sauce over the chicken and continue baking for 15 minutes. Scatter the red pepper, green pepper, and pineapple over the chicken and continue baking 15 minutes before serving. Serves 4.

CALORIES per serving: 196

MG. SODIUM per serving: 116

Roast Turkey

12 pound hen turkey
 2 medium sized onions, chopped
 2 stalks celery and tops, chopped
 2 sprigs parsley, chopped
 2 tablespoons unsaturated margarine ☑
 1 tablespoon unsaturated oil ☑
 4 pieces day old bread, cut in cubes
 1 cup cooked rice
   Salt, pepper, and poultry seasoning to taste
½ cup pecans, pine nuts, or filberts, coarsely chopped
 2 tablespoons brandy
¼ cup skim milk or dry white table wine
 3 tablespoons unsaturated oil ☑
   Paprika

Skin turkey and dry the neck and body cavities with paper towels. Sauté onions, celery, and parsley in the margarine and 1 tablespoon oil until vegetables are limp. Add the bread cubes and continue cooking until they are toasted slightly. Add the rice, salt, pepper, poultry seasoning, and nuts. Stir and cook slowly for 5 minutes. Add the brandy and enough milk or wine to make the dressing slightly moist but not soggy. Pack stuffing loosely in the turkey.

   Place turkey on a rack in a roasting pan. Rub with 2 tablespoons of the oil, sprinkle with paprika, then cover with a cap of aluminum foil. Bake in a very hot oven (450°) for 20 minutes, then reduce heat to 350° and continue cooking for about 3 hours. Test the turkey at the thickest part of the drumstick; it should be soft. Remove the foil the last 20 minutes of cooking and spoon over the remaining 1 tablespoon oil. Do not baste turkey with the drippings from the pan.

   The turkey meat may be used for any number of dishes such as turkey hash, chef's salad, hot turkey sandwiches, or just good meat alone.

CALORIES for 2 slices (4 ounces) of breast meat: 230

CALORIES per ½ cup serving of dressing: 168

MG. SODIUM for 2 slices (4 ounces) breast meat: 60

LOW-SODIUM MODIFICATION: Omit celery in the dressing. Use low-sodium bread ☑ and low-sodium unsaturated margarine ☑. Be sure the rice was cooked in unsalted water. Use salt substitute ☑ and low-sodium skim milk ☑.

MG. SODIUM per ½ cup serving of dressing: 8

MEATS

"Jack Sprat could eat no fat".
   —From an old nursery rhyme—
   When Mrs. Sprat found out that Jack could eat no fat what did she do?
   Mrs. Sprat concocted some special recipes for Jack, not entirely free of fat, but reasonably lower in fat than what Jack had been gobbling up before.
   And here they are!

Veal Marengo

   4 veal cutlets (1 pound)
   3 tablespoons flour
      Salt, pepper, and monosodium glutamate to taste
   1 clove garlic, cut in 3 pieces
   3 tablespoons unsaturated oil ☑
   1 medium sized onion, chopped
   3 tomatoes, sliced
   ⅓ cup water
   ¼ teaspoon basil
   ⅓ cup dry white table wine
   ½ cup sliced mushrooms
   1½ teaspoons unsaturated oil ☑

Season meat with flour, salt, pepper, and monosodium glutamate. Reserve any flour that remains. Sauté the garlic in the 3 tablespoons hot oil until brown. Remove garlic, then brown the seasoned meat along with the onion. Arrange tomato slices in a lightly greased casserole; cover with the browned meat and onion. Add the reserved flour to the pan drippings and stir until blended. Pour in the water slowly, and stirring, cook until smooth and thickened. Add the basil and wine to the gravy then pour over meat. Cover and bake in a moderate oven (350°) for 45 minutes or until meat is tender. Sauté the mushrooms in the 1½ teaspoons oil and add to the meat the last 15 minutes of cooking. Serves 4.

CALORIES per serving: 390

VARIATIONS: If you use veal cut for *Scallopini,* be sure to pound the meat with the edge of a heavy saucer or a mallet to break up the fibers and give the meat its tender succulence. About 2 tablespoons of brandy may be used in the gravy. This will add 18 calories to each serving.

LOW-SODIUM MODIFICATION: Delete salt and monosodium glutamate. Depend upon the brandy, wine, a squeeze of lemon juice, and basil for seasoning.

MG. SODIUM per serving: 118

Breaded Veal Cutlets A L' Italienne

   2 tablespoons unsaturated margarine ☑
   2 tablespoons cornstarch
   4 veal cutlets (1 pound)
      Salt to taste
      Fine dry bread crumbs
   2 teaspoons unsaturated oil ☑
   1 large tomato, cut in 4 thick slices
   ½ lemon

Heat the margarine slowly until it melts but does not brown; remove from heat and blend in the cornstarch. Pound veal and season with salt. Dip in the cornstarch-margarine mixture, then in the bread crumbs. Save any of the cornstarch mixture that remains. Heat oil in a non-stick fluorocarbon coated pan. Cook the meat slowly until tender and browned. Transfer meat to a serving platter and keep hot. Dip tomato slices in the remaining cornstarch mixture, then in bread crumbs. Fry tomatoes in the pan in which you cooked the meat. Place a tomato slice on each piece of meat and add a squeeze of lemon juice. Serves 4.

CALORIES per serving: 330

LOW-SODIUM MODIFICATION: Use low-sodium unsaturated margarine ☑. Substitute low-sodium seasoning ☑ for the salt and use low-sodium bread crumbs ☑.

MG. SODIUM per serving: 105

Veal Meat Balls

    2 slices French bread, cut in small cubes
    ¼ cup skim milk
    1½ pounds ground veal stew meat
    ½ cup dry red table wine
    1 tablespoon dehydrated onion flakes
    2 tablespoons chopped parsley
    ¼ teaspoon each oregano and monosodium gluta-
        mate
        Salt to taste
    1½ tablespoons unsaturated margarine ☑
    ¼ cup water

Soak bread in the milk for a few minutes. Add the ground meat, wine, onion flakes, parsley, oregano, monosodium glutamate, and salt; mix well. Shape into 12 meat balls or 6 patties. Brown meat on all sides in the margarine. Pour the water over meat, cover and simmer for 20 minutes. This is very good with steamed rice or tiny boiled white potatoes sprinkled with paprika and chopped parsley. Serves 6.

CALORIES for 2 meat balls or 1 patty: 330

VARIATIONS: Add 1 cup chopped mushrooms and 1 teaspoon lemon juice to the browned meat when you pour in the water. This will add 8 calories per serving.

LOW-SODIUM MODIFICATION: Use low-sodium bread ☑, low-sodium skim milk ☑, and low-sodium unsaturated margarine ☑. Omit salt and monosodium glutamate; use salt substitute ☑.

MG. SODIUM for 2 meat balls or 1 patty: 106

Veal Italian Style

    4 boned veal steaks (1 pound)
    ¼ cup flour
    2 tablespoons unsaturated oil ☑
    1 can beef consommé
    1 medium sized onion, finely chopped
    1 clove garlic, mashed or minced
    1 pound mushrooms, sliced
    4 tablespoons of dry white table wine, a squeeze
        of lemon, and a bit of grated lemon peel
    ½ teaspoon oregano
        Salt to taste
    1 green pepper, seeded and cut in thin slices

Pound veal and dredge in flour. Heat oil in a large skillet and brown meat on both sides. Remove meat from pan and add 2 tablespoons of the consommé. Toss in the onion, garlic, and mushrooms, and sauté until vegetables are limp. Return the meat to the pan and add the wine, oregano, salt and the rest of the consommé. Cover and cook 30 to 40 minutes or until the meat is tender. Add the green pepper the last 10 minutes of cooking. Serves 4.

CALORIES per serving: 345

LOW-SODIUM MODIFICATION: Use low-sodium beef bouillon ☑. Omit salt and use salt substitute ☑.

MG. SODIUM per serving: 135

Apple Stuffed Veal Rolls

    1 cup finely chopped onion
    5 tablespoons unsaturated oil ☑
    2 cups soft bread cubes
    1 cup chopped peeled green apple
    1 teaspoon salt
    ½ teaspoon poultry seasoning
    6 thinly sliced boned veal steaks (1½ pounds)
    2 tablespoons flour
    1½ cups apple juice or cider

Sauté onion in 3 tablespoons of the oil until golden. Add the bread cubes, apple, salt, and poultry seasoning. Stirring occasionally, cook for 5 minutes. Pound meat slightly. Spoon stuffing on each piece of meat. Roll up meat, tucking in the ends, so the stuffing is held inside; fasten with toothpicks. Dust the meat rolls on all sides with flour. Heat the remaining 2 tablespoons oil in a skillet and brown meat well on all sides. Pour in apple juice. Cover and simmer for 30 to 40 minutes or until meat is tender. Remove toothpicks before serving and spoon the juices over the meat. Serves 6.

CALORIES per serving: 450

VARIATIONS: Substitute 2 tablespoons of Vermouth for 2 tablespoons of the apple juice. There will be little change in calories.

LOW-SODIUM MODIFICATION: Use low-sodium bread ☑. Delete salt and use salt substitute ☑.

MG. SODIUM per serving: 95

Dilled Cold Veal

    3 pound veal roast, boned and rolled
      Water
    2 whole cloves
    2 onions
    2 cups dry white table wine
    2 bay leaves
    1 leek, chopped
    2 carrots, coarsely chopped
    3 sprigs parsley
    5 whole black peppercorns
    4 tablespoons chopped fresh dill or 2 tablespoons
        dill seed
      Salt to taste
      Dill Sauce (See Sauces)

Cover meat with water; bring to a boil and cook 2 minutes. Pour off water and scum. Stick whole cloves in 1 of the onions and place in the kettle with the meat. Coarsely chop the other onion and add to the meat along with the wine, bay leaves, leek, carrots, parsley, black peppercorns, dill, and salt. Pour in enough water to cover meat. Simmer for 2 hours. Allow meat to cool in the stock, then chill.

  Prepare Dill Sauce. Slice the cold veal in thin slices and serve with the sauce. Serve the meat with sliced peeled cucumbers sprinkled with chopped parsley. A hot, broiled tomato is a delicious contrast to the cold veal and cucumber.

CALORIES per 4 ounce serving of meat (2 slices) and 2 tablespoons of sauce: 250

LOW-SODIUM MODIFICATION: Delete salt from both the veal stock and the sauce. Sprinkle with salt substitute ☑ to taste. Add the juice of ½ lemon to the stock.

MG. SODIUM per 4 ounce serving of meat (2 slices) and 2 tablespoons of sauce: 186

Hasenpfeffer

    1 young rabbit, cut in serving-size pieces
    2 large onions, sliced
    2 cloves garlic, mashed or minced
    3 sprigs parsley
    1 bay leaf
    ½ teaspoon salt
    6 whole black peppercorns, crushed
      Pinch each of thyme and rosemary
    1 teaspoon juniper berries, crushed
    2 lemons sliced
    1 large bottle dry red table wine
    2 tablespoons flour
    3 tablespoons vegetable oil
    6 small white boiling onions
    2 tablespoons Cognac or brandy

Wash rabbit pieces and pat dry with paper toweling. Combine the onions, garlic, parsley, bay leaf, salt, peppers, thyme, rosemary, juniper berries, lemons, and wine. Marinate rabbit in this mixture for 2 days, turning occasionally. Remove rabbit from the marinade and dry. Sprinkle with flour. In a heavy skillet, brown the rabbit and onions in the oil. Strain the marinade and pour over rabbit; add the Cognac or brandy. Cover pan and bake in a slow oven (300°) for 1½ hours or until the rabbit is tender. Serve with boiled chopped chestnuts or wild rice and steamed Brussels sprouts and a bottle of Claret. Serves 6.

CALORIES per serving of meat and sauce: 363

Warning: You might like to add the chopped liver when cooking, but it is so easy to have the gallbladder nicked and spill onto the liver, giving an extraordinarily bitter taste, that we do not recommend it. We've eaten it, but it doesn't add that much anyhow.

LOW-SODIUM MODIFICATION: Delete salt and use salt substitute ☑.

MG. SODIUM per serving of meat and sauce: 51

Shish Kebab

(Syrian Style)

Have your meat man bone a leg of lamb and remove as much fat as possible. Cut the meat in cubes approximately 1½ inches square and place in a large bowl. Mix together 1½ cups dry red table wine, 2 mashed cloves garlic, 2 tablespoons unsaturated oil ☑, 1 tablespoon crumbled dried mint or a little chopped fresh mint, and salt and pepper to taste; pour over meat and let it marinate overnight. Thread meat on skewers (the disposable bamboo skewers are good if you soak them first in water) with an assortment of vegetables. For each skewer use 2 pieces of meat, alternating it with a piece of green pepper, a small tomato, and fresh mushroom caps. Broil the meat over low coals or cook under the broiler until it is tender and browned. Don't cook the meat too long or it will dry out.

The edges of the meat may have a few small black spots from charring, but this is fairly routine.

CALORIES per skewer using 2 pieces of lamb: 165

VARIATIONS: Serve Shish Kebab with a flair by arranging the skewers on an oval platter. Heap steaming cracked wheat in the center. Heat 2 tablespoons brandy, spoon it over the skewers, and light. Serve this with a sharply flavored green salad. The brandy will add 73 calories.

LOW-SODIUM MODIFICATION: Avoid salt and use salt substitute ☑ and low-sodium flavoring ☑.

MG. SODIUM per skewer: 50

Lamb Stew

  1 pound lamb stew meat
  2 tablespoons unsaturated oil ☑
1½ cups water
10 small white boiling onions
  1 cup chopped carrot
  1 cup diced potato
  1 can (1 pound) solid pack tomatoes
 ¼ teaspoon rosemary
    Salt and pepper to taste

Trim any visible fat from meat and cut into bite-size pieces. Brown meat in the oil, pour in the water, and cover and simmer 2 hours. Cool meat, then refrigerate overnight. The next day carefully lift off the layer of fat which has solidified on the surface. Peel onions and add to meat along with the carrot, potato, and tomatoes. (Italian style tomatoes are good if you can find them, otherwise add a pinch of basil with the regular tomatoes.) Season with rosemary, salt, and pepper. Reheat stew and cook for 30 minutes or until vegetables are tender. Serves 5.

CALORIES per serving: 294

LOW-SODIUM MODIFICATION: Use salt substitute ☑ in place of salt. Omit carrots and use 1 cup of low-sodium canned peas ☑ or fresh peas. Use low-sodium canned tomatoes ☑.

MG. SODIUM per serving: 95

Roast Leg O' Lamb

  5 pound leg of lamb
 ½ cup chicken stock or water
 ½ cup dry white table wine
  1 teaspoon salt
 ¼ teaspoon pepper
  1 teaspoon minced onion
 ½ cup beef bouillon
  2 teaspoons chopped fresh mint leaves or 1 teaspoon dried mint
  1 tablespoon mint, apple, or wine jelly (optional)

Wash meat quickly and dry with paper towels. Place on a rack in a roasting pan. Sear meat in a very hot oven (500°) for 15 minutes. Combine the chicken stock or water, wine, salt, pepper, and onion. Reduce oven temperature to moderate (350°), spoon a little of the marinade over the meat, and continue cooking for about 2½ hours or until meat is tender. Baste frequently with the remaining marinade but do not baste with any of the drippings in the pan since they contain fat from the meat. For a meat sauce, heat beef bouillon with the mint. Stir in the jelly until it melts.

CALORIES per 3 ounce serving of meat: 160

LOW-SODIUM MODIFICATION: Use water or low-sodium chicken broth ☑ in the marinade. Omit salt and use a salt substitute ☑.

MG. SODIUM per 3 ounce serving of meat: 60

Beef Oriental

1 pound round or flank steak
2 tablespoons soy sauce
2 tablespoons dry white table wine or lemon juice
2 medium sized onions
3 stalks celery
½ green pepper
1 pound fresh spinach
1 small can water chestnuts
1 small can bamboo shoots
1 tomato
2 tablespoons unsaturated oil ☑
1 teaspoon sugar
1 cup beef stock
½ teaspoon monosodium glutamate
2 tablespoons cornstarch
¼ cup water

Be sure the meat is very cold; it will be easier to work with. Trim any visible fat; cut meat across the grain in very thin slices. Combine meat with 1 tablespoon of the soy sauce and wine; let stand at room temperature for 1 hour, turning occasionally in the marinade. Cut onions in small wedges. Slice celery on the diagonal. Cut green pepper in small pieces. Wash spinach, remove stems, and tear the leaves in half. Slice water chestnuts, cut bamboo shoots in small strips, and cut tomato in 8 wedges. Chill vegetables until you are ready to use.

Heat 1 tablespoon of the oil in a large frying pan; add onions and sauté for 10 minutes until they are tender but not browned. Remove onions to a small bowl and mix with the remaining 1 tablespoon soy sauce and sugar. Add the remaining 1 tablespoon oil to the pan and quickly brown the meat. Add the sautéed onions, celery, green pepper, spinach, water chestnuts, and bamboo shoots. Cook 1 minute, then add the tomato. Mix the beef stock and monosodium glutamate, pour over the meat, and cover and cook 3 minutes. Blend the cornstarch with the water; add to pan, and stirring, cook until sauce is clear and thickened. Stir gently so the meat and vegetables are covered with sauce. Serve over hot steamed rice. Serves 4.

CALORIES per serving: 345

LOW-SODIUM MODIFICATION: There is a good deal of sodium in the above recipe so appropriate modifications are in order. Avoid soy sauce and use low-sodium flavoring ☑. Remember there are 50 milligrams of sodium in a stalk of celery and 71 milligrams in ½ cup of spinach. However, there is a lot less sodium in a stalk of broccoli (15 milligrams) so feel free to consult the Appendix at the back of the book to devise some changes. Check the water chestnuts as many are packed in salt water. Use low-sodium bouillon ☑ instead of the beef stock and delete the monosodium glutamate.

MG. SODIUM per serving with these changes: 112

Tomato Beef Stroganoff

1¼ pounds flank or round steak
2 tablespoons unsaturated oil ☑
½ cup chopped onion
1 small clove garlic, mashed or minced
1 can (6 oz.) mushrooms
1 can tomato soup
1 cup buttermilk
6 to 8 drops Tabasco
1 tablespoon Worcestershire
½ teaspoon salt
⅛ teaspoon pepper
2 tablespoons flour
¼ cup cold water

Trim fat from meat; cut meat across the grain in thin strips ¼ inch thick. Heat oil in a large frying pan; add the meat, onion, and garlic. Cook until meat is browned and onion is golden. Drain mushrooms and add to meat. Combine the tomato soup, buttermilk, Tabasco, Worcestershire, salt, and pepper; pour over meat. Cover and simmer for 1 hour or until tender. Blend flour with the water; add slowly to the beef mixture, and stirring, cook until smooth and thickened. Serves 4.

CALORIES per serving: 400

Warning: The classical recipe is much simpler, but contains more fat. Commonly, a *roux* of butter and flour is used along with several tablespoons of sour cream. The meat is generally sautéed in butter. You'll like our version though.

LOW-SODIUM MODIFICATION: Use fresh mushrooms to avoid the salt water used to pack canned mushrooms. Avoid tomato soup; substitute with low-sodium stewed tomatoes ☑ which have been forced through a strainer. Use a can of low-sodium skim milk ☑ in place of the buttermilk. Omit salt and use salt substitute ☑ and cayenne. Omit Worcestershire sauce.

MG. SODIUM per serving: 85

Creamed Chipped Beef

1 small jar (2½ oz.) dried beef
1 tablespoon unsaturated oil ☑
2 tablespoons flour
1 cup skim milk
　White pepper or cayenne

Shred dried beef. Sauté in oil until lightly browned. Sprinkle with the flour and mix lightly. Remove pan from heat, and stirring, add skim milk. Return to heat and continue to stir and cook until sauce is thickened. Simmer for 1 minute. Season with pepper or cayenne. Serves 2.

CALORIES per serving: 200

VARIATIONS: You can add some non fat dried milk to the skim milk to increase the protein and to make the sauce more creamy. One tablespoon of non fat dried milk will add 28 calories. This is excellent on a cold day over a waffle or toasted French bread.

LOW-SODIUM MODIFICATION: Dried beef contains a great deal of sodium in the form of sodium chloride and sometimes a little sodium nitrate. Some dried beef is not cured with salt, but this is difficult to find. If your sodium intake is restricted, it might be best avoided.

Boiled Beef
with Horseradish Sauce

Cook a 2 inch thick piece of round steak in seasoned stock. (See Dilled Cold Veal). The meat is generally served hot after simmering for 3 to 3½ hours. Excellent horseradish comes in jars freshly grated and sometimes it is colored with a little beet juice. German horseradish often contains a *roux* made of butter and flour. This, however, is something you don't need. Use the horseradish directly from the jar. A serving of hot beef is good with sliced cold beets and sliced red Italian onions sprinkled with a teaspoon of oil and vinegar dressing or with a watercress and onion salad.

CALORIES per 4 ounces of boiled round steak with 1 teaspoon horseradish: 280

LOW-SODIUM MODIFICATION: Avoid salt in the stock in which you cook the meat; sprinkle in a salt substitute ☑. Check the horseradish as much of it is packed in or diluted with salt water.

MG. SODIUM per 4 ounces of boiled round steak with 1 teaspoon horseradish: 80

Stuffed Green Peppers

6 large green peppers
1¼ pounds lean ground round
¼ cup minced onion
2 tablespoons unsaturated oil ☑
1½ cups canned tomatoes
3 cups cooked rice
½ teaspoon sage
　Dash of pepper
½ cup dried bread crumbs
2 tablespoons melted unsaturated margarine ☑

Wash pepper, then cut in half lengthwise and remove seeds. Cook peppers in boiling water to cover for 5 minutes; drain. Sauté beef and onion in oil until meat is browned and crumbly. Remove from heat and stir in the tomatoes, rice, sage, and pepper. Mix filling well, then spoon into the green pepper halves. Toss bread crumbs with the melted margarine; sprinkle over the peppers. Arrange peppers in a lightly greased baking pan. Bake in a moderately hot oven (375°) for 40 minutes or until peppers are tender and brown on top. Serves 6.

CALORIES per serving: 410

VARIATIONS: The fat may be cut still further if ground veal is used in place of ground round.

LOW-SODIUM MODIFICATION: Use low-sodium bread crumbs ☑, low-sodium unsaturated margarine ☑, and tomatoes canned without salt.

MG. SODIUM per serving: 72

Chili Con Carne

2 pounds lean ground round
2 cups chopped onion
3 cloves garlic, mashed or minced
2 tablespoons unsaturated oil ☑
1 can (1 lb. 4 oz.) tomatoes
2 cans (1 lb. each) kidney beans, drained
1 teaspoon salt
¼ to ½ teaspoon cayenne
4 teaspoons chili powder
¾ teaspoon oregano

Cook meat in a pan without any fat until browned and crumbly. Spoon off pan drippings. Sauté onion and garlic in the vegetable oil until onion is clear and golden. Add the browned meat, tomatoes, kidney beans, salt, cayenne, chili powder, and oregano. Stirring occasionally, cover and simmer for 30 minutes. Cool, then refrigerate overnight. Lift off any fat that has solidified on the surface. Reheat before serving. Serves 6.

CALORIES per serving: 550

Note: There is a ground beef on the market that is called "hi protein" which means that more fat is removed before the meat is ground. Use this if it is available.

LOW-SODIUM MODIFICATION: Carefully check the canned beans for sodium content. You may need to cook your own dried beans unless you can find a low-sodium brand. Omit salt; use salt substitute ☑ and low-sodium flavoring ☑. Use low-sodium canned tomatoes ☑.

MG. SODIUM per serving: 120

Broiled Flank Steak

Rub 1 tablespoon unsaturated oil ☑ over both sides of a flank steak. Broil or barbecue the meat over low coals until it is done to your liking. For rare meat, allow 4 to 5 minutes on a side. If you like your meat medium well done, cook about 7 minutes on a side, though the meat becomes less juicy and less tender the longer you cook it. When the meat is done, sprinkle with a little salt and freshly ground pepper. Cut across the meat diagonally in very thin slices. Serve with broiled mushrooms and thick slices of tomato sprinkled with oregano and oil and vinegar dressing. Sometimes the meat is cut into strips before cooking, then rolled into a pinwheel and fastened with a wooden skewer.

CALORIES per 4 ounce serving of meat: 280

LOW-SODIUM MODIFICATION: Omit salt and use a salt substitute ☑.

MG. SODIUM per 4 ounce serving: 80

Steak Au Poivre

Crush 1 tablespoon of a mixture of black and white peppercorns or just use whole black peppercorns. Dry a 1¼ pound flank steak with paper towels. Rub and press the crushed pepper into both sides of the meat with your fingers and the palms of your hands. Cover

with waxed paper and let stand for 2 to 3 hours so the flavor of the pepper will penetrate the meat. Heat 1 tablespoon unsaturated oil ☑ in a heavy skillet or a nonstick fluorocarbon coated pan. Sauté meat until tender but still juicy, about 4 minutes on a side. Remove to a hot platter, season with salt, and keep warm. Sauté 2 tablespoons chopped onion or shallots for 2 minutes in the pan in which you cooked the meat. Add 2 tablespoons brandy and swirl around pan, then pour sauce over meat. Serve with broiled whole tomatoes sprinkled with basil and large whole broiled mushrooms sprinkled with oil and lemon. You may also want to add slices of green pepper and serve this on a bed of rice. Serves 4.

CALORIES per serving of meat with sauce: 375

LOW-SODIUM MODIFICATION: Omit salt and use a salt substitute ☑.

MG. SODIUM per serving: 80

Beef Bourguignon

1 pound beef stew meat
2 tablespoons unsaturated oil ☑
2 onions, chopped
1 tablespoon flour
1 clove garlic, mashed or minced
1 cup dry red table wine
2 tablespoons tomato sauce or purée
　Salt and pepper to taste
　Bouquet garni (see below)
6 mushrooms, chopped

Cut meat in cubes; brown slowly in the hot oil. Add onions and sauté until golden. Sprinkle with the flour and stir into the meat and onions. Add garlic, wine, tomato sauce, salt and pepper, and *bouquet garni* (1 stalk of celery, 1 sprig of parsley, 1 bay leaf and a sprig of thyme tied in a piece of cheesecloth). Cover and simmer for 2 hours. Toss in the mushrooms and continue cooking for 30 minutes. Remove the *bouquet garni*. Serve with small peeled roasted potatoes and green beans or Chinese (edible pod) peas mixed with water chestnuts. Serves 4.

CALORIES per serving: 425

LOW-SODIUM MODIFICATION: Omit salt; use salt substitute ☑ and low-sodium tomato sauce ☑.

MG. SODIUM per serving: 82

PASTA AND RICE

Since Marco Polo's walking trip half way around the world to China, pasta or spaghetti in its various forms has been a staple in the diet of several European countries, Italy in particular. Of course, China has been eating it for centuries, but the Italians concocted tasty recipes of their own, some of which are offered here for your choosing. You may want to search in specialty markets or delicatessens to find some of the more unusual pastas.

Rice, the staff of life in the Orient, is also presented in a variety of flavorful dishes.

Spaghettini Marinara

1 large onion, chopped
1 or 2 cloves garlic, mashed or minced
2 tablespoons unsaturated oil ☑
1 can (1 lb.) solid pack tomatoes
1 teaspoon sugar
  Small sprig of fresh oregano and basil or ¼ teaspoon of each dried herb
  Salt and pepper
1 anchovy fillet, chopped
½ pound spaghettini (very thin spaghetti) or vermicelli
4 quarts lightly salted water

In a saucepan sauté the onion and garlic in oil until limp and clear. Add the tomatoes and mash slightly; cover pan and simmer gently for 1 hour. Season sauce with sugar, oregano, basil, salt, and pepper to taste; stir in anchovy and continue cooking for 15 minutes.

Cook spaghettini in rapidly boiling, lightly salted water until barely tender, about 10 minutes. Drain well and turn out onto a platter. Pour the hot anchovy sauce over all. Serves 6.

CALORIES per serving: 184

LOW-SODIUM MODIFICATION: Use 1 tablespoon tuna fish packed in water in place of the anchovy; use low sodium canned tomatoes ☑ or 2 cups fresh tomatoes. Use low-sodium flavoring ☑ instead of salt.

MG. SODIUM per serving: 30

Spaghettini with Chicken Livers

½ pound chicken livers, cut in bite-size pieces
6 medium sized fresh mushrooms, sliced
3 tablespoons unsaturated oil ☑
  Salt
1 large onion, finely chopped
1 cup tomato purée
  Salt
  Pinch of crumbled hot red pepper
4 tablespoons finely chopped parsley
½ pound spaghettini (very thin spaghetti) or vermicelli
4 quarts lightly salted water

In a saucepan, sauté the chicken livers and mushrooms in 2 tablespoons of the oil for 6 minutes; sprinkle with a little salt. In a separate pan, sauté onion in the remaining 1 tablespoon oil until limp and clear. Spoon onion into the chicken livers and add the tomato purée, salt to taste, red pepper, and 2 tablespoons of the chopped parsley. Simmer sauce for a few minutes to blend flavors.

Heat the lightly salted water in a large kettle until the surface is furiously boiling, then add the spaghettini and stir frequently. Cook for about 10 minutes or until the pasta is al dente (very slightly resistant to your teeth). The time will vary with different pasta; the larger varieties naturally cook longer. Drain well and heap the spaghettini on a hot platter. Pour the hot sauce over all and sprinkle with the remaining 2 tablespoons chopped parsley. Serves 8.

CALORIES per serving: 220

LOW-SODIUM MODIFICATION: Use lemon juice in the boiling water for the pasta. Use salt substitute ☑ in the sauce; lemon juice is also good in the sauce.

MG. SODIUM per serving: 27

Linguini
with Clam Sauce

  2 cloves garlic, mashed or minced
  3 tablespoons unsaturated oil ☑
  1 can (7 oz.) minced clams
  1 small hot red pepper, crumbled
  ½ cup finely chopped parsley
  ½ pound linguini (slightly flattened pasta) or tag-
       liarini
  2 tablespoons grated Parmesan cheese (optional)

Sauté garlic in oil until golden. Add the clams, including the liquid, the red pepper, and parsley. Cook just long enough to heat through.

Cook the linguini according to directions given for spaghettini (see preceding recipe). Mound on a warm platter and spoon the clam sauce over all. You may sprinkle the grated cheese over it, but take it easy on the amount. Serves 6.

CALORIES per serving: 200

VARIATIONS: In place of canned clams, you may use 10 to 15 medium sized clams in the shells. Arrange clams in a baking pan and place in a hot oven (400°) for 10 minutes or until the shells open. Let clams cool slightly, then remove from the shells and coarsely chop; continue recipe as above.

LOW-SODIUM MODIFICATION: Delete salt in the cooking water for the linguini and omit the Parmesan cheese. Use some lemon juice to flavor the clam sauce. If the clams are canned with salt, start with raw ones and cook them yourself.

MG. SODIUM per serving: 35

Fusilli
with Herb Dressing

  2 cloves peeled garlic
  ¼ cup fresh basil or 1 tablespoon dried leaf basil
  ¼ cup parsley
  2 tablespoons pine nuts
  ¼ cup unsaturated oil ☑
  ¼ cup grated Parmesan or Romano cheese
       Pepper and salt
  ½ pound fusilli or tagliarini
  3 to 4 quarts lightly salted water
  1 teaspoon chopped parsley

Crush garlic, basil, parsley, and pine nuts in a mortar or chop very finely; work well with a wooden spoon into the oil. Add grated cheese and a little pepper and salt; work it all until it is very smooth. Use a blender to mix the sauce if you're not fortunate enough to own a mortar and pestle.

Put fusilli into rapidly boiling, lightly salted water and cook quickly. Test it repeatedly by pulling out a piece and biting it. When it is al dente, immediately pour off the water. Place fusilli on a hot platter and quickly mix with most of the herb sauce. Ladle the remainder of the sauce over the top and sprinkle with the chopped parsley. Serves 6.

CALORIES per serving: 255

LOW-SODIUM MODIFICATION: Avoid salt in the boiling water and sauce; delete grated cheese. Use some salt substitute ☑ and lemon to taste.

MG. SODIUM per serving: 72

Spanish Rice

  2 tablespoons unsaturated margarine ☑
  1 large onion, chopped
  1 green pepper, seeded and chopped
  1 cup uncooked rice
  6 medium sized mushrooms, sliced
  1 cup canned tomatoes
  1 cup water or consommé
       Salt and pepper
  1 clove garlic, peeled
       Bouquet garni (see below)

Melt unsaturated margarine in a heavy pan, then sauté the onion and green pepper until limp. Add the rice, and stirring occasionally, cook until it is golden. Add the mushrooms, tomatoes, water or consommé, salt and pepper to taste, and the whole garlic. Drop in a *bouquet garni* (a bay leaf, a stem of thyme, two sprigs parsley, and a small branch of celery). Cover pan, bring to a boil, then reduce heat to lowest possible point and steam for 20 to 25 minutes. Discard the *bouquet garni* and garlic. Gently lift rice with a fork, and if it is too moist, replace on the heat for a few minutes to dry slightly. Serve with a nicely browned chicken thigh or breast. Serves 6.

CALORIES per serving: 175

LOW-SODIUM MODIFICATION: Use low-sodium unsaturated margarine ☑, low-sodium consommé ☑, and low-sodium canned tomatoes ☑. Delete salt and use a salt substitute ☑.

MG. SODIUM per serving: 13

Baked Manicotti

  1 large onion, chopped
  3 tablespoons egg substitute ☑ equivalent to 1 egg
  3 tablespoons unsaturated margarine ☑
  2 tablespoons unsaturated oil ☑
  1 clove garlic, mashed or minced
  1 large can (1 lb. 13 oz.) solid pack tomatoes
    Pinch each of basil, oregano, and rosemary
  ½ teaspoon sugar
    Salt and pepper to taste
1½ cups ricotta or dry sieved cottage cheese ☑
  2 tablespoons grated Parmesan or Romano cheese
  1 tablespoon chopped parsley
    Salt and pepper
  8 manicotti shells

In a large pot, sauté the onion in the unsaturated margarine and oil until it is limp and clear. Add the garlic and continue cooking for 1 minute. Pour in the tomatoes and season with basil, oregano, rosemary, sugar, and salt and pepper to taste. Mash tomatoes slightly, then simmer for 20 minutes or until thick; keep sauce hot.

Mix ricotta or dry cottage cheese with grated Parmesan, parsley, and salt and pepper to taste. Beat egg and fold into the whipped cream mixture. This lightens the filling. Fill the uncooked manicotti shells with the cheese filling; arrange in a single layer in an oiled baking dish. Leave space between each manicotti shell to allow for expansion during baking. Spoon the hot tomato sauce over all.

Cover the dish with aluminum foil. Bake in a hot oven (400°) for 45 minutes. Remove foil and bake 5 more minutes. Serve two manicotti to each person and pass around a crisp green salad with lemon and oil dressing. Pour a glass of Chianti or Pinot Noir and you're living. (Avoid ricotta that is not a true whey cheese. It has too much fat!) Serves 4.

CALORIES for 2 manicotti and sauce: 369

LOW-SODIUM MODIFICATION: Use no salt in the sauce; use salt substitute ☑. There is very little sodium in the manicotti shells. Use low-sodium unsaturated margarine ☑, low-sodium cottage cheese ☑, and reduce Parmesan cheese to 2 teaspoons. Add a few sautéed chopped mushrooms to the ricotta filling.

MG. SODIUM for 2 manicotti & sauce: 55

Confetti Rice

  ½ cup chopped onion
  ½ cup chopped green pepper
  2 tablespoons unsaturated margarine ☑
  ½ cup diced pimiento
  2 cups hot cooked rice

Sauté onion and green pepper in unsaturated margarine until onion is golden and pepper is tender; add pimiento and heat through. Stir into hot rice. Serves 6.

CALORIES per serving: 102

LOW-SODIUM MODIFICATION: Use a low-sodium unsaturated margarine ☑ and cook rice in unsalted water.

MG. SODIUM per serving: 4

Pilaff

(Rice usually mixed with something)

¼ cup unsaturated margarine ☑
1½ cups uncooked rice
2 tablespoons each walnuts and raisins
3 cups hot chicken or beef broth

Melt the margarine in a heavy pan. Add the rice and cook, stirring often, until the rice turns golden. Add the raisins and walnuts. Pour in the broth and cover pan tightly. Bake in a hot oven (400°) for 30 minutes. Remove the cover, stir the rice, and bake about 10 minutes longer. Serves 6.

CALORIES per serving: 260

VARIATIONS: Sauté a finely chopped onion in the margarine until the onion is clear, then add the rice and continue as above. Or you may stir in a couple of tablespoons of finely chopped parsley after the rice is done. This adds about 6 calories to each serving.

In the Middle East, a sauce called Khoresh is made to be eaten with rice. This sauce contains ½ pound of sautéed, finely ground beef and 1 cup of mixed fruit, such as dried apricots, prunes, raisins, and pomegranate seeds. (Cook the dried fruit in a little water to soften, then chop before adding to the meat.) To this mixture add 1 tablespoon unsaturated margarine ☑, ¼ teaspoon lemon juice, and 1 teaspoon sugar; cook for 5 minutes and serve the sauce hot over steamed rice as a main dish. Serves 6. This makes 280 calories per serving with ⅔ cup cooked rice.

LOW-SODIUM MODIFICATION: Use low-sodium chicken consommé ☑ or bouillon ☑ and low-sodium unsaturated margarine ☑.

MG. SODIUM per serving of pilaff: 8

MG. SODIUM with meat and fruit sauce on rice: 20

Spanish Paella

This is a dish of rice, chicken, saffron, seafood, sausages, and vegetables cooked in a flat iron pan with two handles called a *paella*. It is delicious to eat, low in saturated fats, and glamorous enough for a festive occasion. You may not have a paella available, so use a large casserole or a heavy iron frying pan or Dutch oven. This is easily made by serving broiled chicken one night and cooking ten extra legs and thighs to use in making paella.

10 medium sized raw shrimp
1 small lobster or lobster tail
3 tablespoons unsaturated oil ☑
1 hot Italian sausage, cut in ½-inch slices
10 broiled skinned chicken legs or thighs
1 large onion, finely chopped
2 cloves garlic, mashed or minced
1 cup canned tomatoes
1 small jar (2 oz.) pimiento, chopped
2 sprigs parsley, chopped
2 cups uncooked long grain rice
⅛ to ¼ teaspoon saffron
3½ cups chicken consommé
1 tablespoon chopped parsley for garnish

Peel shrimp; cut down the rounded back side and remove the sand vein. Split lobster and remove shell; cut meat in bite-size pieces. In a large pan, sauté shrimp and lobster or lobster tail in 2 tablespoons of the oil until the shrimp turn pink. Remove shrimp and lobster and reserve. Sauté the sausage in the pan drippings until lightly browned. Pour off the fat. Reheat chicken in the pan with the sausage.

In a separate pan sauté the onion and garlic in the remaining 1 tablespoon oil. Remove seeds from tomatoes, coarsely chop, and add to onion along with the pimiento and parsley. Cook long enough to heat through, then pour over sausage and chicken in the paella pan. Sprinkle rice on the paella. Dissolve saffron in the chicken consommé and pour over rice. Bring mixture to a boil, then reduce heat and cook, uncovered, for 15 to 20 minutes. Gently stir in the shrimp and lobster, and cook a few more minutes until the rice is dry enough to your liking. Sprinkle with chopped parsley, and dig in. Serves 8.

CALORIES per serving: 286

VARIATIONS: Clams in their shells are often added, and the open shells make the dish very attractive. Scrub the clams well, and steam with a little water until the shells open. Add the clams in the last few minutes of cooking along with the shrimp and lobster. Each clam will add about 10 calories and 30 milligrams of sodium. Stir in some cooked green peas too for color. You really don't need any additional dish with the paella. Serve a bottle of Spanish Rioja or Riesling, and later, black coffee—Magnifico!!

LOW-SODIUM MODIFICATION: Avoid the Italian sausage and lobster. Add a little cayenne pepper to the consommé which should be low-sodium bouillon ☑. Use low-sodium canned tomatoes or use fresh tomatoes if possible. This dish is fairly spicy with the blend of saffron, garlic, sea food, and chicken, so only a little lemon juice and or salt substitute ☑ may be needed.

MG. SODIUM per serving without the clams: 52

Dolmas

This is a dish consisting of grape leaves stuffed with seasoned rice and meat and then steamed. It is served with or without a lemon sauce. (See Sauces.)

      3 to 4 dozen fresh grape leaves
    ½ pound lean ground beef
    1   onion, chopped
    1   cup cooked rice
        Salt and pepper
    1½ cups consommé
        Juice of 2 lemons
    ¼   teaspoon allspice

Select young tender grape leaves from yours or someone else's grapevine; wash well to avoid any residual insecticide. Snip away the stems. Pile leaves in 3 or 4 stacks and place in a large kettle; cover with water. Heat to boiling, boil 1 minute, then remove from heat and let stand 5 minutes; drain.

For the filling, cook the meat slowly until it is brown and crumbly. Add the onion and sauté until it is limp. Spoon off any fat that accumulates. Stir in the cooked rice and salt and pepper to taste.

Depending on the size of the leaf, put about 1 tablespoon of filling across the middle of the grape leaf. From stem end roll up leaf halfway, fold in either side to make a packet, and continue rolling to seal. Continue filling and rolling until all of grape leaves and filling are used. Arrange stuffed grape leaves in solid layers in a heavy kettle. Add the consommé, lemon juice and allspice. Weight the leaves down with a heavy plate; cover pan, and simmer for 30 minutes. Serve these either hot or cold. If cold, they are excellent topped with low-fat yogurt ☑ seasoned with some chopped fresh dill, or, what is probably more available, fresh mint.

CALORIES per grape leaf: 32

VARIATIONS: Sometimes these are cooked with finely ground lean lamb instead of beef. Also the flavor of cinnamon may be added to the stuffing. If grape leaves are not available, the same operation may be carried out with cabbage leaves. No change in calories.

LOW-SODIUM MODIFICATION: Beware of canned grape leaves which are packed in brine and are very difficult to wash free of sodium. Use fresh grape leaves and low-sodium bouillon ☑ to cook the leaves. Use salt substitute ☑ and more lemon, mint, and dill in the flavoring. Fresh cabbage leaves may also be used for the sodium restricted diet.

MG. SODIUM per grape leaf: 7

VEGETABLES OR LEGUMES

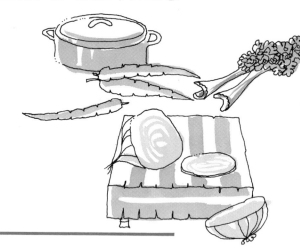

Long scorned by the uninitiated, vegetables properly prepared can be an unsuspected source of gastronomic enjoyment.

The calories are moderate for the most part in these selections.

Artichokes Vinaigrette

Select bright green artichokes with the leaflets closed. Rinse in cold water, remove stems, and cut off about 2 inches of the tops. Rub artichokes well with a cut lemon. Stand in a large pot of boiling water with 2 lemons, sliced, and 3 tablespoons white vinegar. Boil gently for 30 to 45 minutes depending on the size; drain. When an artichoke is cooked you can easily pull away a leaf at the base. Spread artichokes apart slightly and scrape out the fuzzy chokes with a spoon. Do this gently and a smooth concave bottom (heart) remains at the base of the leaves. Place on an attractive dish and garnish with lemon slices. For each artichoke make a dressing of 1½ teaspoons unsaturated oil, 1½ teaspoons lemon juice, salt, and freshly ground pepper; spoon over the vegetable. Chill for 1 hour before serving. Pull each leaf away from the base and pull the fleshy part through the teeth. When the leaves are all cleaned, slice the bottom into nice bite-size morsels and wipe up the little sauce remaining.

CALORIES per plain artichoke: 51

CALORIES per artichoke with dressing: 113

VARIATIONS: Dip leaves and bottom in a highly seasoned unsaturated mayonnaise ☑ mixed with a little extra lemon juice.

CALORIES per 1 tablespoon unsaturated mayonnaise ☑: 92

LOW-SODIUM MODIFICATION: While there is very little fat present, a medium artichoke has about 41 to 45 milligrams sodium, so act accordingly.

MG. SODIUM per artichoke: 45

MG. SODIUM per 1 tablespoon unsaturated mayonnaise: 10

Asparagus with Herbs and Lemon

Look for asparagus spears that do not have any wrinkles which usually result from drying. Snap off tough ends of asparagus stalks and remove scales. Scrub with a brush under running water. Stand stalks upright in a deep pan such as a clean coffee pot or the top of the double boiler. Add 1 inch of water and cover pan. Cook quickly for 15 minutes or just until tender. Check the thicker ends of the stalks with a toothpick or fork. Drain and serve with a little melted unsaturated margarine ☑, lemon juice, and salt and pepper—or just salt and pepper and lemon.

CALORIES per 6 stalks: 26

CALORIES with dressing: 60

VARIATIONS: Cool asparagus. Pour over the stalks a couple of tablespoons of oil and lemon or vinegar dressing to which a little fresh or dried tarragon has been added. Chill for several hours and serve with un-saturated mayonnaise ☑ mixed with a little lemon. Each teaspoon of unsaturated mayonnaise will add 31 calories and 1 teaspoon of oil (for the dressing) will add 41 calories.

LOW-SODIUM MODIFICATION: Use salt substi-tute ☑, low-sodium dressing ☑, and low-sodium un-saturated margarine ☑.

MG. SODIUM per 6 stalks: 2

Negligible sodium in dressing

Asparagus, Chinese Style

1 pound asparagus
2 tablespoons peanut oil
2 slices fresh ginger root, minced
1 teaspoon sugar
   Salt and monosodium glutamate to taste
¼ cup chicken consommé or stock
1 teaspoon cornstarch
2 tablespoons water

Wash asparagus and snap off the lower stalks. Cut diagonally in very thin slices; separate the tender tips from the less tender pieces. Heat oil in a heavy skillet and toss in the ginger root and less tender pieces of asparagus. Stirring often, sauté for a few minutes or until asparagus is crisp tender. Add the tender tips and stir until they are covered with oil. Add the sugar, salt, monosodium glutamate, and chicken consommé. Cover and cook for 2 or 3 minutes or until tender. Blend cornstarch with water, quickly mix into the as-paragus, and stir and cook until sauce is clear and thick. Serves 4.

CALORIES per serving: 85

VARIATIONS: It is often a good idea to parboil the less tender segments of asparagus for 2 minutes, drain well, then stir-fry. Several shrimp, coarsely chopped, may be added for color variation or a few shreds of beef steak or slices of left-over beef. Substitute 1 clove of minced garlic for the ginger, or add 1 teaspoon of rice wine or Sherry to the chicken consommé. Also, a few rinsed black beans crushed with the garlic and wine make an excellent addition. (See Lobster or Shrimp with Black Bean Sauce.) Each variation will add about 50 Calories and 30 milligrams sodium.

LOW-SODIUM MODIFICATION: Delete monoso-dium glutamate and salt. Be sure chicken consommé is a low-sodium type. Rinse black beans well to remove sodium. Use salt substitute ☑ and a squeeze of lemon juice.

MG. SODIUM per serving: 2

Green Beans in Tomato Sauce

1 pound fresh green beans
1 tablespoon unsaturated oil ☑
1 clove garlic, thinly sliced
1 cup peeled tomatoes, mashed
¼ teaspoon pepper
⅛ teaspoon dill
¼ teaspoon monosodium glutamate

Snip ends from beans; cut into 2-inch pieces. Heat oil in a heavy skillet and brown the garlic slightly. Add the beans, tomatoes, pepper, dill, and monosodium glutamate. Stir and simmer 20 minutes or until beans are tender and sauce is slightly reduced and thickened. Serves 4.

CALORIES per serving: 65

VARIATIONS: Use canned Italian-style tomatoes, which usually contain some basil. Cut beans diagonally or cut French style. No change in calories.

LOW-SODIUM MODIFICATION: Delete monoso-dium glutamate; use low-sodium gourmet seasoning ☑ and low-sodium canned tomatoes ☑.

MG. SODIUM per serving: 9

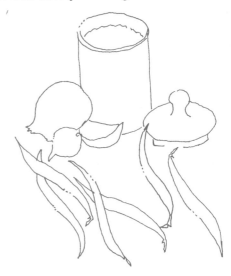

Green Beans with Savory

1 pound fresh green beans
Lightly salted water
1 tablespoon unsaturated margarine ☑
¼ teaspoon monsodium glutamate
Summer savory, sprigs or leaves

Snip ends from beans. Cook whole beans in lightly salted water for 20 minutes or until crisp tender; drain. Melt unsaturated margarine and add monosodium glutamate and enough summer savory to give all a good taste; pour over beans. Keep warm and let stand a few minutes for the flavors to blend. Serve with lean roast beef or broiled chicken. Serves 4.

CALORIES per serving: 58

VARIATIONS: Add 1 tablespoon sugar to the cooking water. For a German taste, mix ½ teaspoon caraway seed in the melted margarine and pour with beans. Substitute unsaturated oil for the margarine and season with rosemary for an Italian flavor. Sprinkle over a few slivered almonds or season with chopped fresh dill and lemon juice. Add a few sliced and sautéed mushrooms and 1 tablespoon of dry white wine. No change in calories or sodium.

LOW-SODIUM MODIFICATION: Delete salt in the cooking water and use sugar instead. Omit monosodium glutamate. Use low-sodium unsaturated margarine ☑, unsalted almonds and know the sodium content of wines you use.

MG. SODIUM per serving: 5

Beets in Orange Sauce

1 can (1 pound) sliced beets
2 tablespoons cornstarch
½ cup orange juice
Sugar substitute ☑ to equal 1 tablespoon sugar
1 tablespoon unsaturated margarine ☑
Red food coloring

Drain beets and save 2 tablespoons of the liquid; blend with the cornstarch. Heat orange juice and sugar substitute in a saucepan; add cornstarch mixture and stir and cook until thickened. Add margarine and enough food coloring to make sauce a light red. Place beets in the sauce and heat through. Serves 4.

CALORIES per serving: 70

VARIATIONS: Use a 1 pound can of small whole beets and marinate beets in the orange juice for 1 hour before proceeding with the above recipe. Or you can flavor the sliced beets with ¼ teaspoon orange bitters or a little grated orange peel.

LOW-SODIUM MODIFICATION: Use low-sodium canned beets or cook your own. Wash raw beets and cut off the tops, leaving a 1-inch stem. Cook in boiling water for 30 minutes to 1½ hours, depending on the size of the beets, or until tender. Cool slightly, then slip off skins and slice or chop. Use low-sodium unsaturated margarine ☑.

MG. SODIUM per serving: 37

Broccoli Italienne

1 bunch (1 pound) broccoli
Salted water
2 tablespoons unsaturated oil ☑
1 clove garlic, mashed or minced
3 pitted ripe olives, sliced

Wash broccoli. Cut off tough ends of stalks; split stems so they will cook as rapidly as the tender top portion. Cook in boiling salted water for 10 to 15 minutes or until crisp tender. Drain and keep hot. Heat oil with garlic for 2 minutes; stir in sliced olives and pour over the broccoli. Serve with a small piece of broiled steak and sour dough French bread. Serves 4.

CALORIES per serving: 95

VARIATIONS: Flavor cooked broccoli with a little lemon juice and oil and a small chopped pimiento; chill and marinate for 12 hours. To cook broccoli Chinese style, parboil until just slightly underdone; drain and finish cooking in a skillet with a tablespoon of hot oil. Add 1 tablespoon rice wine or Sherry and a squeeze of lemon juice, salt, and pepper. No calorie or sodium change.

LOW-SODIUM MODIFICATION: Delete salt in cooking water; omit olives and use lemon juice.

MG. SODIUM per serving: 13

Chinese Cabbage Sautéed with Green Onions

    1 head (1½ pounds) Chinese cabbage
    3 tablespoons peanut oil
    4 green onions, thinly sliced crosswise
       Dash each of salt and sugar
    ¼ teaspoon monosodium glutamate
    ¼ cup consommé, bouillon, or water
    1 teaspoon cornstarch mixed with 1 tablespoon
       water (optional)

Wash cabbage, remove any wilted or tough outer leaves, then cut in convenient sections. Heat oil in a large heavy skillet; add cabbage and cook quickly until it wilts. Add the green onions, salt, sugar, monosodium glutamate, and consommé. Simmer for 5 minutes or until cabbage is crisp tender. Serve at once. If you wish to glaze the cabbage, add the blended cornstarch-water mixture and cook and stir for 1 minute until sauce thickens slightly. Serves 4.

CALORIES per serving: 94

VARIATIONS: Instead of using green onions, thinly slice 1 large onion and simmer with the cabbage. Sprinkle with ½ teaspoon toasted sesame seeds. Use regular cabbage instead of the Chinese cabbage and season with onion, chopped fresh dill or dried dill seeds, and lemon juice. No change in calories or sodium.

LOW-SODIUM MODIFICATION: Delete salt and monosodium glutamate; use low-sodium bouillon ☑ or water. Do use the sesame seeds in the variation and a good squeeze of lemon.

MG. SODIUM per serving: 39

Brussels Sprouts

Select Brussels sprouts that are compact and bright green. Cut off the stems and wash carefully in lightly salted water; drain. Cook in freshly salted water for 8 to 10 minutes or until tender; do not overcook. Drain and serve hot with a little unsaturated margarine ☑ blended with chopped parsley.

CALORIES per 6 Brussels sprouts: 36

VARIATIONS: Cut a gash in the flat side of 10 chestnuts and drop in boiling water. Boil for 10 minutes, then plunge into cold water. Quickly peel off the shells and brown skin. Quarter chestnuts. Make 1 cup White Sauce (see Sauces) and use 2 tablespoons flour to thicken 1 cup milk; season with a little mace. Stir the chestnuts and hot drained Brussels sprouts into the sauce and heat through. Serve with veal or broiled chicken. There are 135 calories for 6 Brussels sprouts in this variation.

LOW-SODIUM MODIFICATION: Omit salt in the cooking water. Use the low-sodium modification for the White Sauce in the variation.

MG. SODIUM per 6 Brussels sprouts, plain: 12

MG SODIUM per 6 Brussels sprouts in sauce with chestnuts: 20

Caraway Cabbage

    2 tablespoons unsaturated margarine ☑
    1 clove garlic, mashed or minced
    6 cups shredded cabbage
    2 tablespoons water
       Sugar substitute ☑ equal to 2 tablespoons sugar
          or 2 tablespoons sugar
       Dash of salt
    2 tablespoons vinegar or lemon juice
    6 tablespoons imitation sour cream ☑
    ½ teaspoon caraway seed

Heat margarine in a large skillet. Add the garlic, cabbage, and water; cover and steam for 10 to 12 minutes. Remove cover and add the sugar substitute, salt, vinegar or lemon juice, and imitation sour cream. Mix well and heat through. Sprinkle with caraway seed before serving. Serves 6.

CALORIES per serving using sugar substitute: 98

CALORIES per serving using sugar: 113

LOW-SODIUM MODIFICATION: Use low-sodium unsaturated margarine ☑ and a dash of salt substitute ☑.

MG. SODIUM per serving: 46

Baked Carrots Julienne

   6 medium sized carrots
   4 tablespoons unsaturated margarine ☑
   1 tablespoon lemon juice
   ½ teaspoon salt
   2 tablespoons water
   1 tablespoon chopped parsley

Peel carrots and cut in narrow strips 3 inches long; arrange in a small baking pan. Melt margarine and combine with the lemon juice, salt, and water; pour over carrots. Cover pan and bake in a moderate oven (350°) for 50 minutes to 1 hour or until carrots are tender. Sprinkle with parsley before serving. Serves 6.

CALORIES per serving: 70

VARIATIONS: Add 1 teaspoon of chopped candied ginger and a bit of grated orange peel to the carrots before baking. Cook peeled carrots in a little water until crisp tender; turn into a baking pan and cover with 2 tablespoons unsaturated margarine ☑ and 2 tablespoons brown sugar. Bake in a hot oven until carrots are tender and glazed. (There are 60 calories per serving for this variation.) Boil carrots in water, then drain and marinate as with the Marinated Cauliflower. Add a slice of fresh ginger to the marinade.

LOW-SODIUM MODIFICATION: A ½ cup serving of carrots contains 23 milligrams sodium so don't be overly generous with yourself. Avoid additional salt; if necessary use low-sodium gourmet seasoning ☑. Use low-sodium unsaturated margarine ☑.

MG. SODIUM per serving: 23

Marinated Cauliflower

   1 head (1½ pounds) cauliflower
     Lightly salted water
   1 tablespoon lemon juice
   3 tablespoons unsaturated oil ☑
   1 tablespoon dry white table wine or white vinegar
     Salt, pepper, and curry powder

Choose a head with no marks on the white surface. Soak cauliflower in cold water for a few minutes, then separate into flowerets. Cook in boiling salted water seasoned with the lemon juice for 9 minutes or just until tender. Drain and cool. Make a dressing with the oil and wine or vinegar. Season to taste with salt, pepper, and curry powder. Pour dressing over cauliflower, cover, and chill overnight. Baste with the marinade several times as it chills. Serves 6.

CALORIES per serving: 74

VARIATIONS: Season the dressing with dry mustard rather than curry powder, or try adding a dash of allspice or dill seeds, a little chopped fresh parsley, and a tomato that has been peeled, cut up, and simmered for a few minutes. The raw flowerets are excellent with a spot of the same dressing or a dressing seasoned with parsley and tarragon. No change in calories or sodium.

LOW-SODIUM MODIFICATION: Delete salt in the cooking water; use salt substitute ☑ and lots of lemon which both seasons and helps to keep the cauliflower white.

MG. SODIUM per serving: 15

Corn On or Off The Cob

Get ears of very fresh corn from the fields so that the sugar has not changed to starch. The change begins rapidly after picking, so the corn in the markets is not nearly so good. Pull down the husks, look for any worms or damage to the ears, remove corn silk, and pull husks back up. Plunge corn into boiling water which is sweetened with a little sugar. (Use 2 tablespoons sugar to cook 8 ears corn.) The green husks and sugar really add to the flavor. After 3 to 5 minutes of simmering, lift out the ears and drain. Using a clean towel to protect your hands, remove the husks. Serve each ear of corn with ½ teaspoon unsaturated margarine ☑ and a bit of salt and pepper.

CALORIES for each 4-inch ear of corn with margarine: 117

VARIATIONS: With a sharp knife cut enough corn from cobs to make 2 cups corn; add ½ cup skim milk, a dash of cayenne, and 1 teaspoon unsaturated margarine ☑. Simmer until corn is tender. For corn Mexicaine, add ½ chopped green pepper and enough pimiento to add some color before cooking the corn. Serves 4. There will be 92 calories per serving.

LOW-SODIUM MODIFICATION: Use salt substitute ☑ and low-sodium unsaturated margarine ☑ on the whole ears. Use low-sodium skim milk and low-sodium unsaturated margarine ☑ in the variation.

Negligible amount of sodium for whole ears

MG. SODIUM per serving of the variation: 2

Corn and Tomato Casserole

   1 can (1 pound) whole kernel corn, drained
   1 can (1 pound) solid pack tomatoes
   ¾ teaspoon salt
   ¼ teaspoon monosodium glutamate
   ¼ teaspoon pepper
   2 tablespoons melted unsaturated margarine ☑
   ½ cup cracker crumbs

Combine the corn, tomatoes, salt, monosodium glutamate, pepper, and melted margarine; turn into a lightly greased casserole. Sprinkle cracker crumbs over the top. Bake in a moderately hot oven (375°) for 30 minutes or until crumbs are brown and mixture is bubbly. Serves 4 as a main dish.

CALORIES per serving: 177

LOW-SODIUM MODIFICATION: Avoid salt and monosodium glutamate and season with a salt substitute ☑. Use low-sodium canned tomatoes ☑ and low-sodium canned corn ☑ or use fresh tomatoes and corn and cook them yourself. You should have 2 cups of each vegetable. Add a little fines herbes to unsalted cracker crumbs for the topping. Fines herbes are good in the corn too. Use low-sodium unsaturated margarine ☑.

MG. SODIUM per serving: 8

Braised Celery

   4 large stalks celery
   2 tablespoons unsaturated margarine ☑
     Salt and pepper
   4 cups chicken consommé or bouillon
   1 small onion, finely chopped
   1 tablespoon flour
   1 cup skim milk
   1 teaspoon chopped parsley
   1 tablespoon chopped chives
   1 tablespoon slivered almonds

Wash celery and cut each stalk in about 4 inch lengths; arrange in rows in a lightly greased baking pan. Dot with 1 tablespoon of the margarine, sprinkle with salt and pepper to taste, and add the consommé. Bake in a moderately slow oven (325°) until tender. Turn pieces of celery several times during baking. While the celery is cooking prepare the following sauce: sauté onion in the remaining 1 tablespoon margarine until limp and clear. Add flour and mix well. Slowly pour in the milk, and stirring, cook until sauce is smooth and thickened. Season with parsley, chives, and salt and pepper to taste. Drain liquid from the cooked celery, spoon the sauce over the celery and sprinkle almonds over the top. Continue baking for 10 minutes or until bubbly. Serve this heavier vegetable dish with a lighter main course such as a piece of broiled fish garnished with lemon. Serves 4.

CALORIES per serving: 95

LOW-SODIUM MODIFICATION: Use low-sodium unsaturated margarine ☑, low-sodium skim milk ☑ and low-sodium consommé or bouillon ☑. Celery has 50 milligrams sodium for 1 large stalk so watch it!

MG. SODIUM per serving: 50

Stir-fried Celery and Black Mushrooms

8 stalks celery
6 dried Chinese mushrooms
2 tablespoons unsaturated oil ☑
1 clove garlic, mashed or minced
¼ cup chicken consommé or bouillon
¼ teaspoon monosodium glutamate
   Salt to taste
1 teaspoon cornstarch
1 tablespoon water

Wash celery, remove any leaves, and cut stalks in diagonal shaped pieces. Soak mushrooms in warm water until they are limp and soft; drain and remove stems, then thinly slice crosswise. Heat oil and garlic in a large skillet; add the celery and stir and cook quickly for 4 minutes. Add the sliced mushrooms and cook 1 minute. Add the consommé or bouillon, monosodium glutamate, and salt. Blend cornstarch with the water, pour into pan, and stirring, cook until sauce is thickened and vegetables are glazed. Serves 4.

CALORIES per serving: 82

VARIATIONS: Peel a cucumber, split in half and scrape out seeds, then cut in thick slices. Add to celery when you add the consommé or toss in a handful of Chinese edible pod peas and cook only until vegetables are crisp tender. Sprinkle a few walnut halves in and heat through. This makes 130 calories per serving.

LOW-SODIUM MODIFICATION: Avoid salt and monosodium glutamate. Use a low-sodium consommé or bouillon ☑.

MG. SODIUM per serving: 110

Fennel Au Gratin

The tender stalks of fennel may be eaten raw or treated like celery in many recipes. Cut a head of fennel in quarters lengthwise and arrange in a casserole. Dot with 1 tablespoon unsaturated margarine ☑, pour on chicken consommé to cover, and sprinkle with salt and pepper to taste. Bake in a moderate oven (350°) until tender. Drain off most of liquid and sprinkle 2 tablespoons grated Romano or Parmesan cheese. Continue baking a few minutes to brown cheese on fennel. Serve with broiled or barbecued chicken breasts. Serves 4.

CALORIES per serving: 45

LOW-SODIUM MODIFICATION: Use low-sodium consommé ☑. Use low-sodium unsaturated margarine ☑. Avoid salt and add a little lemon juice. Be very sparing with the dried cheese—use only 1 tablespoon.

MG. SODIUM per serving: 75

Eggplant Provencal

(Eggplant with Tomatoes and Green Peppers)

3 tablespoons unsaturated oil ☑
1 clove garlic, mashed or minced
1 green pepper, seeded and coarsely chopped
1 can Italian style canned tomatoes or 2 medium sized tomatoes
1 eggplant
2 tablespoons flour
   Salt and pepper
1 bay leaf
¼ teaspoon thyme
½ cup fine dry bread crumbs

Sauté garlic in 1 tablespoon of the oil for 1 minute; add the green pepper and tomatoes and simmer for 20 minutes. If you use fresh tomatoes, peel them first and cut in quarters. Peel eggplant and cut in cubes. Roll in flour seasoned with a little salt and pepper, then slowly sauté in the remaining 2 tablespoons oil until lightly browned. Combine eggplant with the tomato mixture and add the bay leaf, thyme, and salt and pepper to taste. Turn into a casserole and sprinkle bread crumbs over the top. Bake in a moderate oven (350°) for 35 to 45 minutes or until eggplant is tender. Serve with shish kebab and rice. Serves 4.

CALORIES per serving: 140

VARIATIONS: Add a handful of fresh mushrooms or a little dry white table wine to the vegetables. Sprinkle a tablespoon of grated Parmesan or Romano cheese over the top along with the bread crumbs. The cheese will add 12 calories per serving.

LOW-SODIUM MODIFICATION: Use low-sodium canned tomatoes ☑ and low-sodium bread crumbs ☑. Delete salt and use a salt substitute ☑; avoid the grated cheese in the variation.

MG. SODIUM per serving: 7

Kale, Dutch Style

The young crinkly leaves may harbor sand so wash well and remove any tough stems. Cook in lightly salted water 10 to 15 minutes or just until tender. Drain well and add 1 tablespoon unsaturated margarine for each pound of kale and a sprinkle of lemon juice and nutmeg or mace.

CALORIES per ½ cup serving: 20

MG. SODIUM per ½ cup serving: 25

VARIATIONS: Cook 1 pound of small white boiling onions until tender, slip off the skins, and combine with 1 pound of kale that is cooked and chopped. Make a cream sauce as follows: Melt 3 tablespoons unsaturated margarine ☑ and blend in 3 tablespoons flour. Slowly add 1½ cups skim milk, and stirring, cook until smooth and thickened. Simmer for a few minutes to be sure flour is cooked. Season with salt, pepper, and nutmeg. Pour over kale and onions and serve hot. If you want a richer sauce, mix 2 tablespoons non fat dried milk with the skim milk.

CALORIES per ½ cup serving: 129

LOW-SODIUM MODIFICATION: Delete salt; use salt substitute ☑, lemon juice, and a dash of cayenne. Use low-sodium unsaturated margarine ☑ and low-sodium skim milk ☑.

MG. SODIUM per ½ cup serving of the variation: 28

Poached Leeks

    2 dozen young tender leeks
    ¼ cup chopped parsley
    1 clove garlic, mashed or minced
        Dash each of nutmeg, salt, and pepper
    1 bay leaf
        Juice of ½ lemon or 1 tablespoon dry white table
            wine
        Beef bouillon or consommé
    ½ cup fine bread crumbs

Cut away the green tops of the leeks except for a narrow rim at the top of the white. Wash well and remove the outer layer; sand is often harbored in this layer. Arrange leeks in a single layer in a lightly greased baking pan. Sprinkle the parsley, garlic, nutmeg, salt, pepper, bay leaf, and lemon juice or wine on leeks. Pour on enough bouillon to just cover the leeks. Cover pan with aluminum foil, and bake in a moderate oven (350°) for about 30 minutes or until leeks are tender and liquid is absorbed. Remove the foil, sprinkle with bread crumbs, and place under the broiler for a few minutes to brown the crumbs. Serves 6.

CALORIES per serving: 60

MG. SODIUM per serving using low-sodium beef bouillon ☑: 5

VARIATIONS: Make ½ cup White Sauce (See Sauces) and pour over the cooked leeks; broil until bubbly. Or serve the leeks cold with an oil and vinegar dressing which contains some chopped parsley. Add 110 calories and 10 milligrams sodium for the white sauce.

Stir-Fried Mushrooms

    ½ pound medium sized mushrooms
    1 tablespoon peanut oil
        Salt and monosodium glutamate to taste
        Juice of ½ lemon
    1 cup Chinese (edible pod) peas
    ½ teaspoon sugar
    4 tablespoons chicken stock or water
    1 teaspoon cornstarch
    2 tablespoons water

Wash mushrooms quickly in cold water and pat dry with paper toweling. Thinly slice, cutting down through the stems. Heat oil in a large skillet. (If you have any sesame oil, use ½ teaspoon in place of ½ teaspoon of the peanut oil.) Add mushrooms and stir quickly. Sprinkle with salt, monosodium glutamate, and lemon juice, and continue cooking for 5 minutes. Add the Chinese peas, sugar, and chicken stock, and stir and cook for 1 minute. Blend cornstarch with the 2 tablespoons water, add to pan, and stir until sauce thickens. Serves 4.

CALORIES per serving: 110

VARIATIONS: Peel and slice fresh water chestnuts and use them in place of, or in addition to, the Chinese peas. Canned water chestnuts are fine if you can find a brand that is not packed with salt. Use 1 teaspoon soy sauce if you are not sodium restricted. Eight water chestnuts will add 40 calories and 10 milligrams sodium.

LOW-SODIUM MODIFICATION: Delete salt, monosodium glutamate, and soy sauce. Use low-sodium chicken bouillon ☑ and a few drops of low-sodium flavoring ☑.

MG. SODIUM per serving: 19

Stuffed Baked Mushrooms

6 medium-large fresh mushrooms
1 cooked chicken breast
1 sprig parsley, chopped
½ clove garlic, mashed or minced
1 teaspoon chopped cooked ham
1 tablespoon unsaturated mayonnaise ☑
  Salt and pepper to taste
1 tablespoon fine dry bread crumbs
1 tablespoon unsaturated oil ☑
2 tablespoons unsaturated margarine ☑

Rinse mushrooms in cold water and pat dry with a paper towel. It is a waste of time to peel them—it's not necessary. Break off the stems so each mushroom forms a hollow cap. Chop the stems. Skin chicken, remove from the bone, and finely chop. Mix together the mushroom stems, chicken, parsley, garlic, ham, mayonnaise, salt, and pepper. Spoon filling in the mushroom caps so it forms a mound; sprinkle with bread crumbs. Heat oil and margarine in a skillet, add mushrooms, and sauté slowly for 5 minutes. Transfer mushrooms to a baking pan and bake in a very hot oven (450°) for 5 minutes. Serve as a garnish, vegetable, or serve several with a green salad as an entreé. Makes 6 stuffed mushrooms.

CALORIES per mushroom: 90

VARIATIONS: Substitute ¼ cup thick White Sauce for the mayonnaise to bind the filling together. Or use flaked crab meat in the stuffing and flavor with a tablespoon of brandy. Serve with bunches of watercress and lots of lemon wedges. Dust the top with paprika to add to the browning. Little change in calories.

LOW-SODIUM MODIFICATION: Delete salt and ham; use low-sodium unsaturated mayonnaise ☑, low-sodium bread crumbs ☑ and low-sodium unsaturated margarine ☑. Go easy on the crab meat in the variation for ¼ cup contains 148 milligrams sodium. Instead use flaked fresh (not canned) fish such as haddock, halibut, snapper, or salmon.

MG. SODIUM per mushroom: 18

Mushrooms En Brochette

16 medium sized mushrooms
¼ cup unsaturated oil ☑
¼ cup lemon juice
½ teaspoon fines herbes
  Salt and pepper to taste

Wash mushrooms; remove stems and save for another use. Mix together the oil, lemon juice, fines herbes, salt, and pepper; pour over mushroom caps and let stand for 1 hour. Soak thin bamboo skewers in water a few minutes, then thread mushrooms on skewers using 4 mushrooms per skewer. Place under the broiler and cook until mushrooms are tender. Turn several times during cooking. Serve with broiled chicken or broiled lamp chops and steamed rice. Makes 4 servings.

CALORIES per serving: 34

VARIATIONS: Alternate mushrooms with medium sized raw shrimp that have been marinated. Vary the herbs in the marinade by adding garlic, or after broiling, set the skewer aflame with a tablespoon of hot brandy. Two shrimp will add 60 calories.

LOW-SODIUM MODIFICATION: Omit salt in the marinade and use a salt substitute ☑. Do not use the variation.

MG. SODIUM per serving: 7

Onions, Baked and Glazed

Cook 1 pound unpeeled small white onions in boiling water for 15 minutes; drain and cool slightly. Peel onions and place in a casserole with 2 tablespoons unsaturated margarine ☑ and ¼ cup brown sugar. Stir well so the onions are coated with the margarine and sugar mixture. Bake in a moderate oven (350°) for 30 minutes or until onions are glazed and tender. Serves 5.

CALORIES per serving: 113

VARIATIONS: Precook onions as in the recipe above. When peeled, combine with 1 cup White Sauce (see Sauces) and bake until tender. Ten minutes before the end of the cooking, sprinkle dried bread crumbs or a few roasted almonds on the onions. There is little change in calories. There will be about 17 milligrams sodium per serving.

LOW-SODIUM MODIFICATION: Use low-sodium modification to make the White Sauce. Use low-sodium bread crumbs ☑, low-sodium unsaturated margarine ☑ and of course non-salted nuts in the variation.

MG. SODIUM per serving: 12

Mushrooms in Cream Sauce

1 cup White Sauce (see Sauces)
  Few drops caramel coloring
8 medium sized mushrooms
1 tablespoon unsaturated margarine ☑
1 teaspoon unsaturated oil ☑
1 teaspoon lemon juice
  Salt and pepper to taste
4 pieces toast

Prepare White Sauce and use 2 tablespoons flour to thicken 1 cup milk; color with a few drops caramel coloring. Wash mushrooms and slice, cutting down through the stems and the caps. Sauté mushrooms in the margarine and oil for 5 minutes; add lemon juice, salt, and pepper and continue cooking until mushrooms are tender. Add mushrooms to the hot sauce and mix well. Spoon each serving over a piece of hot toast. Serves 4.

CALORIES per serving including toast: 148

VARIATIONS: Add a little curry powder to the sauce before mixing in the mushrooms, or for a spicy bite, season the sauce with cayenne or Tabasco. If you don't want to use the White Sauce, stir the sautéed mushrooms into crisp green beans, or combine them with a little imitation sour cream ☑ or low-fat yogurt ☑. No change in calories.

LOW-SODIUM MODIFICATION: Use the low-sodium modification when preparing the White Sauce. Use low-sodium bread ☑ for toast and low-sodium unsaturated margarine ☑. Omit imitation sour cream and low fat yogurt in the variation.

MG. SODIUM per serving: 13

Okra Gumbo Style

1½ pounds okra
 2 tablespoons olive oil
 1 medium sized onion, chopped
 1 clove garlic, mashed or minced
 1 cup canned tomatoes or 2 fresh tomatoes, peeled and quartered
  Salt, monosodium glutamate, and pepper to taste
  Dash of Tabasco

Wash okra, cut off stem ends, and slice crosswise in 1-inch lengths. Heat olive oil in a heavy skillet; add the sliced okra and brown for a few minutes. Add the onion and garlic and continue cooking until onion is limp. Add the tomatoes, salt, monosodium glutamate, pepper, and Tabasco. Cover and simmer for 20 minutes or until okra is tender. Long cooking tends to make sliced okra slippery. Serves 10.

CALORIES per serving: 56

VARIATIONS: A few pieces of seafood such as small shrimp or flaked crab may be added near the end of the cooking. Each ounce (2 tablespoons) of seafood will add about 30 calories to the recipe.

LOW-SODIUM MODIFICATION: Okra is very low in sodium. Use low-sodium canned tomatoes ☑. Delete salt and monosodium glutamate. Use substitute ☑. Go easy on the crab meat. There are 74 milligrams sodium in 2 tablespoons of crab meat.

MG. SODIUM per serving without crab: 4

Broiled Onion Rings

1 large Bermuda onion
1 tablespoon melted unsaturated margarine ☑
2 tablespoons skim milk
½ cup crushed shredded wheat cereal

Peel onion and cut crosswise in ¼-inch thick slices. Cook onion slices in simmering water for 5 minutes; drain. When cool enough to handle, separate into rings and pat dry with paper toweling. Mix the melted margarine with the milk. Dip onion rings into the milk mixture, then in the crushed cereal. Place on a cooky sheet, and broil for 5 minutes; turn onion rings over and continue cooking for 5 minutes or until golden brown. Serves 2.

CALORIES per serving: 114

LOW-SODIUM MODIFICATION: Use a low-sodium unsaturated margarine ☑ and low-sodium skim milk ☑.

MG. SODIUM per serving: 14

Peas and Mushrooms

You will need 2 pounds of peas in the pod for 2 cups of shelled peas. Cook the shelled peas in lightly salted boiling water for 6 to 8 minutes or until tender. Drain well, then swirl 1 tablespoon unsaturated margarine ☑ through the peas. While peas are cooking, slice 8 mushrooms. Sauté with 1 tablespoon unsaturated margarine, the juice of ½ lemon and ¼ teaspoon monosodium glutamate. When mushrooms are tender, pour over the peas, add a grating of fresh pepper, and mix. Heat through before serving. Serves 4.

CALORIES per serving: 116

VARIATIONS: Cook 10 small white onions until tender, peel, and mix with the peas instead of using mushrooms, or add about 20 almonds which have been lightly sautéed. Chopped fresh mint, chives, and parsley are good seasonings for the plain peas. No change in calories with onions. Add 55 calories for almonds.

LOW-SODIUM MODIFICATION:Substitute lemon juice for salt in the cooking water. Avoid monosodium glutamate. Use low-sodium unsaturated margarine ☑, and be sure almonds are not salted. Remember fresh peas have very little sodium, but frozen peas have as much as 86 milligrams sodium per ½ cup.

MG. SODIUM per serving: 8

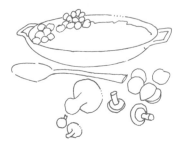

Peas and Rice

 1 tablespoon unsaturated oil ☑
 1 tablespoon unsaturated margarine ☑
 1 small onion, finely chopped
1½ cups shelled peas
 ½ cup uncooked rice
1½ cups chicken consommé or bouillon
 ¼ teaspoon monosodium glutamate
  Salt and pepper to taste
 1 tablespoon grated Romano or Parmesan cheese

Peas and rice mean different things in different locales. For an Italian version, heat oil and margarine in a saucepan. Add the onion and peas and cook gently for 5 to 6 minutes. Add the rice, consommé or bouillon, monosodium glutamate, salt, and pepper. Cover and cook slowly for 20 minutes or until rice is tender and liquid is absorbed. Stir in grated cheese before serving. Serves 6.

CALORIES per serving: 139

LOW-SODIUM MODIFICATION:Omit salt, monosodium glutamate, and Romano or Parmesan cheese. Use salt substitute ☑ and lemon juice for flavoring. Use low-sodium unsaturated margarine ☑ and low-sodium chicken consommé or bouillon ☑.

MG. SODIUM per serving: 5

Carribean Style Beans and Rice

 1 cup dried black beans (not Chinese)
 1 onion, finely chopped
 ½ clove garlic, mashed or minced
 ¼ teaspoon chili powder
  Dash of Tabasco
 1 tablespoon orange marmalade
 2 cups cooked rice

Soak beans overnight in water to cover (or cover with water, boil briskly 2 minutes, then cover and let stand 1 hour). Add a little salt to the soaking water and cook beans until tender. Add the onion, garlic, chili powder, Tabasco, and marmalade, to the cooked beans. Continue cooking slowly until most of the liquid has evaporated. Fold in the cooked rice and heat through before serving. Garnish with wedges of lime. Serves 8.

CALORIES per serving: 138

LOW-SODIUM MODIFICATION: Omit salt in the cooking water for the beans; use salt substitute ☑ and lemon juice. Cook rice in unsalted water.

MG. SODIUM per serving: 10

Red and Green Pepper Sauté

2 sweet red peppers
2 green peppers
2 tablespoons unsaturated oil
1 clove garlic, mashed or minced
Juice of ½ lemon
Salt and pepper to taste

Wash and seed peppers; cut into long strips. Heat oil with the garlic in a large skillet; add peppers and cook very slowly until tender. Stir occasionally during cooking, and when peppers are nearly tender, add the lemon juice, salt, and pepper. Serves 6.

CALORIES per serving: 53

VARIATIONS: When peppers are tender, add 2 peeled and quartered tomatoes and heat through for 5 minutes. Each tomato will add 22 calories and 3 milligrams sodium.

LOW-SODIUM MODIFICATION: Peppers are very low in sodium and they taste good in this Italian way. Delete salt and add an extra bit of lemon.

MG. SODIUM per serving: 8

Baked White Potato

Scrub medium size baking potatoes, and run a metal skewer into the end of each as far as you can. This speeds up the cooking by conducting heat into the middle of the potato. Bake in a hot oven (400°) for 45 minutes to 1 hour. Slash the tops of the potatoes to permit steam to escape and put ½ teaspoon unsaturated margarine ☑ and a little salt and pepper in each potato. Many restaurants now serve baked potatoes wrapped in aluminum foil. This is a dreary method because the skin doesn't get crisp. If you do

not eat the skin it will make little difference, however, unwrapped potatoes develop a delicious taste in the crisp skin which we think should not be missed.

CALORIES per potato with margarine: 100

VARIATIONS: Split the baked potato, scoop out the inside, and whip until smooth with a little skim milk enriched with non fat dried milk, a little unsaturated margarine ☑, and salt and pepper. Pile back in shells, dust with paprika, and put under the broiler for a couple of minutes to brown. Try mixing chopped chives and parsley into the hot potato or use a little imitation sour cream ☑ and chives.

LOW-SODIUM MODIFICATION: Avoid salt, use low-sodium skim milk ☑, low-sodium unsaturated margarine ☑. Omit imitation sour cream.

MG. SODIUM per potato: 3

Boiled Potatoes with Seasoned Sauce

4 medium sized potatoes
2 tablespoons unsaturated margarine ☑
1 whole clove garlic, peeled
½ teaspoon fines herbes
⅛ teaspoon dry mustard
½ teaspoon lemon juice
1 teaspoon chopped parsley
Salt and pepper to taste

Peel potatoes; cook in boiling water until tender. While potatoes are cooking, melt margarine in a saucepan. Remove from heat and stir in the garlic, fines herbes, dry mustard, lemon juice, parsley, salt, and pepper. Let stand at least 30 minutes. Remove garlic, reheat sauce, and serve over hot drained potatoes. Sauce may be strained before serving if desired. Serves 4.

CALORIES per serving: 120

LOW-SODIUM MODIFICATION: Omit salt; use low-sodium unsaturated margarine ☑.

MG. SODIUM per serving: 3

Mashed Potatoes

4 medium sized potatoes
1 minced onion
¼ teaspoon fines herbes
1 tablespoon unsaturated margarine ☑
3 tablespoons hot skim milk
Salt and pepper to taste
⅛ teaspoon mace

Peel potatoes and place in a saucepan with the onion, fines herbes, and boiling water to cover. Cover pan and cook 20 to 40 minutes or until tender; drain. Mash potatoes with a fork, then add the margarine, milk, salt, pepper, and mace. Beat until smooth. Serves 6.

CALORIES per serving: 77

LOW-SODIUM MODIFICATION: Omit salt; use salt substitute ☑, low-sodium skim milk, and low-sodium unsaturated margarine ☑.

MG. SODIUM per serving: 4

Sweet Potatoes with Orange

1 pound yams or sweet potatoes
2 tablespoons unsaturated margarine ☑
1 tablespoon brown sugar
1 tablespoon orange juice
1½ teaspoons grated orange peel

Boil sweet potatoes in their jackets in lightly salted water for 20 to 30 minutes, or until tender. Drain, and when cool enough to handle, peel and arrange in a lightly greased casserole. Cream together the margarine, brown sugar, orange juice, and grated peel. Spoon over sweet potatoes. Bake in a moderate oven (350°) for 30 minutes or until potatoes are hot and glazed. Serves 4.

CALORIES per serving: 176

VARIATIONS: Mash 1 pound cooked sweet potatoes with a little skim milk, 2 tablespoons each margarine and brown sugar, 1 teaspoon grated orange peel, and salt and pepper to taste. Spread in a baking pan and cover the top with 10 marshmallows. Heat in a moderate oven (350°) until marshmallows brown. You can also whip a tablespoon of Cointreau, Grand Marnier, or brandy into the sweet potatoes. There are 11 milligrams sodium in 1 ounce of marshmallows so keep your own helping down. Figure on 235 calories per serving.

LOW-SODIUM MODIFICATION: One small sweet potato has about 10 milligrams sodium whereas ½ cup canned sweet potato has 52 milligrams, so cook your own. Use low-sodium unsaturated margarine ☑ and low-sodium skim milk ☑. Avoid salt; use salt substitute ☑.

MG. SODIUM per serving: 20

Creamed Spinach

1½ pounds spinach
2 tablespoons unsaturated margarine ☑
2 tablespoons flour
1 tablespoon non fat dried milk
½ cup skim milk
¼ teaspoon mace or nutmeg
Salt and pepper to taste

Wash spinach and place in a heavy pan without adding any water. The spinach will steam with only the water that adheres to the leaves. Cover and cook until spinach is tender; drain, keep hot while you prepare the sauce. Melt margarine and blend in flour. Stir non fat dried milk into skim milk; slowly add to margarine and flour mixture, and stirring, cook until smooth and thick. Season with mace or nutmeg, salt, and pepper. Pour sauce over spinach and stir until all the leaves are coated. Serves 6.

CALORIES per serving: 84

VARIATIONS: Coarsely chop the hot cooked spinach before coating with the sauce or whirl in a blender. Sauté a chopped shallot or 1 teaspoon of minced onion in the margarine when you make the sauce. No change in calories.

LOW-SODIUM MODIFICATION: Use low-sodium skim milk ☑ and omit salt. Use low-sodium unsaturated margarine ☑. Spinach contains a moderate amount of sodium, 45 milligrams sodium for ½ cup of the cooked vegetable, hence it is probably best left out of the restricted diet. There is, however, no fat present, and if your restriction is limited to fat and not sodium, then it is a reasonable vegetable and very tasty this way.

MG. SODIUM per ½ cup spinach with 2 tablespoons of sauce: 47

Stuffed Zucchini

  4 zucchini (3 to 4 inches long)
  1 small onion, finely chopped
  1 stalk celery, chopped
  2 tomatoes, peeled, seeded, and coarsely chopped
  ½ clove garlic, mashed or minced
  1 tablespoon melted unsaturated margarine ☑
  1 large slice French bread, lightly toasted and cut into small cubes
  1 tablespoon unsaturated oil ☑
  ¼ teaspoon basil or oregano
  ¼ teaspoon chopped parsley
    Salt and pepper to taste
    Fine dry bread crumbs

Wash zucchini; cook whole zucchini in lightly salted water for 3 minutes; drain. Split in half and scrape out the seeds and discard. Remove pulp leaving a shell ¼ inch thick. Chop pulp and combine with the onion, celery, tomatoes, garlic, margarine. Saute a few minutes until vegetables are crunchy, but partly cooked. Add bread cubes, oil, basil or oregano, parsley, salt, and pepper. Season zucchini shells with a little salt and pepper; spoon filling into the shells. Place zucchini side by side in a lightly greased baking pan; sprinkle a few bread crumbs over the top of the zucchini. Bake in a moderate oven (350°) for 20–25 minutes or until zucchini is tender. Serves 4.

CALORIES per 2 halves: 116

VARIATIONS: Sauté a little chopped meat to put into the stuffing or use finely chopped left-over roast beef or a left-over chicken breast. A few mushrooms or a finely chopped carrot are good too. All these things will vary the taste and texture and contribute vitamins. The calories will vary only slightly.

LOW-SODIUM MODIFICATION: Zucchini is very low in sodium. Omit salt in the cooking water and for seasoning. Use low-sodium bread ☑ and low-sodium unsaturated margarine ☑. Omit celery.

MG. SODIUM per 2 halves: 7

Baked Winter Squash

  3 cups peeled Hubbard or banana squash
  2 cups lightly salted water
  1 tablespoon unsaturated margarine ☑
  1 tablespoon brown sugar
    Dash of ginger, nutmeg, or cinnamon
  1 apple
  1 teaspoon brown sugar

Cook squash in lightly salted water until tender; drain. Mash well, then beat in margarine, the 1 tablespoon brown sugar, and ginger, nutmeg, or cinnamon. Spoon into a casserole. Peel and core apple; cut in thin slices. Overlap slices and arrange in a circle on the squash; sprinkle the 1 teaspoon brown sugar on squash. Bake in a moderate oven (350°) until apple is tender. Serves 6.

CALORIES per serving: 88

VARIATIONS: Cut acorn or butternut squash in half, scrape out seeds, and place in a baking pan with ½ inch of water. Dot each with ½ teaspoon unsaturated margarine ☑ and a little salt and pepper. Bake in a moderately hot oven (375°) for 35 minutes or until tender. Squash soaks up fat, so do not add any more. Sprinkle with a little lemon juice and chopped parsley before serving. Pieces of pumpkin may be cooked the same way. There are 125 calories per serving.

LOW-SODIUM MODIFICATION: Squash of all types has very little sodium and almost negligible fat. As usual, use low-sodium unsaturated margarine ☑. Delete salt and use salt substitute ☑ and lemon juice or a little extra sugar.

MG. SODIUM per serving: 2

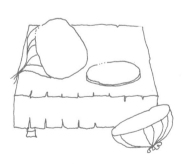

Summer Squash with Dill

    3 cups sliced summer squash
      Salt and pepper to taste
    1½ teaspoons minced onion
    ½ teaspoon crushed dill seed
    ¼ cup water
    1 tablespoon unsaturated margarine ☑

Place the squash, salt, pepper, onion, dill seed, and water in a saucepan. Cover and cook over low heat for 10 minutes or until tender but firm. Drain, then turn into a serving dish and top with margarine. Serves 4.

CALORIES per serving: 50

VARIATIONS: Fold in 1 tablespoon low-fat yogurt ☑. This adds only 2 calories per serving. Very young squash may be cooked without peeling.

LOW-SODIUM MODIFICATION: Omit salt; use a salt substitute ☑ and low-sodium unsaturated margarine ☑.

MG. SODIUM with added low-fat yogurt: 4

Swiss Chard

Choose young curly leaves. Wash several times to remove all of sand. Thinly slice the stalks; keep the leaves whole. Cook in boiling water for 15 minutes or until tender; drain well. Season 2 pounds of Swiss chard with 1 teaspoon unsaturated margarine ☑, the juice of ½ lemon, and a dash each of salt, pepper, and clove. It is important not to cook chard in salted water as this will cause it to darken. Serves 4.

CALORIES per ½ cup serving: 24

VARIATIONS: Season a little White Sauce (see Sauces) with nutmeg and stir into hot cooked chard. Use 1 tablespoon sauce for each ½ cup serving. This will increase calories to 100 calories per ½ cup serving.

LOW-SODIUM MODIFICATION: Delete salt. Chard itself contains a fair amount of sodium so treat it accordingly. Use low-sodium unsaturated margarine ☑.

MG. SODIUM per ½ cup serving: 86

Scalloped Tomatoes and Celery

    1 can (1 pound) solid pack tomatoes
    1½ cups soft bread crumbs
    1 cup diced cooked celery
    2 tablespoons unsaturated margarine ☑
    ¾ teaspoon salt
    ¼ teaspoon monosodium glutamate
      Pepper to taste

Place alternate layers of tomatoes, bread crumbs, and celery, in a lightly greased baking pan. Dot with margarine and season with salt, monosodium glutamate, and pepper. Bake in a moderately hot oven (375°) for 25 to 30 minutes or until hot and bubbly. Serves 6.

CALORIES per serving: 85

VARIATIONS: Substitute 1 tablespoon grated Parmesan or Romano cheese for 1 tablespoon of the bread crumbs, or sprinkle the grated cheese over the top before baking. Change the seasoning with a little curry powder, basil, or onion. The cheese will add about 50 calories.

LOW-SODIUM MODIFICATION: Delete salt and monosodium glutamate. Use low-sodium bread crumbs ☑, low-sodium unsaturated margarine ☑ and low-sodium canned tomatoes ☑. Reduce grated cheese to 1 teaspoon.

MG. SODIUM per serving: 28

MG. SODIUM per serving with cheese: 60

Stuffed Baked Tomatoes

  6 tomatoes
¼ cup minced onion
  2 tablespoons unsaturated oil ☑
  1 cup bread crumbs (use day old bread)
⅛ teaspoon each thyme and pepper
½ teaspoon sugar
    Salt to taste

Cut the tops off tomatoes and scoop out pulp. Drain the juice and seeds; chop pulp and reserve. Sauté onion in oil until limp and clear. Stir in reserved tomato pulp, bread crumbs, thyme, pepper, sugar, and salt. Spoon filling into tomato shells. Place in a lightly greased baking pan and pour a little water in the bottom of the pan. Bake in a moderate oven (350°) for 20 minutes or until tomatoes are tender. Serves 6.

CALORIES per serving: 47

LOW-SODIUM MODIFICATION: Delete salt; use salt substitute ☑ and low-sodium bread crumbs ☑.

MG. SODIUM per serving: 6

Broiled Tomatoes Italienne

Grease a cookie sheet with a little unsaturated oil. Dip thick slices of ripe firm tomatoes in a dish of dry bread crumbs mixed with a little finely chopped parsley and a chopped shallot, chopped chives, or a sliver of garlic. Place tomatoes on cookie sheet, then put under the broiler for 2 minutes; turn and brown the other side. Sprinkle with monosodium glutamate, fresh black pepper, and a little salt before serving.

CALORIES for 2 thick slices: 45

VARIATIONS: Sugar the tomatoes first or mix chopped fresh basil leaves with the chives. Each teaspoon of sugar adds about 20 calories.

LOW-SODIUM MODIFICATION: Delete salt and monosodium glutamate. Use low-sodium bread crumbs ☑.

MG. SODIUM for 2 thick slices: 4

Turnips and Rutabaga

Cut off the top and bottom and peel; cut into medium size pieces. Simmer in lightly salted water until tender. Allow about 20 minutes for turnips and 30 minutes for rutabaga. Drain and serve with a little freshly ground pepper and unsaturated margarine ☑.

CALORIES per ⅔ cup serving: 57

VARIATIONS: Mash cooked turnips and add a little sugar substitute along with the other seasonings. Mash cooked rutabaga and combine with mashed potato and a little skim milk. No change in calories or sodium.

LOW-SODIUM MODIFICATION: Omit salt; use salt substitute ☑ and low-sodium unsaturated margarine ☑.

MG. SODIUM per ⅔ cup serving: 35

Mixed Vegetables Sautéed, Italian Style

  1 pound zucchini, sliced
  1 cup diced green pepper
½ clove garlic, mashed or minced
  4 tablespoons unsaturated margarine ☑
½ pound mushrooms, sliced
⅛ teaspoon pepper
    Salt and monosodium glutamate to taste

Sauté zucchini, green pepper, and garlic, in unsaturated margarine until almost tender. Add mushrooms, pepper, salt, and monosodium glutamate. Continue cooking for 10 minutes or until all the vegetables are tender. Serve at once. Serves 6.

CALORIES per serving: 105

VARIATIONS: Add 1 peeled and chopped tomato with the mushrooms. Or use a few dried black Italian-style mushrooms, soaked first in consommé or water. Little change in calories and sodium.

LOW-SODIUM MODIFICATION: Delete salt and monosodium glutamate; use low-sodium unsaturated margarine ☑. Soak dried mushrooms in low-sodium consommé ☑ in the variation.

MG. SODIUM per serving: 10

Salads instill a freshness into the meal. They provide a moment of respite to the palate, between the heavier entrée and the sweet dessert.

However, in some parts of the world such as in California, salads are often eaten before the main course. A hangover, no doubt, from the days of our Gold Rush when fresh vegetables and lettuce were so scarce as to be worth more than their weight in gold!

Needless to say, certain salads are a meal in themselves and a habit among certain socially active, middle aged women who keep a "sharp eye on their middle aged middles!"

SALADS

Alice Salad

> 1 well-flavored red or yellow apple
> ½ teaspoon lemon juice
> 1 small banana, sliced
> 1 stalk celery, chopped
> 1 tablespoon Sauterne or Chablis
> 2 tablespoons imitation sour cream ☑
> Watercress

For each individual salad, cut the top off the apple; scoop out the meat, leaving a shell one-fourth inch thick. Swirl half of the lemon juice around inside the apple to prevent discoloration. Chop the apple you have removed (discard core) and combine with the banana and celery. Blend the other half of the lemon juice with the wine and imitation sour cream; stir into fruit. Spoon filling into the apple shell; replace top. Serve on a bed of watercress.

CALORIES per apple: 320

LOW-SODIUM MODIFICATION: Substitute 1 tablespoon low-sodium unsaturated mayonnaise ☑ for the imitation sour cream ☑.

MG. SODIUM per apple: 28

Molded Apple Salad

> 1 envelope (1 tablespoon) unflavored gelatin
> 1¼ cups apple cider
> ½ cup unsweetened pineapple juice
> Sugar substitute ☑ to equal 1 tablespoon sugar
> 1 tablespoon lemon juice
> 1 teaspoon grated orange peel
> ¼ cup chopped walnuts
> ½ cup unsweetened pineapple tidbits
> ¾ cup chopped apple
> Greens

Soften the gelatin in ¼ cup of the cider for about 5 minutes. Heat the remaining 1 cup cider; add the gelatin and stir until thoroughly dissolved. Stir in the pineapple juice, sugar substitute, lemon juice, and orange peel. Chill until syrupy. Fold in the walnuts, pineapple, and apple, and turn into a 1-quart mold. Chill until firm. Unmold on crisp greens. Serves 6.

CALORIES per serving: 88

MG. SODIUM per serving: 2

Apple Walnut Salad

 2 medium sized apples
 ¼ cup chopped walnuts
 2 teaspoons lemon juice
   Dash each of cinnamon and nutmeg
 2 tablespoons unsaturated mayonnaise ☑
   Endive, escarole, or lettuce

Core and chop the unpeeled apples. Combine with the walnuts, lemon juice, cinnamon, nutmeg, and unsaturated mayonnaise; chill. Serve on endive, escarole, or other feathery lettuce. Serves 4.

CALORIES per serving: 100

VARIATIONS: Substitute other nuts such as filberts or pecans for the walnuts; or use bananas instead of apples. To make a Waldorf salad, slice a small celery heart and add to the apple and nut mixture. A few raisins are a good addition too.

LOW-SODIUM MODIFICATION: Use low-sodium unsaturated mayonnaise ☑. Do not add celery heart in the variation.

MG. SODIUM per serving: 5

Chicken Salad Supreme

   Apple Walnut Salad
 1 cup diced cooked chicken
 ⅛ teaspoon curry powder
   Salt and pepper

Prepare Apple Walnut Salad to serve 4 persons. Add the chicken, curry powder, and salt and pepper to taste. You may wish to add a little more unsaturated mayonnaise ☑. Serves 4.

CALORIES per serving: 190

VARIATIONS: Marinate the diced chicken with 2 teaspoons French dressing (oil and lemon juice or tarragon vinegar), then add the unsaturated mayonnaise and delete the curry powder. A bit of chopped tarragon or parsley is a good addition too. The French dressing will add about 15 calories per serving.

LOW-SODIUM MODIFICATION: Delete salt and use low-sodium unsaturated mayonnaise ☑.

MG. SODIUM per serving: 22

Marinated Bean Salad

 1 can (1 lb.) green beans, kidney beans, or garbanzos
 1 tablespoon chopped green onion
 1 tablespoon chopped green pepper
 1 tablespoon chopped pimiento
 ½ cup unsaturated oil ☑
 ¼ cup vinegar
   Sugar substitute ☑ to equal 1 tablespoon sugar
 ½ teaspoon salt
 ¼ teaspoon pepper
   Greens

Drain beans; reserve liquid for the marinade. Combine beans, green onion, green pepper, and pimiento. Mix together ⅓ cup reserved bean liquid (add water if there is not enough), oil, vinegar, sugar substitute, salt, and pepper; pour over beans and chill for at least 2 hours. Drain marinade before serving and garnish with crisp greens. Serves 4.

CALORIES per serving using green beans: 100

CALORIES per serving using kidney beans or garbanzos: 200

VARIATIONS: Use fresh green beans or yellow wax beans and cook just until tender, then add to other ingredients. Or delete pimiento and add caraway seeds, basil, or a little rosemary. No change in calories or sodium.

LOW-SODIUM MODIFICATION: Delete salt; use salt substitute ☑ and lemon juice in the marinade. Avoid canned beans unless they are a low-sodium pack.

MG. SODIUM per serving: 6

Cucumber Salad

 2 medium sized cucumbers
   Salt
 ½ cup imitation sour cream ☑
 ½ teaspoon each chopped parsley, chives, and fresh mint

Peel cucumbers; split lengthwise and scrape out seeds, then thinly slice crosswise. Sprinkle with a little salt; chill over night. (The salt brings the water out of the cucumbers.) The next day, pour off the water; rinse cucumbers quickly with ice water, and drain. Season the imitation sour cream with parsely, chives, and mint; combine with cucumbers and serve at once. Serves 4.

CALORIES per serving: 25

VARIATIONS: Dress the sliced cucumbers with ½ cup imitation sour cream ☑ seasoned with 1 teaspoon onion juice, ¼ teaspoon dry mustard, and salt and pepper to taste. No change in calories.

LOW-SODIUM MODIFICATION: Do not use salt to pull the water out of the cucumbers. Season the dressing with a salt substitute ☑.

MG. SODIUM per serving: 22

Cool Cucumber Mold

 ¾ cup boiling water
 1 envelope lime-flavored low calorie gelatin ☑
 ¼ cup lemon juice
 1 teaspoon onion juice
 1 cup imitation sour cream ☑
 1 cup chopped peeled cucumber
   Watercress or parsley and lime wedges for garnish

Pour boiling water over gelatin and stir until completely dissolved. Add lemon juice and onion juice. Chill until syrupy; fold in imitation sour cream and cucumber. Pour into a mold and chill until firm. Unmold on a serving plate and garnish with watercress or parsley and lime wedges. Serves 6.

CALORIES per serving: 148

VARIATIONS: If calories are of no immediate concern, use regular lime-flavored gelatin. This will increase calories to 205 per serving.

LOW-SODIUM MODIFICATION: use low-fat yogurt ☑ instead of imitation sour cream.

MG. SODIUM per serving: 24

Coleslaw

 ½ cup imitation sour cream ☑
 1 tablespoon vinegar
 2 to 3 drops liquid sugar substitute ☑ or 1 teaspoon sugar
   Dash of paprika
 1 teaspoon minced onion
 4 cups finely shredded cabbage

Mix together the sour cream, vinegar, sugar substitute, paprika, and onion; pour over cabbage and toss lightly. Chill before serving. Serves 6.

CALORIES per serving, using sugar substitute: 32

VARIATIONS: Shred a small head of bright green cabbage. Chop 1 stalk celery and add to cabbage along with a little chopped apple. Or toss the cabbage with chopped scallion and chopped green pepper. Make a dressing with 3 tablespoons unsaturated oil ☑, the juice of half a lemon, a sprinkle of sugar, salt, and pepper, and a few mustard seeds. Pour over cabbage and mix lightly; chill. No change in calories.

LOW-SODIUM MODIFICATION: Skip the salt and use low-sodium gourmet seasoning ☑. Omit celery in the variation.

MG. SODIUM per serving: 50

Macédoine of Fruit

 1 envelope (1 tablespoon) unflavored gelatin
 1¼ cups water
 ½ cup orange juice
   Sugar substitute ☑ equal to ¼ cup sugar
 2 cups cut fresh fruit (grapes, oranges, bananas, pears, peaches, melon balls)
   Greens

Soften the gelatin in ¼ cup of the water. Heat the remaining 1 cup water; add the gelatin and stir until thoroughly dissolved. Stir in the orange juice and sugar substitute. Chill until syrupy. Fold in the fruit and turn into a 1-quart mold or 6 individual molds. Chill until firm. Unmold on feathery greens. Serves 6.

CALORIES per serving, using sugar substitute: 40

VARIATIONS: Omit the gelatin and merely mix the fresh fruit with a little orange juice, sugar or sugar substitute ☑, and a couple of tablespoons of sharp vinegar and oil dressing. Add some fresh pineapple or grapefruit. (These fruits have very little sodium so they may be used for many recipes.) Drain the fruit well and serve it on a few tender romaine leaves.

CALORIES per serving: 75

MG. SODIUM for Macédoine of Fruit and variation: 2

Wilted Endive Salad

    1 head curly endive (chicory)
    2 tablespoons unsaturated mayonnaise ☑
    1 teaspoon sugar
    1 teaspoon Dijon mustard
       Wine vinegar
       Salt and pepper

Wash endive, dry, and tear into bite-sized pieces. In a small saucepan blend the unsaturated mayonnaise, sugar, and mustard. Add wine vinegar, salt, and pepper to taste. Heat slowly without boiling; pour over endive and mix gently until the leaves are coated. Serves 6.

CALORIES per serving: 29

VARIATIONS: Other greens may be used in the same way. Lettuce and escarole are excellent, or try a mixture of some bitter (dandelion) and some sweet (romaine). No calorie change.

LOW-SODIUM MODIFICATION: Use low-sodium unsaturated mayonnaise ☑ and salt substitute ☑. Prepared mustards contain a fair amount of salt so instead use ¼ to ½ teaspoon dry mustard.

MG. SODIUM per serving: 6

Mixed Green Salad

      Mixture of greens (see below)
    3 tablespoons unsaturated oil ☑
    1 tablespoon lemon juice
    1 tablespoon wine vinegar or cider vinegar
  ¼ teaspoon each dry mustard, monosodium gluta-
        mate, and freshly ground pepper
      Salt

Use any mixture of greens which might include one or several of the following: romaine, leaf lettuce, head lettuce, Boston or butter lettuce, endive, escarole, dandelion greens, spinach, chives, watercress, fennel, or whatever else your market has to offer. Wash greens quickly in cold water, gently shake off any moisture, then wrap greens in a clean dish towel or put them in a plastic bag and refrigerate until chilled and crisp.

For the dressing mix together the oil, lemon juice, vinegar, dry mustard, monosodium glutamate, and pepper. Add salt to taste. When serving time comes, tear the greens into bite-sized pieces and place in a salad bowl. Shake the dressing until blended; pour just enough over the greens to coat all the leaves well. Toss salad lightly and serve it with pumpernickel or other dark bread and a glass of very cold dark beer.

CALORIES for 1 cup of tossed greens and dressing: 110

VARIATIONS: Try different fruit vinegars. Delete the mustard in the dressing and add curry powder. Or add garlic or chopped onion to the dressing. For an unusual salad, toss the dressing with finely shredded Chinese cabbage or red cabbage; toss in a few sliced cooked beets or a few sections of grapefruit or orange. No appreciable calorie or sodium change.

LOW-SODIUM MODIFICATION: It's best not to use dandelion greens or spinach leaves. Check sodium content of any vinegar or spice used. Delete salt and monosodium glutamate; use salt substitute ☑. Remember beer has 17 milligrams sodium per 8 ounces which will roughly fill a pilsner. Use low-sodium breads for toast.

MG. SODIUM for 1 cup of tossed greens and dressing: 10

Raw Mushroom Salad

1 pound medium sized mushrooms
⅓ cup unsaturated oil ☑
⅓ cup lemon juice or vinegar
¼ teaspoon dried leaf tarragon
   Salt and pepper
   Boston lettuce

Wash mushrooms quickly in cold water and pat dry with paper toweling. Cut off the dry end of the stems; thinly slice mushrooms. Make a dressing with the oil, lemon juice or vinegar, tarragon, and salt and pepper to taste. Pour over mushrooms and chill for 1 to 2 hours. Pour off any extra dressing, and serve the marinated mushrooms in lettuce cups. Serves 4.

CALORIES per salad: 53

VARIATIONS: Put a thin slice of lemon or lime on the dish with the mushrooms or add a few capers; garnish with watercress. No calorie change.

LOW-SODIUM MODIFICATION: Delete salt and use low-sodium gourmet seasoning ☑. Avoid capers.

MG. SODIUM per salad: 5

Fluffy Orange Mold

½ cup boiling water
1 envelope orange-flavored low calorie gelatin ☑
½ cup ice water
½ cup orange-flavored low-fat yogurt ☑
1 banana, diced
½ cup artificially sweetened pineapple, cut in small
     pieces
   Fresh mint or watercress

Add boiling water to gelatin and stir until completely dissolved. Add ice water. Chill until syrupy; fold in yogurt, banana, and pineapple. Pour into a 1-quart mold and chill until firm. Unmold on a bed of mint or watercress. Serves 6.

CALORIES per serving: 60

VARIATIONS: If you are not counting calories, use regular orange-flavored gelatin and regular canned pineapple. Fold in a can of drained mandarin oranges. This variation makes 86 calories per serving.

LOW-SODIUM MODIFICATION: Check sodium in low-fat yogurt; the salad is still good if it is omitted. Do not use regular orange-flavored gelatin in the variation.

MG. SODIUM per serving without yogurt: 8

MG. SODIUM per serving with yogurt: 20

Perfection Salad

1 cup boiling water
1 envelope lime-flavored low calorie gelatin ☑
½ cup ice water
1 tablespoon lemon juice
¼ teaspoon salt
¼ cup each chopped celery and green pepper
½ cup finely shredded cabbage
¼ cup chopped pimiento

Add boiling water to gelatin and stir until completely dissolved. Add ice water, lemon juice, and salt. Chill until slightly thickened; fold in celery, green pepper, cabbage, and pimiento. Pour into individual molds or into a small pan and chill until firm. Unmold or cut in squares to serve. Serves 4.

CALORIES per serving: 16

VARIATIONS: Again, if you aren't presently concerned with calories, use a regular lime-flavored gelatin and 2 cups liquid. If you want to heighten the green color slightly, add a drop of green food coloring.

CALORIES per serving: 52

LOW-SODIUM MODIFICATION: Delete salt and use low-sodium gourmet seasoning ☑ or more lemon juice. Be sure the pimiento is not canned with salt. Do not use regular gelatin.

MG. SODIUM per serving: 28

Potato Salad

3 medium sized potatoes
Dash of pepper
1 teaspoon vinegar
2 teaspoons minced onion
¼ teaspoon salt
½ cucumber, peeled and chopped
½ teaspoon fines herbes
3 tablespoons unsaturated mayonnaise ☑
½ teaspoon lemon juice
Salt and pepper

Peel potatoes; boil in water seasoned with a dash of pepper until they are tender but still hold their shape. Cool potatoes, then cut in small cubes. Season with vinegar, onion, and ¼ teaspoon salt; chill for 30 minutes. Mix in the cucumber, fines herbes, mayonnaise, lemon juice, and salt and pepper to taste. Chill again before serving. Serves 4.

CALORIES per serving: 135

VARIATIONS: Boil potatoes with skins on. Peel potatoes while still hot, slice, and mix with the following dressing: 1 tablespoon chopped chives, 1 tablespoon chopped parsley, 1 teaspoon dry leaf tarragon or 1 tablespoon chopped fresh tarragon, 5 tablespoons unsaturated oil ☑, 1 tablespoon white vinegar, and salt and white pepper to taste. Chill before serving. There are 215 calories and 4 milligrams sodium in each serving.

LOW-SODIUM MODIFICATION: Omit salt and use salt substitute ☑. Use low-sodium unsaturated mayonnaise ☑.

MG. SODIUM per serving: 5

Seafood Mold with Walnuts

1 envelope (1 tablespoon) unflavored gelatin
1½ cups water
½ cup lemon juice
1 cup flaked poached salmon, halibut, or other fish
⅓ cup unsaturated mayonnaise ☑
¼ cup chopped walnuts
Greens

Soften gelatin in ¼ cup of the water. Heat the remaining 1¼ cups water and pour over the softened gelatin; stir until it is dissolved. Add lemon juice. Chill until syrupy; fold in flaked fish, mayonnaise, and walnuts. Turn into a 1-quart mold and chill until firm. Unmold and garnish with crisp greens. Serves 4.

CALORIES per serving: 205

VARIATIONS: Substitute a little dry white table wine for part of the water used to make the gelatin.

LOW-SODIUM MODIFICATION: Do not use frozen fish and do not use salted nuts. Use low-sodium unsaturated mayonnaise ☑.

MG. SODIUM per serving: 27

Tomato Aspic

1 envelope (1 tablespoon) unflavored gelatin
½ cup cold water
1½ cups hot tomato juice
1 teaspoon sugar
1 tablespoon minced onion
Dash of paprika
¼ teaspoon thyme or basil
1 tablespoon vinegar or lemon juice
Greens

Soften gelatin in cold water. Add hot tomato juice and stir until gelatin is dissolved. Add remaining ingredients. Pour into a 1-quart mold and chill until set. Unmold on crisp greens. Serves 4.

CALORIES per serving: 30

VARIATIONS: When heating the tomato juice, add a couple of whole cloves to the juice, then discard cloves before mixing the liquid with the gelatin. You can line the bottom of the mold with various garnishes before pouring in the gelatin mixture; use cold cooked carrots, small shrimp, or a few slices of cucumber. Indulge your fancy and cut the vegetables in interesting shapes. You might want to use one of your limited eggs, hard-cooked and sliced, to arrange in a decorative pattern in the bottom of the mold. If your sodium is not limited, add a little monosodium glutamate and salt to the tomato juice. Check Appendix for calorie and sodium content of your chosen garnish.

LOW-SODIUM MODIFICATION: Use unsalted tomato juice; season with salt substitute ☑.

MG. SODIUM per serving: 4

Turkey Salad

2 cups diced cooked turkey
1 cup sliced celery
1 cup pineapple tidbits, well drained
½ cup toasted, slivered almonds
  Unsaturated mayonnaise ☑ to moisten
  Salad greens

Combine ingredients and toss lightly. Serve chilled on lettuce or other greens. Serves 6.

CALORIES per serving: 175

VARIATIONS: Marinate the turkey first with a little low calorie French dressing. Mix pink grapefruit sections with the turkey instead of pineapple, or put a dash of curry in the mayonnaise. No calorie change.

LOW-SODIUM MODIFICATION: Use turkey meat that was cooked without additional sodium. Do not use salted nuts. Use low-sodium unsaturated mayonnaise ☑ and reduce the amount of celery to ½ cup.

MG. SODIUM per serving: 85

Shrimp Louis

  Lettuce
  Endive
  Sliced radishes
  Sliced celery
⅓ cup small cooked shrimp for each salad
  Tomato wedge
  Cooked asparagus spear
  Pickled beet slice

To make each individual salad, form a lettuce cup on a salad plate. Toss broken endive with radishes and celery and spoon in lettuce cup. Place shrimp over top of salad. Garnish with tomato, asparagus, and beet. Serve with a generous amount of Louis Dressing (see Sauces).

CALORIES per salad without dressing: 75

LOW-SODIUM MODIFICATION: Be sure to use fresh shrimp, or substitute large segments of poached fresh fish for shrimp. Omit celery. Use the Louis Dressing with low-sodium modification. Sprinkle greens liberally with lemon juice and add some chopped watercress to heighten the spicy taste.

MG. SODIUM per shrimp salad without dressing: 120

MG. SODIUM per fish salad without dressing: 80

Tomatoes in Herb Vinegar

3 tomatoes
½ cup wine vinegar
1 tablespoon chopped parsley
1 tablespoon chopped fresh dill or 1 teaspoon dill
    seed
1 bay leaf
  Salt, monosodium glutamate, and pepper

Wash tomatoes, remove stems, and quarter. Combine vinegar, parsley, and dill; season with salt, monosodium glutamate, and pepper to taste. Pour over tomatoes and marinate at least 1 hour. Drain marinade before serving. Serves 3.

CALORIES per serving: 30

VARIATIONS: Peel the tomatoes and slice. Alternate tomato slices with slices of purple Italian onions. Sprinkle with a little oregano and a tablespoon or two of French dressing (4 parts unsaturated oil ☑ and 1 part wine vinegar). Chill for 2 hours; sprinkle with freshly ground pepper before serving. Increase calories to 75. No change in sodium.

LOW-SODIUM MODIFICATION: Avoid, of course, the salt and monosodium glutamate. Use a little salt substitute ☑ and lemon juice.

MG. SODIUM per serving: 18

SNACKS AND COCKTAIL FOODS

Although you may not be the "frivolous cocktail type", you may be forced, by social convention, to have a cocktail party now and then for your friends. If this is the case, thumb through some of these enticing recipes —they will titillate your palate. However, go easy on the cocktails themselves.

Should you raid the refrigerator at night, make it a habit to choose a piece of fruit or a bowl of low calorie cereal topped with a bit of artificial sweetener and skim milk.

Raw Vegetables

Set out a large handsome glass or pottery bowl and fill it with cracked ice, or ice cubes. Arrange in it a mixture of raw vegetables such as celery, sections of cauliflower, carrot curls, cherry tomatoes, pieces of fennel, small fresh mushrooms, peeled slivers of white turnip, thin green scallions, and radishes. Try a few vegetables that are not often served as nibbles, such as Chinese (edible pod) peas, sliced zucchini, or parsnips. Make a sharp French dressing of ½ cup unsaturated oil ☑ and ½ cup wine vinegar or lemon juice. Add a little salt and fresh ground pepper, ⅛ teaspoon curry powder, and 1 teaspoon finely chopped onion. Dunk the vegetables in the dressing before eating. See Appendix for food values of all vegetables.

CALORIES per tablespoon of dressing: 60 to 70

LOW-SODIUM MODIFICATION: Delete salt and make dressing sharper by adding more lemon and less oil.

MG. SODIUM: negligible

Fresh Fruit

Most fresh fruits are relatively low in fat and sodium so they are an excellent type of snack or dessert. Use cantalope, casaba, Crenshaw, Persian, or honey dew melon with a big squeeze of lemon or lime juice. Vary this with a half papaya (if you can get one) served with lemon or eat a freshly quartered peach. Don't forget at this point you are denying yourself a number of things, so spend some time picking out the piece of fruit you like best. Enjoy the piece like a true gourmet, savor its aroma, feel the texture on your tongue. Take delight in quality selection rather than filling your abdomen with a half peck of mediocre pieces.

If it is available in your locality, try the beautiful and unusual Kiwi fruit (also called Chinese goose-berries) in a salad. It has brilliant green flesh speckled with tiny jet black seeds. Scatter bright red pomegranate seeds in a salad, or late some afternoon in the Fall, sit down with a large, just-ripe persimmon, and quietly eat it all yourself. The flat type that resembles the tomato may be eaten while still crisp without puckering the mouth. The globe type of persimmon, however, must be soft and ripe. If you live in the Eastern part of the United States, you may find the delicious small ones in the woods after a frost.

The Mexicans have a root like a big turnip (Jicama), which is delicious sliced raw, eat it without salt and use a tiny sprinkle of chili powder. An excellent snack is a beautiful fresh black or green fig. They are also good simmered with a little wine or water, sugar substitute ☑, and lemon. A succulent ruby grapefruit costs more than a white one, but it's worth it; and don't forget, this is a treat, not the daily vitamin C requirement. Have the less expensive grapefruit mostly, but once in a while sneak a great one!

For finger food, have a small bunch of Ribier or Malaga grapes. A Comice pear is so juicy that you will need a bib—eat one with a spoon. If the Comice is unavailable, the gorgeous red Bartlett pear or the small tasty Seckle pear will fill the bill. Don't forget lemon or lime juice is wonderful on fresh fruit. Folks with their own strawberry plants are able to pick strawberries with the stems still on—roll them in powdered sugar and sink their teeth into this tasty treat. For a real treat spoon a tablespoon of Kirsh or Brandy over the berries, then roll in the sugar—Luscious!!

CHECK THE CALORIES IN APPENDIX

Curried and/or Chili Flavored Nuts

Season ½ pound of unsalted nuts (almonds, filberts, pecans, walnuts), or if you have no sodium restriction, use regular nuts. Beat 1 egg white with 1 tablespoon water. Stir nuts in egg white, then remove with a slotted spoon and spread out in a baking pan. Sprinkle over a little curry powder and salt or chili powder and salt. Bake in a slow oven (300°) for 15 minutes or until dry. Shake off any excess seasoning. Have a couple when your taste or spirit lags. Makes 1½ cups.

CALORIES per 2 tablespoons: 75

LOW-SODIUM MODIFICATION: Omit the salt from the seasoning and use a little salt substitute ☑.

MG. SODIUM per 2 tablespoons: 6

Wine Marinated Prunes

1½ pounds large prunes
1½ cups Port or other sweet red wine
 1 cinnamon stick
 6 whole cloves
 ½ teaspoon allspice
 ½ cup brown sugar
 3 pieces lemon peel

Wash prunes, shake off water, and place in a small crock or jar that has a lid. Heat the Port with the cinnamon stick, cloves, allspice, brown sugar, and lemon peel; stir until sugar dissolves. Pour the hot marinade over the prunes. Cover and let stand until the prunes are plump and show only a few wrinkles. Serve cold with cottage cheese and lettuce or serve as a garnish for roast or baked chicken. The prunes may be kept for 1 week in the refrigerator.

CALORIES per prune: 46

LOW-SODIUM MODIFICATION: There are roughly 20 milligrams sodium in 1 cup Port. However, in this receipe the prunes absorb only a little of the marinade so with 2 to 3 prunes you are not getting much.

MG. SODIUM per prune: 2

Broiled Stuffed Mushrooms

 1 small onion, finely chopped
 1 sliver of garlic, minced
 1 tablespoon unsaturated margarine ☑
 1 tablespoon flour
 ¼ cup skim milk
 1 teaspoon lemon juice
 1 teaspoon chopped parsley
    Salt and pepper
 8 medium-large mushrooms
 ¼ cup flaked cooked fish
    Bread crumbs

Sauté onion and garlic in unsaturated margarine until limp and clear. Blend in flour and cook a few minutes to brown flour slightly. Pour in milk, and stirring, cook until smooth and thick. Stir in lemon juice, parsley, and salt and pepper to taste. Wash mushrooms; remove stems and finely chop. Mix together the sauce, chopped stems, and fish (not a highly flavored one like salmon). Spoon filling into the mushroom caps; sprinkle with bread crumbs. Place filled mushrooms on a lightly greased baking sheet. Bake in a moderate oven (350°) for 15 to 20 minutes or until hot and bubbly. Serve plain or on toast rounds. Serves 4.

CALORIES per 2 stuffed mushrooms: 175

VARIATIONS: Instead of fish, use finely chopped cooked chicken; put a bit of curry powder in the sauce.

If you make the fish-stuffed mushrooms, flame with 2 tablespoons warm brandy. The brandy will add 73 calories.

LOW-SODIUM MODIFICATION: Be sure that the left-over fish or chicken was cooked without extra salt. Use low-sodium unsaturated margarine ☑ and low-sodium skim milk ☑; delete salt and add more lemon juice or teaspoon of dry white wine. Instead of bread crumbs, sprinkle crushed unsalted matzohs over the filled mushrooms.

MG. SODIUM per 2 stuffed mushrooms: 18

Fruit Kebabs

Use several kinds of melon (cantalope, Persian, Crenshaw) and cut fruit in 1-inch cubes. Marinate the melon in sweet or dry white wine, champagne, or just a little lemon flavored syrup. Alternating kinds of melon, thread on small bamboo skewers. Decorate the end of each skewer with a maraschino cherry. Garnish with fresh mint.

CALORIES per skewer: 20

MG. SODIUM per skewer: 10

Swordfish Kebabs

    1 pound swordfish
  16 small mushrooms
    3 tablespoons unsaturated oil ☑
    1 tablespoon tarragon vinegar or lemon juice
    1 tablespoon dry white table wine
      Salt and pepper
      Chopped fresh tarragon or chopped parsley
      Lemon wedges

Cut fish in 1-inch cubes. Wash mushrooms and remove stems (save for another use). Toss the fish and mushrooms in a bowl with the oil, vinegar, wine, and salt and pepper to taste; marinate for 30 minutes. Alternate 2 pieces of fish and 2 mushrooms on small bamboo skewers. Cook under the broiler or grill over charcoal until the fish is tender, about 8 minutes. When it is cooked, arrange the skewers on a chop plate, sprinkle with tarragon or parsley, and garnish with lemon wedges. Makes about 8 skewers.

CALORIES per skewer with 2 pieces swordfish: 80

VARIATIONS: Use cherry tomatoes instead of or in addition to the mushrooms. Arrange the cooked kebabs on a plate lined with freshly washed parsley. No change in calories.

LOW-SODIUM MODIFICATION: Do not use frozen fish as it contains too much sodium. Omit salt and use salt substitute ☑.

MG. SODIUM per skewer with 2 pieces swordfish: 45

Raw Clams on the Half Shell

Treat these similarly to raw oysters (see Entrées). Scrub clams well; open with a sharp knife or clean screw driver. Cut the muscle away from the shell, being careful not to spill the juice. Place the clams in the half shell on a bed of cracked ice and garnish with parsley, watercress, or other bright greens. Squeeze a little lemon juice over the clams and dot with horseradish. Serve with a split of cold white wine.

CALORIES per small clam: 10

LOW-SODIUM MODIFICATION: Clams are high in sodium and should be omitted from a low-sodium diet.

Cheese

There are some cheeses coming on the market with a low-sodium content, and in some cases, attempts have been made to decrease the saturated fat. However, they have been disappointing, so far. Perhaps the taste and smell of Cheddar, Stilton, Brie, and Roquefort will soon be added to farmer's cheese, cottage cheese, or even Monterey jack which contains less saturated fat than many others. Still, they all contain large amounts of sodium. So forego cheese except for a small piece on a rare occasion. If you are a compulsive eater, and you can't stop once the stuff passes your lips avoid these altogether.

Fish Bites
With Chili Dip

¼ cup finely chopped onion
6 tablespoons unsaturated oil ☑
1 clove garlic, mashed or minced
1 teaspoon dry mustard
5 tablespoons chili sauce
1 pound fish fillets or steaks (cod, haddock, swordfish, halibut, snapper)
½ cup lemon juice
½ small bay leaf, crumbled
  Paprika

Sauté the onion in 2 tablespoons of the oil until limp but not brown. Add the garlic and cook for 30 seconds. Remove from heat and blend in the mustard and chili sauce. Spoon sauce into a small serving bowl. Remove any skin and bones from fish. Cut in 1-inch cubes. Place fish in a bowl with the remaining 4 tablespoons oil, lemon juice, and bay leaf; marinate 1 hour, then pour off marinade. Thread 2 pieces of fish on each small skewer and dust with paprika. Broil for 8 to 10 minutes, turning several times during cooking. To serve arrange the skewers on a serving plate or stand them in a sheet of cork. Dip the fish in the sauce and eat. Makes about 20 small skewers.

CALORIES per skewer with small amount of sauce: 60

LOW-SODIUM MODIFICATION: Use low-sodium chili sauce ☑.

MG. SODIUM per skewer with small amount of sauce: 18

Garlic Tomatoes

1 box cherry tomatoes
6 tablespoons unsaturated oil ☑
2 tablespoons wine vinegar
2 cloves garlic, slivered
1 bay leaf
1 sprig parsley
  Few celery leaves
½ lemon, thinly sliced
  Monosodium glutamate
  Salt and pepper

Wash tomatoes, remove stems, and pat dry with paper towels. Place tomatoes in a jar with a tight fitting lid; add the oil, wine vinegar, garlic, bay leaf, parsley, celery leaves, lemon slices, and monosodium glutamate

and salt and pepper to taste. Cover and let stand in the refrigerator 1 day before using. Invert jar occasionally to keep the tomatoes coated with the marinade. These will keep for at least a week in the refrigerator. Serve as a garnish in a salad or arrange with escarole or curly endive to serve as a snack.

CALORIES per 6 cherry tomatoes: 25

LOW-SODIUM MODIFICATION: Delete monosodium glutamate and salt. Use salt substitute ☑ and some dill seed or chopped fresh dill.

MG. SODIUM per 6 cherry tomatoes: 5

Chicken Livers
and Water Chestnuts

1 pound chicken livers
3 tablespoons unsaturated oil ☑
2 tablespoons soy sauce
1 teaspoon sugar
1 small clove garlic, mashed or minced
2 pieces slivered fresh ginger or a dash powdered ginger
1 flat can water chestnuts

In the classic Rumaki, a strip of bacon is wrapped around a marinated chicken liver and water chestnut, and broiled. This has too much fat, so try this adaptation. Use fresh chicken livers—frozen ones tend to be mushy and watery when they thaw. Remove any tough bits of membrane and fat. Place whole livers in a bowl with the oil, soy sauce, sugar, garlic, and ginger; let stand 30 minutes. Wrap 1 marinated liver around a water chestnut and spear with a small bamboo skewer. You should end up with 14 to 16 filled skewers. Broil about 5 minutes or until the livers are cooked. Turn several times during cooking. These have a wonderful taste and aroma! Makes 14 to 16 servings.

CALORIES per skewer: 65

LOW-SODIUM MODIFICATION: An ounce of plain chicken liver (about one liver) contains about 20 milligrams sodium, so take it easy. Do not use soy sauce in the marinade; substitute with low-sodium flavoring ☑, a little wine, and a small amount of salt substitute ☑. The canned water chestnuts may or may not contain sodium; if they do, you'll have to resort to the fresh variety from a Chinese or other specialty market. The sacrifice is not great since the fresh ones are so much better.

MG. SODIUM per skewer: 24

BREADS, CAKES, COOKIES, AND PIES

The staff of life in its many guises greets you from these pages. Careful on the size of the servings though, for the calories add up!

Remember, use this section in moderation, always keeping in mind the kind of well-balanced meal included in the 14 day menu guides.

"Man Cannot Live by Bread Alone".

Cereals

Cereals have been used from the days of pre-history as a major source of food. Ever since man found that certain wild grasses could be domesticated, he has thrashed and gleaned them at harvest time and has learned to store them through the next season.

Today we do not need to go through this laborious process, for they are available neatly packaged on our grocery shelves.

Most cereals that have to be cooked in the home such as oatmeal, cornmeal, cream of wheat, and farina, are usually low in fat and sodium. Be sure to avoid the "quick cooking" varieties as they are processed with the addition of sodium. Remember, of course, not to add salt while cooking; instead add a few teaspoons of raisins or a few chopped dates. To avoid increasing calories, use granulated sugar substitute ☑ on top.

Dry cereals can also be a source of breakfast enjoyment or eaten as a snack. If you are restricted in the use of sodium use shredded wheat, puffed wheat, or puffed rice. Other prepared dry cereals contain too much sodium except for a few low sodium brands that have appeared on the market. (See list of products in Appendix).

Cut up fresh fruits such as bananas, strawberries, or apples sprinkled with a little sugar or sugar substitute, will make your breakfast a cereal treat. For those on the low sodium modification, use low-sodium skim milk.

Baking Powder Biscuits

    2 cups flour
    3 teaspoons baking powder
 ¼ cup non fat dried milk
    1 tablespoon sugar
 ⅓ cup unsaturated oil ☑
 ⅔ cup water

Sift flour, measure, then sift again with baking powder, dried milk, and sugar into a bowl. With a fork, beat the oil and water together; pour all at once into flour mixture and stir lightly until the dough holds together. Knead about 10 times in the bowl until smooth. Place ball of dough between 2 pieces of waxed paper and press or roll out until it is ¼ inch thick. Cut out with unfloured cutter. Place on ungreased baking sheet; for crusty sides allow space between biscuits. Bake in a very hot oven (475°) for 10 to 12 minutes. If higher biscuits are desired, roll out dough ½ inch thick. Makes 14 biscuits.

CALORIES per biscuit: 100

VARIATIONS: Use half the recipe, roll out into a sheet to cover a small beef stew for 4 people. You'll get a slightly raised tender crust. If your sodium is not restricted, brush the crust with a teaspoon of milk to help make it shiny brown. Put a few coriander seeds or a pinch of ground coriander into the dough or add a few caraway seeds to the basic mix. Fines herbes and poppy seeds are good too.

LOW-SODIUM MODIFICATION: Use low-sodium skim milk ☑ and low-sodium baking powder ☑.

MG. SODIUM per biscuit: ½

Yeast Rolls

  2 packages yeast, active dry or compressed
½ cup warm water (lukewarm for compressed yeast)
⅓ cup sugar
  4 cups regular all-purpose flour (sift before measuring)
  1 cup unsaturated oil ☑
  4 egg whites

Dissolve yeast in warm water; add sugar and stir mixture well. Add half of the flour and all the oil to the yeast mixture; beat until very smooth. Add remaining flour to yeast mixture and blend well. Beat egg whites until stiff but not dry; mix with dough. Turn dough out on a board and knead. Add a little flour to the board as you knead, until the dough no longer sticks. Knead until dough is smooth and satiny. Put dough in a lightly greased bowl and rub a little oil over the top. Cover bowl and place in the refrigerator overnight; dough will rise. In the morning take out dough and shape into rolls as desired such as clover leaf, Parker house, braids, fan tans, and bowknots. Place on lightly greased baking sheets or muffin tins. Let rise in a warm place until almost doubled in size. Bake in a hot oven (400°) for 30 minutes or until golden brown. Makes 2 dozen rolls, depending of course, on size and shape.

CALORIES per roll: 60

LOW-SODIUM MODIFICATION: Omit egg whites. A nice variation which doesn't add sodium is the cinnamon roll. Put 1 tablespoon melted low-sodium unsaturated margarine ☑, 2 tablespoons brown sugar, 2 tablespoons dark corn syrup, and ½ teaspoon cinnamon in the bottom of the baking pan; mix well, then place bun shaped rolls in the pan. Let dough rise, bake, then turn the pan over so the rich glaze shines on the top.

MG. SODIUM per roll: negligible

Stone Ground Whole Wheat Bread

  2 packages yeast, active dry or compressed
½ cup warm water (lukewarm for compressed yeast)
  3 cups skim milk
½ cup melted unsaturated margarine ☑
  1 tablespoon salt
  3 tablespoons molasses
  6 cups stone ground whole wheat flour
  2 cups regular all-purpose flour
¼ cup wheat germ—if desired

Dissolve yeast in warm water. Scald milk and cool. Add the cooled milk to the yeast along with melted margarine, salt, and molasses; stir until well blended. Add 5 cups of flour, 1 cup at a time. Add the 6th cup of flour and beat until dough is smooth and elastic. Add wheat germ if desired. Mix the 7th cup of flour in to make a stiff dough. Measure the 8th cup of flour and sprinkle about half of it on a board. Turn out dough onto the floured board and knead. Add more flour as needed until dough no longer sticks. Knead until dough is smooth and satiny. Put dough in a greased bowl, grease top lightly, cover and let rise in a warm place until almost doubled in bulk. Test by inserting two fingers down into the dough—the indentation should remain. Punch dough down; divide into 3 equal parts and shape each part into a loaf. Place in greased loaf pans. Cover and let rise in a warm place until almost doubled. Brush tops with a little skim milk. Bake in a hot oven (400°) for 15 minutes, then reduce heat to 350° and continue baking 45 minutes or until lightly browned. Makes 3 loaves

CALORIES per loaf with wheat germ: 1552

CALORIES per slice: 86

LOW-SODIUM MODIFICATION: Omit salt; use low-sodium skim milk ☑ and low-sodium unsaturated margarine ☑. The molasses will make up for the "unsalted" taste.

MG. SODIUM per loaf: 163

MG. SODIUM per slice: 9

Pancakes

    2 cups flour
    2½ teaspoons baking powder
    1½ tablespoons sugar
    1½ cups skim milk
    2 tablespoons unsaturated oil ☑

Sift flour, measure, then sift again with baking powder and sugar into a bowl. Combine the milk and oil; add to dry ingredients, stirring only enough to moisten. Bake on a hot griddle lightly greased with unsaturated oil, turn to brown both sides. Makes 12 pancakes

CALORIES per pancake: 102

VARIATIONS: Beat 2 egg whites until stiff but not dry and fold into the batter. (This will add 8 milligrams sodium to each pancake.) Because the basic recipe for pancakes is made without eggs, the batter tends to be slightly dense. You might like to try flavoring these "tortillas" this way. Bake thin pancakes and spread each one with 1 tablespoon of low-calorie apricot jam ☑, roll up, and place side by side in a flame-proof dish. Shake a little powdered sugar over pancakes. Broil for 2 minutes, then pour 2 tablespoons of warm brandy over pancakes and light. When the blue flames die, serve one or two pancakes with café expresso. There are 120 calories and 5 milligrams sodium per rolled pancake.

LOW-SODIUM MODIFICATION: Use low-sodium baking powder ☑ and low-sodium skim milk ☑. Go easy on the egg whites in the variation.

MG. SODIUM per pancake: 2

Blueberry Pancakes

Prepare the recipe above for plain pancakes or the low-sodium modification; fold ½ cup well drained canned unsweetened blueberries into the batter. Save the juice. Bake pancakes on a hot griddle. To make a syrup, stir 1 teaspoon cornstarch into ½ cup unsweetened blueberry juice; cook and stir until slightly thickened. Remove from heat and add sugar substitute equal to ¼ cup sugar. Makes 12 pancakes

CALORIES per pancake: 120

CALORIES for ½ cup syrup: 80

VARIATIONS: Any sweetened, flavored, slightly thickened fruit may be used as a filling if you want to roll up the plain pancakes. Peaches, apricots, cherries, strawberries, and other berries are all good. If you make the plain pancakes without the sugar, you can use them to roll around creamed chicken, mushrooms, asparagus, or tuna. Flavor the creamed fillings with curry powder or chili powder—this is especially good with chicken. Remember you are allowed a couple of eggs a week, so reserve them and use in cakes or other situations where the special qualities of the egg are useful.

Waffles

    2 cups flour
    2 teaspoons baking powder
    ¼ teaspoon salt
    2 eggs
    1¼ cups skim milk
    6 tablespoons unsaturated oil ☑
    2 tablespoons sugar (optional)

Sift flour, measure, and sift again with baking powder and salt into a bowl. Separate the eggs; beat yolks until light, then combine with milk and oil. Add to dry ingredients, beating until smooth. Stir sugar into the batter if desired; however, it will tend to make the waffle less crisp. Beat egg whites until stiff but not dry; carefully fold into batter. Bake in a hot waffle iron. Makes 8 waffles.

CALORIES per waffle: 228

VARIATIONS: To serve sweet waffles for dessert, add grated orange peel to the batter and shake powdered sugar over the hot waffle. Cinnamon, clove, and cardamom may also be added. One teaspoon powdered sugar will add 20 calories to each waffle. Unsweetened waffles become an entrée when topped with creamed chicken or fish.

LOW-SODIUM MODIFICATION: Omit salt. Use low-sodium baking powder ☑ and low-sodium skim milk ☑.

MG. SODIUM per waffle: 20

Special Breads

(Zweibach and Melba Toast)

Zweibach is best purchased in fresh boxes. Melba toast is easy to make. Thinly slice low-fat white bread and place on a baking sheet; bake in a very slow oven (250°) until brown.

CALORIES per slice: 60

LOW-SODIUM MODIFICATION: Use low-sodium melba toast ☑ or make your own with low-sodium bread slices.

MG. SODIUM per slice: 7

French Toast

   1 egg white
   1 tablespoon skim milk
   1 teaspoon flour
     Dash of salt
   2 slices day-old bread
   1 teaspoon unsaturated oil ☑

Beat egg white slightly. Combine with milk, flour, and salt, and mix until smooth. Dip slices of bread in the mixture, and **sauté** in oil, turning to brown both sides. Shake on powdered sugar before serving or top with a spoonful of apricot or raspberry jam. You can also use the toast as a main part of an evening meal and serve it with vegetables such as broccoli, sautéed celery and carrots, or mushrooms. Serves 1 (2 slices).

CALORIES per serving: 200

VARIATIONS: You may want to use your weekly egg allowance here and beat up the whole egg instead of just using the egg white. This will add 60 calories and 14 milligrams sodium.

LOW-SODIUM MODIFICATION: use low-sodium bread ☑. Omit the milk and use 1 tablespoon water to beat with the egg white. Use a salt substitute ☑. Omit celery.

MG. SODIUM per serving: 62

Cinnamon Toast

   4 tablespoons unsaturated margarine ☑, softened
     Sugar substitute ☑ equal to ¼ cup sugar
   1 teaspoon cinnamon
   8 slices bread

Blend the unsaturated margarine, sugar substitute, and cinnamon. Toast bread on one side. Spread the cinnamon mixture over the other side and broil until browned. Serves 4.

CALORIES per serving: 235

VARIATIONS: Make a piece only for yourself in the afternoon for tea. Just use a little brown sugar and cinnamon sprinkled over and delete the margarine. This is really good with a cup of hot tea that has a little dried orange peel and spice in it. Add a spot of sweetener, put your feet up, and relax. No change in calories or sodium.

LOW-SODIUM MODIFICATION: Use low-sodium bread ☑ and low-sodium unsaturated margarine ☑.

MG. SODIUM per serving: 15

Muffins

   2 cups flour
   3 teaspoons baking powder
   2 tablespoons sugar
   1 teaspoon salt
   1 egg white
   ⅓ cup unsaturated oil ☑
 1¼ cups skim milk
   2 drops yellow food coloring (optional)

Sift flour, measure, and sift again with baking powder, sugar, and salt. Beat egg white with the oil until well mixed; stir in milk and food coloring if desired. Add to flour mixture, stirring only until mixed. Batter will still be lumpy. Spoon into greased muffin pans and bake in a hot oven (400°) for 25 minutes or until lightly browned. Makes 12 large muffins.

CALORIES per muffin: 135

VARIATIONS: Nut Muffins: Add ½ cup coarsely chopped walnuts to the mixed dry ingredients.

CALORIES per muffin: 162

Blueberry Muffins: Add sugar substitute equal to 3 tablespoons sugar. Combine 1 cup of fresh, frozen, or canned berries with the mixed dry ingredients. Drain berries well to avoid staining all the dry ingredients. The frozen ones with no added syrup are beautiful.

CALORIES per muffin: 142

Apple Muffins. Add 1 cup chopped peeled apple and ½ teaspoon cinnamon to the mixed dry ingredients.

CALORIES per muffin: 146

Orange Muffins: Add 1 tablespoon grated orange peel to dry ingredients. Use half orange juice and half milk for the liquid.

CALORIES per muffin: 135

Whole Wheat Muffins: ⅔ cup whole wheat flour and 1⅓ cups white flour.

No calorie change

LOW-SODIUM MODIFICATION: Use low-sodium baking powder ☑; delete salt and add a little salt substitute ☑, grated lemon peel, nutmeg, or cinnamon, and sugar. Use low-sodium skim milk ☑.

MG. SODIUM per muffin: 6

Cornmeal Muffins

    1 cup flour
    ¾ cup yellow cornmeal
    2½ teaspoons baking powder
    ½ teaspoon salt
    2 tablespoons sugar
    2 egg whites or 1 whole egg
    1 cup skim milk
    ¼ cup unsaturated oil ☑

Sift flour, measure, then sift again with cornmeal, baking powder, salt, and sugar. Beat egg whites or egg with the milk and oil; add to dry ingredients and stir only enough to barely mix. Do not beat. Drop batter into greased muffin tins and bake in a hot oven (425°) for 20 to 25 minutes. Makes 12.

CALORIES per muffin: 158

VARIATIONS: Shave some fresh corn from the cob and mix a little into the batter to add to the texture; bran flakes may be used in this way. To make a hush puppy variation, add a small chopped onion. Buttermilk may be used in place of the skim milk.

No appreciable change in calories

LOW-SODIUM MODIFICATION: Delete salt. Use low-sodium baking powder ☑ and low-sodium skim milk ☑. Do not use buttermilk. Instead of using egg whites, use one of the eggs in your allowance here! It will be extensively diluted in the recipes.

MG. SODIUM per muffin: 19

Buttermilk Biscuits

    2 cups flour
    2½ teaspoons baking powder
    ¼ teaspoon soda
    ½ teaspoon salt
    1 tablespoon sugar
    ¼ cup powdered buttermilk ☑ (hard to find, but
        it comes in a box)
    ⅓ cup unsaturated oil ☑
    ⅔ cup water

Sift flour, measure, then sift again with baking powder, soda, salt, sugar, and powdered buttermilk. Stir the oil and water together; pour all at once into the dry ingredients. Stir with a fork until the dough rounds up into a ball. Knead dough in the bowl about 10 times or until smooth; do not add extra flour. Place ball of dough between two pieces of waxed paper and press or roll out until ¼ inch thick. Cut with an unfloured biscuit cutter and place on an ungreased baking sheet. For crusty sides, allow space between biscuits. Bake in a very hot oven (475°) for 10 to 12 minutes. If higher biscuits are desired, roll out dough to ½ inch thickness. Makes 14 biscuits.

CALORIES per biscuit: 100

VARIATIONS: Try adding a little curry powder or saffron to the dry ingredients or add some chopped parsley or chives. A few raisins or currents are another good addition. Substitute ½ teaspoon scasame oil for ½ teaspoon of the vegetable oil to get a nutty flavor.

LOW-SODIUM MODIFICATION: These biscuits have a very low fat content, but they have a very large quantity of sodium. It is impractical to modify this for low-sodium diets, so use the other biscuit recipe.

Buttermilk Scones

3 cups flour
2 teaspoons baking powder
1 teaspoon salt
2 cups buttermilk
1 teaspoon egg white
1 teaspoon water
Sugar

Sift flour, measure, then sift again with baking powder and salt. Add buttermilk and stir lightly to make a soft dough. Press or roll out dough on a lightly floured board to ¾ inch thickness. Using a large round cutter, cut out 12 scones. Beat egg white with the water; brush over tops of scones. Sprinkle each with a pinch of sugar. Bake in a hot oven (400°) for 15 minutes or bake on an ungreased griddle or in an electric frying pan over medium heat. Serve hot, or cool scones, split in half, and toast before serving. Makes 12 scones.

CALORIES per scone: 80

LOW-SODIUM MODIFICATION: Use low-sodium baking powder ☑ and low-sodium buttermilk ☑. If buttermilk is unavailable, use low-sodium skim milk and add 2 tablespoons white vinegar to make the milk sour. Do not brush with egg white.

MG. SODIUM per scone: 25

Date Raisin Nut Loaf

1 cup raisins
1 cup pitted dates, cut in small pieces
½ cup unsaturated margarine ☑
1½ cups boiling water
½ cup sugar
  Sugar substitute ☑ to equal ½ cup sugar
1 teaspoon soda
2 cups flour
2 teaspoons baking powder
½ cup chopped walnuts
1 teaspoon vanilla

Place raisins, dates, and margarine in a mixing bowl; pour boiling water over and stir. Add sugar, sugar substitute, and soda, and stir until sugar is dissolved. Sift flour, measure, then sift with baking powder. Add to raisin mixture; stir until well mixed. Add the walnuts and vanilla. Turn into a greased loaf pan and bake in

a moderately slow oven (325°) for 1 hour. (Bake covered for 15 to 20 minutes, then remove cover and finish baking. The bread is more moist that way. Makes 1 loaf or 20 slices.

CALORIES per slice: 162

VARIATIONS: Substitute dried apricots, dried peaches, or dried apple slices for the dates. Use brown sugar for part of the sugar. Vary the nuts by using pecans or filberts. After the loaf is baked, sprinkle with 1 tablespoon warm brandy; cover pan with aluminum foil for several hours to allow the flavor to permeate the loaf. This type of loaf is often served in place of cake or other dessert, but it may also be used for afternoon tea or to vary lunches. Spread it with cottage cheese or a little jam.

LOW-SODIUM MODIFICATION: Use low-sodium unsaturated margarine ☑. Omit soda; use 3 teaspoons low-sodium baking powder ☑. In the variation use a low-sodium cottage cheese ☑.

MG. SODIUM per slice: 3

Cranberry Nut Loaf

2 cups flour
2 teaspoons baking powder
½ cup sugar
1 egg
  Sugar substitute ☑ equal to ½ cup sugar
¼ cup unsaturated oil ☑
¾ cup orange juice
¼ cup water
1 cup uncooked cranberries, chopped
½ cup chopped walnuts

Sift flour, measure, then sift again with baking powder and sugar into a bowl. Beat egg slightly, then combine with the sugar substitute, oil, orange juice, and water. Pour liquid into the dry ingredients and stir only until well mixed. Quickly stir in the cranberries and walnuts. Turn into a greased loaf pan and bake in a moderate oven (350°) for 1 hour or until golden brown. Makes 1 loaf or 20 slices.

CALORIES per slice: 113

VARIATIONS: Add some grated orange peel. These fruit breads keep a surprising length of time if well wrapped with aluminum foil or with a small clean dish towel dampened with Sherry.

Basic Pie Crust

  2 cups flour
½ teaspoon salt
½ cup unsaturated oil ☑
  3 to 4 tablespoons cold water

There are many ways to make a pie crust, but most use saturated fat. This recipe has virtually none. Sift flour, measure, then sift again with salt into a bowl. Add the oil and mix thoroughly with a fork. Add water by the tablespoonful, sprinkling over top of mixture. Toss with a fork to moisten evenly. Press into a ball; divide dough almost in half. Flatten the large portion of dough and roll out to a 12-inch circle between 2 pieces of waxed paper. Peel off paper and fit pastry loosely into a 9-inch pie pan. Fill as desired. Roll out remaining dough for top crust. Cut slits in top pastry to allow steam to escape; place pastry over filling and press the edges together with a fork to seal. Brush the top crust with a teaspoon of skim milk and water to glaze. Bake according to the specific recipe. Makes 1 (9-inch) double crust pie or 2 pie shells.

For a 1-crust pie, make half of recipe. Fit into a 9-inch pie pan, trim edge of pastry with scissors, leaving about a 1-inch overhang. Fold edge under and flute. If pastry is to be used in a recipe calling for a baked pastry shell, prick shell well and bake in a hot oven (450°) for 10 to 12 minutes. Another way to keep the shell from bubbling as it bakes is to put a piece of aluminum foil in the unbaked shell; fill with beans or rice to keep flat. When baked, remove the beans or rice and save for another time.

CALORIES per whole recipe: 1775

VARIATIONS: A little flavoring may be put into the crust such as cinnamon and/or sugar or a sugar substitute ☑.

LOW-SODIUM MODIFICATION: Delete salt; add a little lemon peel and ½ teaspoon sugar. Brush top crust with low-sodium skim milk ☑.

MG. SODIUM per recipe: 4

Fresh Peach Pie

    Pastry for 2-crust pie
  1 tablespoon non fat dried milk
  6 peaches
  3 tablespoons cold water
  1 tablespoon cornstarch
½ cup sugar
  2 tablespoons unsaturated margarine ☑
¼ teaspoon cinnamon

Line a 9-inch pie pan with pastry. Sprinkle dried milk over bottom of crust. This helps absorb some of the peach juice. (As an alternate you can paint the bottom crust with ½ egg white or 1 teaspoon of jam.) Peel and slice peaches; place in pastry shell. Blend the water, cornstarch, and sugar; spoon evenly over peaches. Dot with unsaturated margarine; sprinkle with cinnamon. Cover with top crust, seal, and flute edge. Bake in a very hot oven (425°) for 15 minutes; reduce heat to 375° and continue baking 25 minutes longer. Serves 8.

CALORIES per serving: 316

VARIATIONS: Make the pie with less crust by making a lattice top from strips of dough and placing it over the peaches. Add a few slivered almonds. Try not to use canned fruit; if it is necessary, reduce cooking time about 10 minutes.

LOW-SODIUM MODIFICATION: Use low-sodium unsaturated margarine ☑. Do not brush bottom crust with egg white.

MG. SODIUM per serving: 6

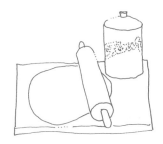

Dutch Apple Cake

1 recipe Baking Powder Biscuits
1 egg
5 green apples
2 tablespoons brown sugar
2 tablespoons granulated sugar
½ teaspoon cinnamon
2 tablespoons unsaturated margarine ☑

Follow the recipe for Baking Powder Biscuits with this change: Beat the whole egg with the oil and water, then add to the dry ingredients. Roll out dough to ½ inch thickness and place in a long rectangular pan or 2 pie pans. Peel, core, and thinly slice apples. Arrange apple slices over the biscuit dough; sprinkle with the brown sugar, granulated sugar, and cinnamon. Dot with unsaturated margarine. Bake in a hot oven (400°) for 15 minutes or until apples are tender and crust is golden. Makes 20 pieces.

CALORIES per piece: 105

VARIATIONS: Substitute fresh peaches, cherries, or apricots for the apples. No change in calories or sodium.

LOW-SODIUM MODIFICATION: Prepare biscuits with the low-sodium modification and omit egg. Use low-sodium unsaturated margarine ☑.

MG. SODIUM per serving: 5

No Bake Pumpkin Pie

1 envelope (1 tablespoon) unflavored gelatin
¼ cup cold water
1½ cups canned pumpkin
¼ cup sugar
Sugar substitute ☑ equal to ¼ cup sugar
2 teaspoons pumpkin pie spice mix
2 tablespoons rum
2 tablespoons unsaturated margarine ☑
½ teaspoon grated orange peel
1 (9-inch) baked pastry shell (See Basic Pie Crust)

Soften gelatin in cold water. In a saucepan mix together the pumpkin, sugar, sugar substitute, pumpkin pie spice mix, rum, unsaturated margarine, and orange peel. Cook slowly until hot and slightly thickened; add the softened gelatin and stir until it is dissolved. Cool filling slightly, then pour into baked pastry shell. Chill for several hours or until firm. Serves 8.

CALORIES per serving: 194

VARIATIONS: Use an equivalent amount of fresh cooked pumpkin, yellow winter squash, cooked sweet potatoes, or mashed cooked carrots. Pumpkin pie spice mix is made up of ginger, cinnamon, and nutmeg, and occasionally allspice. You can mix your own according to your own taste. No change in calories.

LOW-SODIUM MODIFICATION: Omit salt in pastry and substitute with a little sugar. Use low-sodium unsaturated margarine ☑.

MG. SODIUM per serving: 2

Angel Food Cake

1 cup sifted cake flour
1¼ cups sugar
1 cup (8 to 10) egg whites
1 teaspoon cream of tartar
¼ teaspoon salt
1 teaspoon vanilla
½ teaspoon grated lemon peel

Sift flour several times with ¼ cup of the sugar. Put the egg whites in a large bowl. Beat with a rotary or electric beater or wire whisk until foamy. Sprinkle with the cream of tartar and salt and continue beating until the egg whites appear glossy. Gradually beat in the remaining 1 cup sugar and beat until the mixture stands in peaks. Gently fold in flour sifted with sugar. Add vanilla and lemon peel and fold batter gently but thoroughly until no flour can be seen. Pour into an ungreased tube pan and bake in a slow oven (300°) for 1 hour or until the top of the cake springs back when you touch it. Cool in inverted pan, then remove by gently loosening the sides with a spatula. Serves 16.

CALORIES per slice: 79

VARIATIONS: For a spicy cake, add ¾ teaspoon cinnamon, ¼ teaspoon cloves, and ¼ teaspoon allspice. For a fruity cake, finely chop ½ cup of well drained maraschino cherries. Scatter cherries in layers as you spoon the batter into the pan.

CALORIES per slice with cherries: 86

LOW-SODIUM MODIFICATION: Delete salt. Remember that each egg white contains about 47 milligrams sodium, so if you use 8 to 10 egg whites, the cake will contain 376 to 470 milligrams sodium. However, you are not going to sit down and eat the entire cake unless you are "gargantua", so unless your restriction is great you will be able to eat some.

MG. SODIUM per slice: 24

Angel Food Cake is fairly bland, but takes very well to an additional garnish. Try pouring a tablespoon of Kirsch, Cognac, or rum over a slice. Serve this with cooked apples or apricots and a cup of rich black coffee laced with brandy.

Coffee Cake

    1 package yeast, active dry or compressed
    ½ cup warm water (lukewarm for compressed
        yeast)
    6 tablespoons sugar
    ½ cup skim milk
    3 tablespoons unsaturated margarine ☑
    2 eggs
 3½ cups all-purpose flour (sift before measuring)
    ⅓ cup raisins or currants
    1 teaspoon cinnamon

Dissolved yeast in warm water with 1 tablespoon of the sugar. Scald milk; stir in the margarine and remaining 5 tablespoons sugar and then cool. Add the cooled milk mixture to the yeast. Beat eggs and stir in. Add the flour and blend well. Knead lightly until dough is smooth and elastic. Place dough in a lightly greased bowl and rub the top with a little unsaturated oil. Cover and let rise in a warm place until almost doubled in bulk. Roll out dough on a lightly floured board into a rectangle. Sprinkle raisins and cinnamon over dough. Roll jelly-roll fashion from one of the long sides. Shape into a ring on a greased baking sheet, seam side down. Slash top at 1-inch intervals with scissors. Let rise again in a warm place. Bake in a hot oven (400°) for 20 to 25 minutes. Serve hot or cooled. Makes 24 servings.

CALORIES per serving: 93

VARIATIONS: Vary the shape of the dough. Use chopped nuts, citron, or orange or grapefruit peel in the filling. Shape dough into buns and make a deep depression in the center of each bun; fill the center with sweetened vanilla or lemon flavored cottage cheese or fruit preserves, or low calorie jam. The filling will add about 15 calories per serving. The top can be painted with a little egg white and sprinkled with chopped nuts.

LOW-SODIUM MODIFICATION: Use low-sodium skim milk ☑ and low-sodium unsaturated margarine ☑. Be sure the various fruits and peels do not contain sodium. Use low-sodium cottage cheese ☑ in the variation.

MG. SODIUM per serving: 6

Orange Refrigerator Cookies

    ½ cup unsaturated margarine ☑
    ½ cup sugar
        Sugar substitute ☑ equal to ½ cup sugar
    2 egg whites
    3 tablespoons orange juice
    ¼ teaspoon grated orange peel
    2 cups flour
    1 teaspoon baking powder
    ¼ teaspoon salt
    1 cup dry cereal flakes

Cream unsaturated margarine with the sugar and sugar substitute. Add egg whites and beat well. Beat in the orange juice and orange peel. Sift flour, measure, then sift again with baking powder and salt. Work into the creamed mixture along with the cereal flakes until well mixed. Shape into 2 rolls, 2 inches in diameter and wrap in waxed paper; chill. When firm, cut in ⅛-inch thick slices and bake on a lightly greased cookie sheet. Bake in a hot oven (400°) for 12 minutes or until golden. Makes 5 dozen cookies.

CALORIES per cookie: 36

VARIATIONS: Add a few chopped raisins, dates, or nuts or substitute wine or brandy for the orange juice. Substitute toasted rolled oats for the cereal flakes. Here is another version for an oatmeal cookie. Sift together 1½ cups flour, 2 teaspoons baking powder, ½ cup sugar, and ¼ teaspoon each cinnamon, allspice, and nutmeg. Combine ¼ cup unsaturated oil, 1 cup puréed bananas (baby food bananas are excellent), and 5 tablespoons water; add to dry ingredients and mix well. Stir in 1¾ cup toasted rolled oats and ¼ cup chopped walnuts. Drop by teaspoonfuls on a lightly greased baking sheet and bake in a moderately hot oven (375°) for 10 minutes or until browned. No appreciable change in calories or sodium.

LOW-SODIUM MODIFICATION: Delete salt and use low-sodium baking powder ☑ and low-sodium unsaturated margarine ☑.

MG. SODIUM per cookie: 5

SAUCES, DRESSING, AND VINEGARS

Here you finally come into your own! You are the chef at your own Cordon Bleu restaurant.

These sauces will make the food "sing". Your family will too if you don't watch the wine or liqueurs used in your cooking.

Seriously though, the sauces, all low in fat and some low in sodium, will provide your stomach with all the varied rich continental flavor that a true gourmet dreams about; and they are not difficult to prepare.

Natural Juice

When beef, chicken, or veal are sauteed, there will be some brown bits sticking to the pan. Remove the meat and pour off all the fat. To the pan drippings add 3 tablespoons wine and ⅔ cup bouillon, and swirl it about, scraping in all the brown bits. Cook a few minutes until the juice is reduced to ½ the original volume; skim off visible fat, then pour over the meat. As a variation, finely chop 2 shallots or a very small onion and cook in the sauté pan a few minutes, then add the wine and bouillon and stir in all the brown bits. A handful of mushrooms may be added also. Tomato juice can be used in place of the bouillon or wine. Flavor the sauce with a little salt if you are not restricted, or lemon juice.

CALORIES per 1 tablespoon of basic sauce: 9

MG. SODIUM per 1 tablespoon of basic sauce: 1

Caper Sauce

Prepare Velouteé Sauce. After sauce is strained, add 1 tablespoon chopped parsley and 1 tablespoon chopped capers. Serve with broiled or sautéed fish.

CALORIES per cup sauce: 119

LOW-SODIUM MODIFICATION: Capers are packed in salt and vinegar, so unless you find a brand that is packed only in vinegar, avoid these if your diet is so restricted.

White Sauce

(Bechamel Sauce)

2 tablespoons unsaturated margarine ☑
1 small onion, finely chopped
4 tablespoons flour
2 tablespoons non fat dried milk
3 cups skim milk
   Salt and white pepper
   Nutmeg

Although this is classically made with butter, this version will give good results. Heat the unsaturated margarine in a saucepan; sauté the onion until limp and clear. Stir in the flour and cook slowly until it takes on a slight golden color. Combine the dried milk and skim milk; gradually add to saucepan, stirring with a spoon or whisk. A whisk is inexpensive and actually works wonders with blending that you won't get with a spoon. Cook, stirring constantly, until sauce is smooth and thick. Season with salt, white pepper, and nutmeg to taste. Cook slowly for 10 minutes to be sure the flour is cooked. Strain. Makes 3 cups sauce.

CALORIES per cup: 220

VARIATIONS: If you wish to have a thicker sauce, decrease the milk a little.

LOW-SODIUM MODIFICATION: Delete salt; use a salt substitute ☑ or a little lemon juice. Use low-sodium skim milk ☑ and low-sodium unsaturated margarine ☑.

MG. SODIUM per cup: 18

Veloutée Sauce

½ cup chopped mushrooms
2 tablespoons unsaturated margarine ☑
4 tablespoons flour
3 cups chicken or veal stock
1 tablespoon chopped parsley
  Dash each of salt, white pepper, and monosodium glutamate

Sauté mushrooms in the unsaturated margarine until tender; add the flour and cook a few minutes. Slowly add the chicken or veal stock, and stirring constantly, cook until sauce is smooth and thick. Stir in the parsley, salt, pepper, and monosodium glutamate. Continue cooking a few minutes until the flour has lost its raw taste, then strain. If you wish to make a fish sauce, substitute fish stock for the chicken or veal stock Makes 3 cups sauce.

CALORIES per cup: 119

LOW-SODIUM MODIFICATION: Delete salt and monosodium glutamate. Use low-sodium chicken stock ☑ or bouillon and low-sodium unsaturated margarine ☑.

MG. SODIUM per cup: 18

Curry Sauce

Prepare Veloutée Sauce but substitute 1 small chopped onion for the mushrooms. Reduce parsley to ½ teaspoon, and add curry powder to taste. This is excellent with cut-up cooked chicken, shrimp, or broiled fish.

CALORIES per cup sauce: 119

LOW-SODIUM MODIFICATION: Follow Veloutée Sauce modification. Add a little lemon juice.

MG. SODIUM per cup sauce: 18

Court Bouillon

2 quarts water
1 cup dry white table wine
¼ cup wine vinegar
2 onions, sliced
2 carrots, cut in chunks
4 stalks celery, cut in chunks
2 bay leaves
2 sprigs parsley
½ teaspoon thyme
2 tablespoons salt
¼ teaspoon white pepper

Place all ingredients in a kettle and bring to a boil. Cover the pot, reduce the heat, and simmer for 30 minutes. Strain through a fine sieve and set aside to cool. This bouillon is excellent for poaching fish or as the basis for a good fish chowder. Freeze part of it if you like, and use as needed. Makes 2 quarts.

CALORIES for total recipe: 248

LOW-SODIUM MODIFICATION: Omit salt. Add a little lemon peel and low-sodium seasoning ☑.

MG. SODIUM for total recipe: 30

Cucumber Sauce

1 cup low-fat yogurt ☑
  Juice of ½ lemon
1 tablespoon each chopped parsley and chopped chives
¼ teaspoon monosodium glutamate
  Salt and cayenne to taste
1 cucumber, peeled and finely chopped

Combine all the ingredients and let stand a few minutes for the flavors to blend. This is good with certain Arabic or Greek dishes. Makes 1 cup.

CALORIES per recipe: 136

VARIATIONS: If you have a tarragon plant growing, add 1 teaspoon chopped fresh tarragon, or omit the chives and add 1 tablespoon chopped fresh mint or watercress. In place of the yogurt you can use imitation sour cream ☑ or unsaturated mayonnaise ☑.

CALORIES per 1 cup using imitation sour cream: 400

CALORIES per 1 cup using unsaturated mayonnaise: 1475

LOW-SODIUM MODIFICATION: Delete salt and monosodium glutamate.

MG. SODIUM per recipe using low-fat yogurt: 150

MG. SODIUM using imitation sour cream: 600

MG. SODIUM using low-sodium unsaturated mayonnaise: 160

CHILI MUSTARD SAUCE: See Fish Bites with Chili Dip (Snacks and Cocktail Foods)

Lemon Sauce

¼ cup unsaturated oil ☑
2 tablespoons lemon juice
1 tablespoon chopped parsley
 Salt and white pepper to taste

Place all the ingredients in a saucepan and heat together for several minutes; do not boil. Good with fish and green vegetables. Makes ⅓ cup sauce.

CALORIES per tablespoon: 82

VARIATIONS: Add 2 tablespoons prepared mustard, or substitute 3 tablespoons dry white table wine for the lemon juice and add 2 tablespoons minced chives and 1 tablespoon chopped fresh dill. No change in calories and sodium.

LOW-SODIUM MODIFICATION: Delete salt. Use low-sodium prepared mustard ☑ or a little dry mustard in the variation.

MG. SODIUM per tablespoon: 2

Tomato Sauce

1 medium sized onion, chopped
1 tablespoon unsaturated margarine ☑
1 clove garlic, mashed or minced
1 can (1 pound) solid pack tomatoes or 1 large can
  tomato purée
½ teaspoon sugar
¼ teaspoon oregano or basil
¼ teaspoon rosemary
 Salt and cayenne to taste
1 tablespoon chopped parsley

Sauté the onion in the margarine until it is limp and clear; add garlic and continue cooking 1 minute. Pour in tomatoes or tomato purée and season with sugar, oregano or basil, rosemary, salt, and cayenne. Cook slowly until sauce is reduced by one-third. Strain and push through a sieve; add parsley. This is a good sauce for meatless spaghetti or ravioli, broiled fish, or eggplant cooked with onion and zucchini. Makes 1½ cups sauce.

CALORIES per recipe: 340

VARIATIONS: For a meat sauce, sauté ½ pound chopped round steak; drain off fat then add to tomato sauce. For a richer flavor add beef extract to either the meat sauce or plain tomato sauce. If you add meat, chill sauce and remove any additional fat that comes to the surface. Much of this may be avoided, however, if you buy meat that is extra lean and ask your meat man to grind it. The meat will add 460 calories and 136 milligrams sodium.

LOW-SODIUM MODIFICATION: Use low-sodium unsaturated margarine ☑, low-sodium canned tomatoes ☑ and low-sodium gourmet seasoning ☑. Avoid meat extract in variation.

MG. SODIUM per recipe: 29

Tartar Sauce

1 cup unsaturated mayonnaise ☑
1 teaspoon prepared mustard
1 teaspoon chopped parsley
1 tablespoon chopped sweet
  pickle
1 teaspoon minced onion
1 tablespoon lemon juice (optional)

Mix all ingredients together but lemon juice. If you prefer a thinner sauce, stir in lemon juice. Makes 1 cup.

CALORIES per 2 tablespoons: 180

LOW-SODIUM MODIFICATION: Use low-sodium unsaturated mayonnaise ☑, low-sodium mustard ☑ or dry mustard and low-sodium pickles ☑. Use low-sodium gourmet seasoning ☑ to taste.

MG. SODIUM per 2 tablespoons: 21

Remoulade Sauce

   5 tablespoons unsaturated mayonnaise ☑
   1 teaspoon Dijon mustard
   1 teaspoon chopped dill pickle
   ½ teaspoon mashed or chopped anchovy
   2 teaspoons capers
   1 tablespoon chopped fresh tarragon or 1 teaspoon
       crumbled dried tarragon
   1 tablespoon chopped parsley

Combine the mayonnaise and mustard, then add the remaining ingredients and stir well. Use a small amount with fish, shrimp, or lobster. This is also good with cold lean meat. Makes ⅔ cup sauce.

CALORIES per tablespoon: 47

LOW-SODIUM MODIFICATION: Use low-sodium unsaturated mayonnaise ☑, low-sodium pickles ☑, and low-sodium mustard ☑ or a little dry mustard. The essence of anchovy paste is salty fish so you will have to delete this if your sodium restriction is too stringent —after all, there are 686 milligrams sodium in 1 teaspoon of anchovy paste. Capers, too, are preserved with salt, so use a healthy dash of freshly ground black pepper and lemon juice instead.

MG. SODIUM per tablespoon with anchovy and capers omitted: 6

Mock Hollandaise Sauce

   2 tablespoons hot water
   ½ cup unsaturated mayonnaise ☑
   1 tablespoon lemon juice

In a small saucepan, blend hot water into mayonnaise. Cook over hot water until sauce is heated through; stir in lemon juice. Serves 4.

CALORIES per serving: 180

VARIATIONS: Mock Hollandaise may be made more elaborate by adding chopped fresh herbs such as parsley, tarragon, chives, or basil. Or you may lighten the sauce by folding in 2 stiffly beaten egg whites. For a good vegetable sauce, substitute 2 tablespoons hot orange juice for the 2 tablespoons hot water and add ½ teaspoon grated orange peel. Serve with asparagus, artichokes, or broccoli. There are 190 calories per serving with the added egg whites.

LOW-SODIUM MODIFICATION: Use low-sodium unsaturated mayonnaise ☑. Don't "slather" the food with sauce; use only a small amount to serve as a taste break. Do not add egg whites in the variation.

MG. SODIUM per serving: 6

Vinegar and Oil Dressing

   ¾ cup unsaturated oil
   ¼ cup lemon juice
   ¼ cup wine vinegar or cider vinegar
   1 teaspoon each of dry mustard, and monosodium
       glutamate
   ½ teaspoon freshly ground pepper
   1 crushed clove of garlic
   ½ teaspoon salt

Mix all ingredients together. Serve on quartered heads of lettuce or toss with mixed greens. Makes 1¼ cups.

CALORIES per tablespoon: 75

VARIATIONS: Add 1 tablespoon sugar (45 calories) or the equivalent sugar substitute for an Italian taste twist.

LOW-SODIUM MODIFICATION: Delete salt and monosodium glutamate. Use salt substitute ☑.

MG. SODIUM per tablespoon: 5

Brown Sauce

- 1 medium sized onion, finely chopped
- 1 carrot, finely chopped
- 1 tablespoon unsaturated oil ☑
- 3 tablespoons flour
- 1 cup beef bouillon (canned or beef tea concentrate ☑ and hot water)
- ¼ cup dry red table wine
  Salt and pepper to taste
- ½ teaspoon monosodium glutamate
  Caramel color (optional)

Sauté onion and carrot in the oil until onion is limp and lightly golden. Sprinkle with the flour, blend well, and cook slowly for a few minutes to brown flour slightly. Add the bouillon slowly and stir. Add the wine, continue stirring, and cook until sauce is smooth and thick. Season with salt, pepper, and monosodium glutamate. Add a drop or two of caramel color to make the sauce a richer brown. Makes 1½ cups sauce.

CALORIES for total recipe: 265

VARIATIONS: Other flavorings may be added such as basil, chili powder, garlic, rosemary, or a bit of brandy.

LOW-SODIUM MODIFICATION: Delete salt and monosodium glutamate. Use low-sodium beef bouillon ☑ and low-sodium unsaturated margarine ☑.

MG. SODIUM for total recipe: 60

Anchovy Sauce

Blend ½ teaspoon anchovy paste with ½ cup Brown Sauce. Heat and serve with fish or with small boiled potatoes. You need only a small amount of this to add a sharp piquant flavor.

CALORIES per ½ cup sauce: 95

LOW-SODIUM MODIFICATION: If your diet is really restricted you will have to avoid the anchovy paste. The anchovy is greatly diluted in this recipe, but there is still a lot of sodium in this sauce, so in the final analysis, your physician will decide.

MG. SODIUM per ½ cup sauce: 363

Barbecue Sauce

- ⅓ cup vinegar
- ⅓ cup lemon juice
- ⅓ cup melted unsaturated margarine ☑
  Salt and pepper to taste

Combine ingredients and use to baste fish or poultry while on the grill. Makes 1 cup sauce.

CALORIES per cup sauce: 550

VARIATIONS: Use unsaturated oil in this instead of margarine and you have a sort of French dressing. For variety, add different herbs such as chopped shallots, onions, or chives, fresh basil, oregano, rosemary, savory, tarragon, garlic, or even mint. A little dry Vermouth will add an elusive but interesting new taste. No calories or sodium change.

LOW-SODIUM MODIFICATION: Use low-sodium unsaturated margarine ☑.

MG. SODIUM per cup sauce: 15

Smoky Basting Sauce

- 1 cup vinegar
- ½ cup unsaturated oil ☑
- ½ teaspoon liquid smoke
- 2 tablespoons grated lemon peel
- ¼ cup lemon juice
- 2 teaspoons brown sugar
- 2 bay leaves
  Black pepper and salt to taste

Combine ingredients and bring to a boil. Use to baste lean beef or chops while cooking. Makes 1¾ cups.

CALORIES for total recipe: 1075

VARIATIONS: Add ¼ cup catsup or chili sauce; replace the vinegar with dry Vermouth. This will add 180 calories to the total recipe.

LOW-SODIUM MODIFICATION: Omit liquid smoke. Use low-sodium gourmet seasoning ☑ in place of salt and low-sodium catsup ☑ in the variation.

MG. SODIUM

Low Calorie Tomato Barbecue Sauce

¼ cup tomato purée
¼ cup water
   Sugar substitute equal to 2 teaspoons sugar
2 tablespoons lemon juice
1 teaspoon Worcestershire
1 teaspoon prepared mustard
½ teaspoon celery salt

Mix all ingredients together and simmer for 15 minutes. Use it to baste meat, fish, or poultry. Makes ½ cup sauce.

CALORIES per ½ cup: 30

LOW-SODIUM MODIFICATION: Use ¼ teaspoon dry mustard in place of prepared mustard, and ½ teaspoon celery seed rather than celery salt. Omit Worcestershire. Omit the water and tomato pureé, and use ¼ cup low-sodium catsup, ¼ cup unsalted tomato juice.

MG. SODIUM per ½ cup: 5

Louis Dressing

1 cup unsaturated mayonnaise ☑
2 tablespoons catsup
2 tablespoons chili sauce
2 tablespoons prepared horseradish
2 tablespoons chopped pimiento
¼ cup finely chopped green onion tops

Mix together until smooth the mayonnaise, catsup, chili sauce, and horseradish. Stir in the pimiento and green onion tops; chill. Serve on fish or shrimp. Makes 1½ cups.

CALORIES per 3 tablespoons: 190

LOW-SODIUM MODIFICATION: Use low-sodium catsup ☑, low-sodium chili sauce ☑, and low-sodium unsaturated mayonnaise ☑.

MG. SODIUM per 3 tablespoons: 21

Lamb Mint Sauce

Heat 3 tablespoons mint or apple jelly with 1 tablespoon water until the jelly melts; stir in 1 to 2 tablespoons chopped fresh mint. Serve with roast lamb. Makes ¼ cup.

CALORIES per tablespoon: 50

VARIATIONS: If mint jelly is not to your liking, make an English sauce by mixing 2 tablespoons sugar with 2 tablespoons vinegar. Heat until sugar dissolves; add 2 tablespoons of finely chopped mint. Cool before serving. No change in calories or sodium.

LOW-SODIUM MODIFICATION: Follow basic recipe.

MG. SODIUM per tablespoon: 1

Dessert Lemon Sauce

1 cup water
1 tablespoon cornstarch
½ teaspoon grated lemon peel
   Sugar substitute ☑ equal to ½ cup sugar
1½ tablespoons lemon juice
2 tablespoons unsaturated margarine ☑
   Dash of salt
   Few drops yellow food coloring

Mix water, cornstarch, and lemon peel in top of double boiler. Stirring often, cook over hot water 5 minutes, or until thickened. Remove from heat and add remaining ingredients. Stir until margarine melts. Serves 6.

CALORIES per serving: 38

LOW-SODIUM MODIFICATION: Delete salt and add a little salt substitute if you find it neccessary. Use low-sodium unsaturated margarine ☑.

MG. SODIUM per serving: 1

Orange Sauce

3 tablespoons unsaturated margarine ☑
½ cup sugar
1½ teaspoons grated orange peel
6 tablespoons orange marmalade
6 tablespoons orange juice
¼ cup orange liqueur

This is good over cake made without icing, rolled pancakes, or bananas flambé. Place in a saucepan the margarine, sugar, orange peel, marmalade, orange juice, and liqueur such as Cointreau, Triple Sec, or Curacao. Heat together until blended; do not boil. Spoon over plain cake. If you use this sauce with rolled pancakes or baked bananas, you might want to add 2 tablespoons warm brandy and set aflame. Makes 1½ cups sauce.

CALORIES per 2 tablespoons: 98

LOW-SODIUM MODIFICATION: Follow basic recipe. Use low-sodium unsaturated margarine ☑.

MG. SODIUM per 2 tablespoons: 4

Marinade for Beef

- 1 carrot
- 1 onion
- 1 stalk celery
- 1 clove garlic
- 1 bay leaf
- 2 sprigs parsley
- 1 tablespoon salt
  Freshly ground pepper
- ¼ cup unsaturated oil ☑
- 3 cups dry red table wine

Wash carrot and coarsely chop. Peel and chop onion. Slice the celery. Leave the skin on the garlic and partially crush. Place all the vegetables in a large bowl with the bay leaf, parsley, salt, several turns of freshly ground pepper, oil, and wine. Put a piece of lean beef in this, cover, and keep cool. Marinate meat for 24 hours, turning several times. Drain meat, pat dry with paper toweling, then roast or grill over a barbecue.

Marinade for Lamb

Prepare Marinade for Beef and add 1 teaspoon rosemary and 2 lemons, sliced. This is excellent for shish kebab. Cut lamb in 1½-inch pieces and marinate overnight. Thread meat on skewers and use the marinade as a basting sauce too. Meat will absorb only a small amount of marinade, about 1 teaspoon per serving.

CALORIES per serving for either marinade: 50

VARIATIONS: Dry Vermouth may be used in place of the wine in the Marinade for Beef.

LOW-SODIUM MODIFICATION: Delete salt; use low sodium flavoring ☑.

MG. SODIUM: negligible

Dill Sauce

- 1 cup low-fat yogurt ☑
- 1 tablespoon chopped chives or green onions
- 1½ teaspoons lime or lemon juice
- 1 teaspoon salt
- 1 teaspoon sugar
- 1 tablespoon chopped fresh dill or 1 teaspoon dill seed
  Sprig of fresh dill

Blend the yogurt with the chives, lime or lemon juice, salt, sugar, and chopped dill. Serve the sauce over cold veal or cold boiled fish and garnish with a sprig of fresh dill. Makes 1 cup sauce.

CALORIES per tablespoon: 10

LOW-SODIUM MODIFICATION: Delete salt; use salt substitute ☑ to taste.

MG. SODIUM per tablespoon: 10

Creamed Low Sodium Herb Dressing

- 1 cup imitation sour cream ☑
- 1 teaspoon dry mustard
- ½ teaspoon paprika
- 1 teaspoon celery seed
- ¼ teaspoon dill seed
- ½ teaspoon summer savory
- ½ teaspoon basil
- 1 teaspoon chopped chives
- 1 tablespoon lemon juice

Combine ingredients and chill. Use on greens, tomato slices, and raw vegetable combinations. Makes 1 cup dressing.

CALORIES per tablespoon: 30

LOW-SODIUM MODIFICATION: Follow basic recipe.

MG. SODIUM per tablespoon: 38

Cranberry-Kumquat Relish

This is a good uncooked relish. Using the medium blade on the food chopper, grind 4 cups fresh cranberries and ½ pound kumquats (grind skin and all). Stir in 2 cups sugar. Chill before serving. Makes 1¼ quarts.

CALORIES per 2 tablespoons: 58

VARIATIONS: Use 2 large peeled oranges instead of the kumquats. Or try mixing the chopped raw cranberries with chopped apples and a few chopped walnuts. One-half cup walnuts will add 325 calories and 1 milligram sodium.

LOW-SODIUM MODIFICATION: For basic relish recipe.

MG. SODIUM per 2 tablespoons: 1

Cranberry Sauce

To make the jellied sauce, bring 2 cups water to a boil. Add 4 cups fresh cranberries and cook until all the skins pop open. Push fruit through a sieve. Place the sieved berries over heat, stir in 2 cups sugar, and bring to a rolling boil. Remove from heat and when slightly cool, pour into a serving bowl. Chill in refrigerator until jelly is firm. Makes 1 quart.

To make the whole cranberry sauce boil 2 cups sugar and 2 cups water together for 5 minutes; add 4 cups fresh cranberries and boil without stirring for 5 minutes or until all the skins pop open. Remove from heat and let cool in the pan. You can also mix this with drained pineapple bits. Makes 1 quart.

CALORIES per 2 tablespoons of either sauce: 55

VARIATIONS: If you wish to add a spice, try cinnamon, clove, or nutmeg.

LOW-SODIUM MODIFICATION: Follow either recipe.

MG. SODIUM: negligible

Whipped Topping

    1 envelope (1 tablespoon) unflavored gelatin
    2 tablespoons water
    ¼ cup non fat dried milk
    ¾ cup skim milk
    ¼ teaspoon vanilla
    2 tablespoons sugar
    ½ teaspoon lemon juice

Soften gelatin in water. Mix the dried milk and skim milk in the top of a double boiler; heat over hot water until the milk is scalded. Add the softened gelatin and stir until it is dissolved. Add the vanilla, sugar, and lemon juice. When the sugar is dissolved, remove from heat and cool until syrupy. Beat until the gelatin mixture is the consistency of whipped cream; chill. Serve as a topping for fruit compotes, gelatin desserts, prune whip, or rice pudding. Prepare the topping only a short time before you need it; it will lose volume on standing too long. Serves 8.

CALORIES per serving: 18

VARIATIONS: For a good lemon topping, add 1 tablespoon of lemon juice and 1 tablespoon grated lemon peel. This may be served alone as a dessert, or to spoon over fruit or un-iced cakes. For a topping on apple cherry desserts, add ¼ teaspoon each nutmeg and cinnamon to the basic recipe. No calorie or sodium change.

LOW-SODIUM MODIFICATION: Use low-sodium skim milk ☑.

MG. SODIUM per serving: 15

Vanilla Sauce

    1¼ cups skim milk
    1 tablespoon cornstarch
    ½ cup sugar
    1 tablespoon unsaturated margarine ☑
    1½ teaspoons vanilla

Heat milk slowly until it is lukewarm. Mix the cornstarch and sugar; add to the warm milk, and stirring, cook until sauce is smooth and thick. Remove from heat and stir in the margarine and vanilla. Serve warm or cold. This is delicious over a baked apple or apple crisp. Makes 1½ cups.

CALORIES per 2 tablespoons sauce: 63

LOW-SODIUM MODIFICATION: Use low-sodium skim milk ☑ and low-sodium unsaturated margarine ☑.

MG. SODIUM per 2 tablespoons sauce: 2

DESSERTS

From now on you will encounter some recipes to which more sugar has been added. It is necessary for the production of certain syrups and for use in certain cakes, pies, and desserts.

Dr. Sampson, in his introduction, points out that excessive amounts of sugar are used in formation of one type of blood fat called "triglycerides".

We have, therefore, attempted to cut down to a minimum the amount of sugar in the recipes. We have found through experience that adding sugar substitutes to regular sugar, permits the right degree of sweetness without sacrificing the desirable texture obtained by the use of sugar.

Since sugar substitute is used wherever possible, the number of calories is reduced. This gives you a chance to try a greater variety of desserts, beverages, cookies, cakes, and pies than you might otherwise be able to.

Your sweet tooth can finally be satisfied without conscious stomach pangs.

These delicacies have been carefully chosen to give a low fat, low sodium, sweet farewell to your culinary "repast", and a lingering taste of satisfaction will remain to be savored with your favorite beverage at the end of the meal.

Applesauce

    2 pounds apples
    2 cups cider
       Sugar substitute ☑ equal to 1 cup sugar or 1 cup
         sugar
       Cinnamon

Peel, core, and quarter good cooking apples. Place in a saucepan with the cider, sugar substitute or sugar, and cinnamon to taste. Simmer slowly until the apples are tender and sauce is thickened. If you like a smoother sauce, mash with a potato masher. This is an excellent sauce with baked or roast chicken. If you wish to serve it as a dessert, give it a topping of Vanilla Sauce (see Sauces). Makes 5 cups sauce.

CALORIES per ½ cup sauce using sugar substitute: 95

CALORIES per ½ cup sauce using sugar: 133

VARIATIONS: Learn the individual tastes of the many wonderful apples in the market and vary the sauce and sharpen your discriminating tongue by mixing the different types. For a starter, look for Winesaps, Delicious, Jonathans, Pippins, McIntosh, Gravensteins, Cortlands, and crab apples. You can make the sauce slightly pink by cooking the apples with a few strawberries. No calorie or sodium change.

LOW-SODIUM MODIFICATION: Follow basic recipe.

MG. SODIUM per ½ cup sauce: 1

Baked Apple

Select a firm cooking apple for each serving; core apples without cutting through the stem end and peel about one-third down from the top. Place in a deep pan. Fill the center of each apple with 1 teaspoon raisins, ½ teaspoon unsaturated margarine ☑, a dash of cinnamon and a sprinkle of sugar substitute ☑. Pour in enough water to just cover bottom of pan. Bake in a moderate oven (350°) for 30 to 45 minutes or until apples are tender. Baste several times during baking. Serve hot or cold. Try it with Vanilla Sauce (see Sauces).

CALORIES per apple: 100

VARIATIONS: Try different things in the center of the apples such as nuts, bits of dried fruit, brown sugar, or maple sugar. Here is another way to bake apples that won't add any calories. Do not fill the center of the apples with sugar, fruit, or nuts, but pour over a can of low-calorie carbonated drink (lemon-lime is good). Baste during baking.

CALORIES per apple: 76

MG. SODIUM per apple: 11

LOW-SODIUM MODIFICATION: Use low-sodium unsaturated margarine ☑ in the standard baked apple. Be sure not to use salted nuts in the variation.

MG. SODIUM per apple: 7

Ricotta Cream Filling

(Whey Type)

Ricotta is delicious plain or with a few variations you can serve it as a dessert. Add small bits of sweetened cooked apple and a little cinnamon to ricotta. Or flavor 1½ cups of ricotta with 1 teaspoon lemon juice, ¼ teaspoon grated lemon peel, and 1 tablespoon honey. To make Italian Cannoli, prepare Basic Pie Crust with these changes: Substitute 3 tablespoons of sweet wine for 3 tablespoons of the water and add ½ teaspoon cinnamon along with the flour. Roll out dough and cut in 8 strips each 3 inches wide. Wrap dough loosely around clean wooden dowel sticks 1 inch in diameter and bake. Slip the shells off the sticks while hot; then cool. Fill each shell with 4 tablespoons of the honey and lemon flavored ricotta and dip the ends in crushed cooky crumbs. Cannoli shells are generally deep fried, but baking is preferable as too much fat is absorbed in the frying. Dry cottage cheese may be used in place of the ricotta. Sieve it first and then flavor with honey, grated orange peel, and a little rum. Some ricotta has extra cream added, as does cottage cheese. Avoid this because the fat and calorie content is greatly increased. This is especially true in the Eastern United States where ricotta is almost as heavy as cream cheese. In the West, ricotta is whey cheese and mostly protein.

CALORIES per 2 filled cannoli: 530

LOW-SODIUM MODIFICATION: Dry cottage cheese is unfortunately not too low in sodium so use low-sodium dry cottage cheese if it is available. Use low-sodium modification for the Basic Pie Crust.

MG. SODIUM for 2 filled cannoli using unsalted, low-fat cottage cheese: 20

Pommes Chateaubriand

(Poached Apples)

6 firm cooking apples
½ lemon
1 tablespoon unsaturated margarine ☑
Water (about 1½ cups)
6 tablespoons sugar
3 tablespoons currant jelly
3 tablespoons Kirsch or Cognac
Red food coloring

Core apples and peel about one-third down from the top; cut the top of the peel to give a scalloped effect. Rub the lemon over the cut portion of the apples to prevent discoloration. Place apples in a casserole or deep pan. Put ½ teaspoon unsaturated margarine in each apple. Bring the water to a boil; add sugar and any juice that is left in the lemon. Pour over apples; the water should come to the level of the peeled skin. Bake in a moderate oven (350°) for 30 minutes or until apples are tender, but still maintain their shape. Remove fruit from pan with a slotted spoon and arrange in a serving dish; cool. Pour the liquid in the pan into a saucepan; cook until it is reduced by one-third. Add the current jelly, Kirsch or Cognac, and a few drops of red food coloring. When the jelly has melted, pour the sauce over the apples. Chill fruit, basting frequently. Serve a chilled apple followed by good black coffee. Serves 6.

CALORIES per apple with sauce: 200

LOW-SODIUM MODIFICATION: Use low-sodium unsaturated margarine ☑.

MG. SODIUM per apple: 2

Minted Fruit Cup

Prepare 2 cups of sliced or cubed fresh fruit. Stir in 2 drops peppermint extract. Service in dessert bowls and garnish with a sprig of fresh mint. Serves 4.

CALORIES per serving: 40

VARIATIONS: If you are serving pineapple or pears, you might flavor the fruit with a tablespoon of Creme de Menthe instead of peppermint extract. Other liqueur and fruit combinations are also good such as Kirsch with pineapple or strawberries, Cointreau with oranges, tangerines, and grapefruit, and Port with grapes.

CALORIES per 1 tablespoon of liqueur: 47

LOW-SODIUM MODIFICATION: Most fruit is fairly low in sodium. Check the Appendix for specific sodium values of various fruits.

MG. SODIUM per serving: 1

Baked Apple Dessert with Lemon Sauce

½ cup unsaturated margarine ☑
    Sugar substitute ☑ equal to ⅓ cup sugar
       cup sugar
 2 egg whites
 1 teaspoon vanilla
1¼ cups flour
 2 teaspoons baking powder
 1 teaspoon cinnamon
¼ teaspoon nutmeg
½ teaspoon salt
 2 apples, peeled and grated
½ cup chopped walnuts

Cream unsaturated margarine and sugar substitute or sugar; beat in egg whites and vanilla. Sift flour, measure, then sift again with baking powder, cinnamon, nutmeg, and salt. Add dry ingredients to creamed mixture and stir until blended. Mix in the apples and walnuts. Turn into a greased 8-inch square baking pan and bake in a moderately hot oven (375°) for 40 to 45 minutes. Cut in squares while still warm and serve with Dessert Lemon Sauce (see Sauces). Serves 9.

CALORIES per serving using sugar substitute without sauce: 203

CALORIES per serving using sugar without sauce: 246

VARIATIONS: Add a few raisins. Use brown sugar for half of the sugar. Serve with Vanilla Sauce.

LOW-SODIUM MODIFICATION: Use low-sodium baking powder ☑ and low-sodium unsaturated margarine ☑. Omit salt; do not use salted nuts.

MG. SODIUM per serving: 14

Apple Crisp

⅓ cup flour
¾ cup rolled oats
⅓ cup unsaturated margarine ☑
    Sugar substitute ☑ equal to ⅓ cup sugar
 1 cup water
⅓ cup sugar
1½ tablespoons cornstarch
¼ teaspoon salt
⅛ teaspoon each cinnamon and nutmeg
 4 large green apples
½ teaspoon grated orange peel

Combine flour and rolled oats; cut in unsaturated margarine until mixture is crumbly. Add sugar substitute and mix lightly. Combine water, sugar, cornstarch, salt, cinnamon, and nutmeg. Stirring, cook over low heat until thick and clear; remove from heat. Peel, core, and slice apples; arrange in an 8-inch square baking pan. Sprinkle with the grated orange peel. Pour cornstarch sauce over the apples and sprinkle the rolled oats mixture over the top. Bake in a hot oven (400°) for 30 minutes. Serve with Whipped Topping (see Sauces). Serves 9.

CALORIES per serving of recipe only: 173

LOW-SODIUM MODIFICATION: Delete salt and add a little salt substitute ☑. Use low-sodium unsaturated margarine ☑. Avoid quick cooking rolled oats for they contain sodium.

MG. SODIUM per serving: 2

Oriental Oranges

This delicious fresh fruit dessert can be made a day ahead of time. Using a vegetable peeler, remove the zest (thin orange skin on the surface) from 8 medium sized oranges. Sliver the zest. Peel the oranges; arrange, side by side, in a saucepan. Sprinkle on the zest. Pour in enough water to cover oranges half way. Add 2 tablespoons sugar and sugar substitute ☑ to equal 3 tablespoons sugar. Bring the water to a boil and cook rapidly for 2 minutes. Turn fruit over and continue cooking for 2 more minutes. Remove oranges with a slotted spoon and place in a deep casserole. Cook the remaining syrup in the pan, with the zest, until it is reduced to one-third of its volume. Add a few drops of red food coloring and 2 tablespoons of orange flavored liqueur (Cointreau, Triple Sec, or Curacao). Cool the syrup and pour over fruit. Chill and baste fruit several times. Serve the cold oranges with some of the zest and syrup. Serves 8.

CALORIES per serving: 80

VARIATIONS: To make Greek oranges, use a good brandy in place of an orange flavored liqueur. This variation is refreshing on a warm day. Cut off the tops of oranges and scoop out the pulp, keeping the skin intact. Fill shells with orange or tangerine sherbet and replace the top. Place in freezer until sherbet is firm. Add Brandy. Garnish with fresh mint. Each sherbet filled orange will have 130 calories and 10 milligrams sodium.

LOW-SODIUM MODIFICATION: Follow basic recipe.

MG. SODIUM per serving: 1

Broiled Grapefruit

Cut grapefruit in half. Top each half with 1 teaspoon brown sugar, ½ teaspoon unsaturated margarine ☑, and a dash of cinnamon, nutmeg, or mace. Broil until the edges are lightly browned and the fruit is bubbly. These are best served hot, but they may also be served cold.

CALORIES per ½ grapefruit: 90

VARIATIONS: Omit the margarine. Pierce the cut surface of the grapefruit and pour on 1 tablespoon of sweet dessert wine (Port, Tokay, sweet Sherry) before broiling. No calorie or sodium change.

LOW-SODIUM MODIFICATION: Use low-sodium unsaturated margarine ☑.

MG. SODIUM per ½ grapefruit: 2

Spiced Applesauce Cupcakes

    1 cup flour
    1 teaspoon baking powder
 1½ teaspoons cinnamon
  ¼ teaspoon each nutmeg, ginger, and cloves
  ⅛ teaspoon allspice
  ½ cup raisins
  ½ cup artificially sweetened applesauce
  ¼ cup unsaturated oil ☑
    1 egg
    1 teaspoon vanilla
    2 tablespoons sugar plus sugar substitute ☑ equal to 2 tablespoons sugar

Sift flour, measure, then sift again with baking powder, cinnamon, nutmeg, ginger, cloves, and allspice. Mix in the raisins. Combine the applesauce, oil, egg, vanilla, sugar, and sugar substitute. Add to dry ingredients and stir just until flour is dampened. Drop by spoonfuls into muffin pans lined with paper cupcake liners. Bake in a moderate oven (350°) for 20 to 25 minutes. Makes 10 cupcakes.

CALORIES per cupcake: 125

LOW-SODIUM MODIFICATION: Use low-sodium baking powder ☑.

MG. SODIUM per cupcake: 10

Broiled Bananas

    4 bananas
  ½ cup Sherry
  ⅛ teaspoon cloves
    1 tablespoon lemon juice
    2 tablespoons sugar
    2 tablespoons melted unsaturated margarine ☑

Peel firm bananas and cut in half lengthwise. Place, cut side up, in a greased baking pan. Combine the Sherry, cloves, lemon juice, sugar, and margarine; pour over bananas. Broil until golden brown, basting frequently. Serves 4.

CALORIES per serving: 182

VARIATIONS: Warm 3 tablespoons brandy or rum, ignite, and pour over the broiled fruit. This will add about 100 calories to recipe.

LOW-SODIUM MODIFICATION: Use low-sodium unsaturated margarine ☑.

MG. SODIUM per serving: 3

Melon au Liqueurs

Select 1 firm ripe melon such as cantaloupe, casaba, honeydew, or Persian. Cut a small plug in one end of the melon. Using a long handled spoon, carefully remove the seeds. Pour 4 tablespoons of a fruit liqueur into the opening (Kirsch, Cointreau, Curacao, Fruit Cordial), replace plug, and seal edges with a little margarine. Chill melon for several hours. To serve, open the plug and pour off the juice and reserve. Slice the melon and spoon a little juice over each serving. Serves 4.

CALORIES per serving: 82

VARIATIONS: Dice 1 cup of melon and slide the fruit into the plugged melon before pouring in the liqueur. Seal and serve as above. No change in calories or sodium.

LOW-SODIUM MODIFICATION: Follow basic recipe.

MG. SODIUM per serving: 12

Spicy Fruit Compote

   1 cup artificially sweetened pears ☑, quartered
   1 can (1 lb.) water-pack sour cherries, drained
   1 cup artificially sweetened apricot halves ☑, drained
   ½ cup water
      Sugar substitute ☑ equal to ¼ cup sugar
   2 tablespoons lemon juice
   ½ teaspoon ginger
   2 cinnamon sticks
   4 whole cloves

Pour canned pears and liquid in a large saucepan; add the cherries and apricots. Combine the water, sugar substitute, lemon juice, ginger, cinnamon, and cloves; pour over fruit. Simmer for 5 minutes; cool fruit in the syrup. Remove cinnamon and cloves. Serve warm or cold. Serves 6.

CALORIES per serving: 50

VARIATIONS: Use a combination of fresh fruit to make the compote or use several dried fruits such as prunes, apricots, peaches, pears, and figs. Simmer the dried fruit in a little water with a bit of lemon until tender. Flavor the compote with a dry or sweet wine, liqueurs, brandy, or lemon and honey. Don't forget fresh or canned berries or frozen fruit. Fresh fruit won't change calories or sodium—liqueurs will.

LOW-SODIUM MODIFICATION: Be sure artificially sweetened fruits have calcium sweetners—not sodium.

MG. SODIUM per serving: 2

Gingered Pears

   1 cup orange juice
   ¼ cup lemon or lime juice
      Sugar substitute ☑ equal to ¼ cup sugar
   ⅛ teaspoon ginger or 4 thin slices fresh ginger root
   2 pears

Combine orange juice, lemon or lime juice, sugar substitute, and ginger; chill for 1 hour. Peel, core, and slice pears into 4 dessert dishes. Pour the ginger syrup over them and chill again before serving. The fresh ginger is superior to the dried ginger and may be obtained from any Chinese or Japanese grocery store or a large supermarket. Serves 4.

CALORIES per serving: 56

LOW-SODIUM MODIFICATION: Follow basic recipe.

MG. SODIUM per serving: 3

Papaya

Select ripe papaya and cut in half lengthwise. Remove the tiny black seeds. Serve one-half of the fruit to each person with a lemon quarter to squeeze over. This is delicious for breakfast or as a dessert. Papaya from Mexico is very large, and is usually sliced for serving. The Hawaiian variety, which is found in most produce stores, is much smaller and tastes better. For variety you can fill each papaya half with a spoonful of fresh blueberries or raspberries or drained mandarin oranges.

CALORIES per ½ papaya: 40

LOW-SODIUM MODIFICATION: Follow basic recipe.

MG. SODIUM per ½ papaya: 3

Poached Pears

    ¾ cup sugar
    ¾ cup water
    6 firm, ripe pears (Bosc, d'anjou, or Bartlett)
    ½ lemon
       Small piece of vanilla bean or 1 teaspoon vanilla

Cook the sugar and water in a saucepan for 5 minutes. While the syrup is cooking, peel and core pears; rub with the cut lemon to prevent discoloration. Place the pears in the syrup with the vanilla bean or vanilla and poach just until tender. Remove pears from syrup and place in a bowl. Pour ¾ cup of the syrup over the fruit and chill. Serves 6.

CALORIES per 1 pear with 2 tablespoons syrup: 130

LOW-SODIUM MODIFICATION: Follow basic recipe.

MG. SODIUM per pear with syrup: 4

Poached Peaches

    6 large freestone peaches
    1 cup Sauterne
    ½ cup sugar
    ¼ cup water
    ¼ cup rum or brandy

Dip peaches in boiling water for 1 minute to loosen skins; plunge in cold water and slip off skins. Cut peaches in half and remove pits. Place peaches in a saucepan with the Sauterne, sugar, and water. Simmer just until tender. Place peaches in a serving dish, add the rum or brandy, and half of the cooking syrup. Chill before serving. Serves 6.

CALORIES for 1 peach with 2 tablespoons syrup: 93

LOW-SODIUM MODIFICATION: Follow basic recipe.

MG. SODIUM for 1 peach with 2 tablespoons syrup: 2

Rhubarb Compote

Select 6 tender, but large stalks of rhubarb; wash and cut in 3-inch lengths. Place in a saucepan with sugar substitute ☑ equal to 1 cup sugar or 1 cup sugar and 1 cup water. Heat to boiling, then lower heat and simmer until the stalks are just tender; keep the rhubarb sections whole. Remove rhubarb from the syrup with a slotted spoon and place in a serving bowl. Continue cooking the syrup to reduce about one-third; add a few drops red food coloring and 3 tablespoons brandy. Pour over fruit and chill before serving. Serves 6.

CALORIES per serving using sugar substitute: 34

CALORIES per serving using sugar: 128

LOW-SODIUM MODIFICATION: Follow basic recipe.

MG. SODIUM per serving: 1

Strawberry Bavarian

Prepare 1 envelope (1 tablespoon) low-calorie strawberry flavored gelatin ☑ according to package directions. Chill until syrupy. Prepare Whipped Topping (see Sauces) and chill. When gelatin mixture is syrupy, whip until foamy; fold in Whipped Topping and ½ cup artificially sweetened crushed fresh strawberries. Pour into 6 sherbet glasses and chill until set. Serves 6.

CALORIES per serving: 20

LOW-SODIUM MODIFICATION: Follow basic recipe.

MG. SODIUM per serving: 18

Cherry Crisp

⅓ cup flour
¾ cup rolled oats
⅓ cup unsaturated margarine ☑
  Sugar substitute ☑ equal to ⅓ cup sugar
1 can (1 pound) pitted sour cherries
⅓ cup sugar
1½ tablespoons cornstarch
¼ teaspoon salt
⅛ teaspoon each cinnamon and nutmeg
1 tablespoon lemon juice

Combine flour and rolled oats. Cut in margarine until mixture is crumbly; add sugar substitute. Drain cherries; combine cherry liquid with sugar, cornstarch, salt, cinnamon, nutmeg, and lemon juice. Cook over low heat, stirring constantly, until thick and clear. Stir cherries into sauce, then pour all into a lightly greased 8-inch square pan. Sprinkle with topping mixture. Bake in a moderately hot oven (375°) for 30 minutes. Serve with Whipped Topping (see Sauces). Serves 9.

CALORIES per serving: 168

LOW-SODIUM MODIFICATION: Use low-sodium unsaturated margarine ☑ and regular rolled oats. If you use the topping, be sure it has no added salt.

MG. SODIUM per serving: 2

Prune Whip

Beat 2 egg whites until foamy, then gradually add ½ cup powdered sugar and continue beating until stiff. Fold in 1 cup cooked prune pulp. Spoon into sherbet glasses and chill. Serve within 2 or 3 hours. Serves 4.

CALORIES per serving: 119

LOW-SODIUM MODIFICATION: There are 48 milligrams of sodium in each egg white. If this recipe is reasonably divided, the individual intake of sodium is fairly small.

MG. SODIUM per serving: 26

Pineapple Tapioca

2 cups unsweetened pineapple juice
½ cup water
  Sugar substitute ☑ equal to ½ cup sugar or ½ cup sugar
¼ cup quick-cooking tapioca
1 cup unsweetened pineapple tidbits, well drained

Combine the pineapple juice, water, sugar substitute or sugar, and tapioca in the top of the double boiler. Cook over hot water, stirring occasionally, until mixture thickens slightly, about 5 to 8 minutes. Remove from heat and cool. Stir in pineapple and chill. Serves 6.

CALORIES per serving using sugar substitute: 75

CALORIES per serving using sugar: 123

VARIATIONS: Use strawberries, fresh peaches, or a can of drained mandarin oranges in place of the pineapple. Bits of cooked sweetened apple are also excellent in tapioca. No change in sodium.

LOW-SODIUM MODIFICATION: Follow basic recipe.

MG. SODIUM per serving: 1

Chocolate Pudding

3 tablespoons cornstarch
  Pinch of salt
1½ tablespoons cocoa
2 cups skim milk
  Sugar substitute ☑ equal to ½ cup sugar or ½ cup sugar
1 teaspoon vanilla

Combine cornstarch, salt, and cocoa. Add milk slowly and stir until blended. Stirring, cook over medium heat until smooth and thick. Remove from heat and stir in sugar substitute and vanilla. If you use sugar rather than the substitute, be sure it is completely dissolved in the hot pudding. Pour into sherbet glasses and chill. Serves 6.

CALORIES per serving using sugar substitute: 50

CALORIES per serving using sugar: 114

LOW-SODIUM MODIFICATION: Delete salt and add a bit of salt substitute ☑. Use low-sodium skim milk ☑. Be sure you do not use Dutch process cocoa.

MG. SODIUM per serving: 4

Apple Brown Betty

1 cup bread crumbs
3 tablespoons unsaturated margarine ☑
1 teaspoon grated orange peel
½ cup sugar or ¼ cup sugar and ¼ cup honey
1 teaspoon cinnamon
5 cooking apples
¼ cup cider or apple juice

Mix together the bread crumbs, unsaturated margarine, orange peel, sugar, and cinnamon. Peel, core, and slice apples. Arrange half of sliced apples in a greased baking pan; cover with half of crumb mixture. Cover with the rest of the apples and top with rest of crumb mixture. Pour the cider over apples. Bake in a moderate oven (350°) for 40 to 50 minutes or until apples are tender. Serve hot or cold with a Vanilla Sauce or Dessert Lemon Sauce. Serves 8.

CALORIES per serving: 156

LOW-SODIUM MODIFICATION: Use low-sodium bread crumbs ☑ and low-sodium unsaturated margarine ☑.

MG. SODIUM per serving: 5

Rice Pudding

3 cups skim milk
¼ cup uncooked rice
¼ teaspoon salt
1 egg white
1 teaspoon vanilla
  Sugar substitute ☑ equal to ½ cup sugar or ½ cup sugar
  Cinnamon or nutmeg

Combine milk, rice, and salt in a saucepan and simmer, uncovered, for 1 hour; stir occasionally. Combine egg white, vanilla, and sugar substitute or sugar. Beat until foamy and moderately stiff, then fold into the rice mixture. Cook 1 minute, stirring constantly. Pour into serving dishes and sprinkle with cinnamon or nutmeg. Serves 4.

CALORIES per serving using sugar substitute: 110

CALORIES per serving using sugar: 206

VARIATIONS: Do not cook the beaten egg white mixture in the pudding for the last minute, but fold in gently after the pudding has been removed from the heat. This will lighten the pudding. Or you can pour the cooked rice mixture into a casserole and spread the beaten egg white mixture over the top. Brown in a hot oven a few minutes until the edges and peaks of the egg white are golden.

LOW-SODIUM MODIFICATION: Delete salt; add a little salt substitute ☑ and/or a little grated lemon peel. Use low-sodium skim milk ☑.

MG. SODIUM per serving: 21

Bread Pudding

1 teaspoon unsaturated margarine ☑
4 slices day-old white bread
1 egg
  Sugar substitute ☑ equal to 5 tablespoons sugar or 5 tablespoons sugar
2 cups lukewarm skim milk
1 teaspoon vanilla
  Nutmeg

Spread margarine over the bread, then arrange bread in a 1-quart baking dish. Beat the egg; stir in the sugar substitute or sugar, milk, and vanilla. Pour over bread. Sprinkle with nutmeg. Set the baking dish in a pan to come halfway up the sides of the baking dish. Bake in a moderate oven (350°) for 45 minutes or until a knife inserted in the center comes out clean. Remove dish from the hot water and cool slightly before serving. Serves 4

CALORIES per serving using sugar substitute: 100

CALORIES per serving using sugar: 140

VARIATIONS: Sprinkle ¼ cup of raisins or chopped dried apricots in the pudding before baking. Or stir 1 teaspoon of grated orange or lemon peel into the milk before pouring over the bread. Raisins add 17 calories and apricots 7 calories per serving. No change in sodium.

LOW-SODIUM MODIFICATION: Use low-sodium skim milk ☑, low-sodium unsaturated margarine ☑, and low-sodium bread ☑.

MG. SODIUM per serving: 30

Glorified Rice

Prepare Whipped Topping (see Sauces) and chill. Gently fold into the chilled topping 1 cup cooked, cooled rice, 1 small can artificially sweetened crushed pineapple ☑, drained, and ⅓ cup chopped walnuts. Spoon into sherbet glasses and serve. Serves 6.

CALORIES per serving: 95

LOW-SODIUM MODIFICATION: Use rice cooked without salt.

MG. SODIUM per serving: 3

Meringue Shells

    4 egg whites
    ¼ teaspoon cream of tartar
    ¼ teaspoon salt
    1 cup sugar
    1 tablespoon liqueur
    1 tablespoon cocoa or instant coffee

Beat egg whites until foamy, then sprinkle cream of tartar and salt over the top and continue beating until stiff. Gradually add the sugar 1 tablespoon at a time. Add the liqueur and cocoa or instant coffee and continue beating until stiff. Using a large spoon, shape into 4-inch nests on greased aluminum foil on a cooky sheet. Don't be concerned if they look a little rough—they'll taste good! If you use a pastry bag with a fluted tip, they will look more professional. However, that may be too much trouble. Bake in a slow oven (300°) for 45 minutes or until dry. Remove at once from the foil; cool. Just before serving, fill with a slightly thickened fresh fruit compote. Makes 8 shells.

CALORIES per shell: 104

LOW-SODIUM MODIFICATION: One egg white contains 48 milligrams sodium, so make the shells small. Omit salt. Do not use Dutch process cocoa.

MG. SODIUM per shell: 24

Gelatin Desserts

Gelatin desserts are refreshing, though rather bland when served plain. You can heighten interest in this dessert with the addition of fruit, or other things. Prepare a package of flavored gelatin according to package directions. When the gelatin is syrupy, fold in the addition and chill until set. Here are some suggestions. Add ¾ cup pitted sweet cherries to black raspberry gelatin; fold a can of drained mandarine oranges and ¼ cup shredded carrot in orange or lemon gelatin; add ½ cup sliced strawberries to cherry gelatin; add ½ cup of canned pineapple tidbits to pineapple gelatin; slice 2 bananas and fold into strawberry gelatin. Nuts may also be added along with the fruit. One package gelatin serves 4.

CALORIES per serving (plain): 81

LOW-SODIUM MODIFICATION: Use low-sodium flavored gelatin ☑ or plain unflavored gelatin which is a low sodium type. Generally one envelope (1 tablespoon) of gelatin will set 2 cups of liquid. Use ¼ cup less liquid if orange, pineapple, or other acidic juice is added. Follow the directions on the package.

MG. SODIUM per serving (plain): 1

Sherbets

These iced foods are often served within a meal as an "aid" to digestion or as a refresher to help you eat more. They are a great finale however, to any meal, and that is the role they are meant to play here. Their variety is infinite and depends only on your imagination for combining new flavors.

Strawberry Sherbet

Combine 2½ cups mashed strawberries (pulp and juice) with ½ cup sugar and a pinch of salt; stir until sugar is dissolved. Pour into a refrigerator freezing tray and freeze until mushy. Beat 2 egg whites until stiff, then gradually beat in ¼ cup sugar. Scrape partially frozen mixture into a well-chilled bowl; blend in egg whites. Return to freezing tray and freeze until firm, stirring once with a fork. When sherbet is firm, spoon into 6 sherbet glasses, and return to freezer until serving time. Do not let the sherbet become "rock hard". Garnish each serving with a whole strawberry and a sprig of mint. Serves 6.

CALORIES per serving: 124

VARIATIONS: You can make this with frozen strawberries. They generally are packed with sugar so eliminate the ½ cup sugar mixed with the fruit and beat only 2 tablespoons sugar into the egg whites. Raspberries may be used in the same way.

LOW-SODIUM MODIFICATION: Omit salt and add a little lemon juice to the berries. If you make any sherbet or ice cream with a hand or electric freezer, be sure that none of the rock salt and ice freezing mixture seeps into the sherbet. Each egg white in this recipe contains 48 milligrams sodium.

MG. SODIUM per serving: 16

Lemon or Lime Sherbet

    1 teaspoon unflavored gelatin
    2 cups water
    1 cup sugar
    6 tablespoons unstrained lemon or lime juice
      Grated peel of 1 lemon
      Yellow or green food coloring (optional)

Soften gelatin in ¼ cup of the water. Place the remaining 1¾ cups water in a saucepan with the sugar, lemon or lime juice, and lemon peel. Boil together for 2 minutes. Add the softened gelatin and stir until dissolved. Add a few drops food coloring, if desired. Cool, then turn into a refrigerator freezing tray and freeze until firm. Stir several times with a fork during freezing to help keep ice crystals from forming. Serves 6.

CALORIES per serving: 149

Orange Sherbet

Follow directions for making Lemon Sherbet, but instead cook 1 cup sugar, 1 cup orange juice, ¾ cup water, the juice of ½ lemon, and the grated peel of 1 orange together for 2 minutes. Add the 1 teaspoon gelatin softened in ¼ cup water and continue as above. No change in calories.

VARIATIONS: Serve 1 teaspoon of Creme de Menthe over lime sherbet or 1 teaspoon Chartreuse over lemon or orange sherbet. You can make your own variations on the basic Lemon Sherbet by using apple or cranberry juice.

LOW-SODIUM MODIFICATION: Use unflavored gelatin for sherbet recipes. You can add beaten egg whites, such as in the Strawberry Sherbet, to keep the mixture from becoming grainy, but if your sodium intake is restricted, they are best left out.

MG. SODIUM per serving for sherbet made with unflavored gelatin: 1

Melon and Grapes with White Wine

Cut a melon in half; remove and discard seeds. Cut fruit into balls using a melon ball cutter or teaspoon, or cube the fruit. Mix with 2 cups of large juicy grapes. Select the kind of melon and grape for an appropriate color contrast. For example, with green honeydew melon use dark purple Ribier grapes; with Persian melon or cantaloupe use large green sweet Malaga grapes; with green white casaba melon use Thompson Seedless grapes. Pour ½ cup of Sauterne, White Port, or champagne over the fruit and chill before serving. Serves 8.

CALORIES per serving: 34

LOW-SODIUM MODIFICATION: Follow basic recipe.

MG. SODIUM per serving: 7

CANDIES

Eating a low fat or low fat sodium restricted diet does not mean that you can't satisfy your sweet tooth!

Candy manufacturers, realizing that more and more people have been placed on one of these diets by their physicians, have anticipated the revolution in candy making and have concocted delicious (we have enjoyed them ourselves) hard candies and gum drops. They are without fat and low in sodium and in some the refined sugar have been reduced.

BEVERAGES

A plea is made to introduce a little variety into what you drink.

We are not "air hostesses" walking down the aisle offering you only coffee, tea, or milk. We urge you to discover for yourselves the quenching hot, cold, sweet and slightly tart beverages in this section of our book.

Fruit Juices

Many fruit juices are excellent. Try them alone as a pick-me-up or to assure adequate vitamin C intake. These juices are especially good in winter season in areas where fresh fruit is either unavailable or is at best, unappealing in appearance and freshness.

Don't neglect mixtures of juices and the juices that are relatively uncommon in the every day diet. There are pineapple and orange juice mixtures sold already canned, but fresh fruit such as oranges, lemons, limes, or grapefruit may also be squeezed and added to pineapple, grape, or cranberry juice. Fresh juices are also useful to blend with the thicker apricot or peach nectar. Or use either a fresh or frozen fruit juice to make lemonade or orangeade. Squeeze the juice of lemon into a tall glass; add 1 teaspoon sugar or an equivalent amount of sugar substitute ☑, and a little water; stir to dissolve sugar and put in a generous branch of fresh mint (if available) and crushed ice. Pour in either carbonated water or ice water to fill the glass. Do the same with orange juice to make orangeade, but add a bit of lemon juice to sharpen the drink.

There are many varieties of mints besides peppermint, and they are easy to grow. Use lemon mint with pineapple. Add some ginger ale to grape juice and pour over cracked ice, chilled cranberry juice makes an excellent fruit drink. Cranberry has also been combined with apple. Or try frozen tangerine juice with apricot nectar.

See Appendix for calorie content and sodium values for different fruit juices.

Carbonated Drinks

In general, 8 ounces (1 cup) of carbonated drinks contain 80 to 100 calories. Unflavored carbonated drinks, (club soda) contain no calories. There are many carbonated drinks now available that contain as little as 1 calorie and of course no fat. Perk up the flavor of these artificially sweetened drinks with a little lemon juice. The sodium content per 8 ounces amounts to approximately 25 to 35 milligrams. See mineral waters.

Tea

Try a variety such as Orange Pekoe, Japanese green tea, English breakfast, spiced tea which contains bits of dried orange peel and spices, smoky Lapsang Souchong, Chinese tea which often contains flower smells and tastes such as jasmine, tea with dried mint leaves mixed in, or a delicious blend of black India and Ceylon. Try them all.

Fill a porcelain or earthenware pot with boiling water let stand 5 minutes to heat pot, then discard water and place 1 teaspoon of tea leaves per cup in the pot and pour in the desired amount of boiling water. Allow to steep, covered, for 3 to 5 minutes; strain into thin warm tea cups or strain into another hot tea pot so the tea infusion does not continue to extract material from the leaves and become bitter. Some teas are more pronounced in taste than others and may require more or less than 1 teaspoon of tea leaves to make each cup. In many areas, milk is added with sugar or a thin lemon slice. Some of the spiced teas and Lapsang Souchong are really spoiled by adding milk and should be savored alone or taken slightly sweetened. Hot flavorful tea mixed with an equal amount of light rum, a little sugar, a strip of lemon peel, and a clove is a really great hot toddy. Serve it on a cold day after a brisk walk through the park or over a nearby field or woods. Try drinking from a small bowl held with both hands to warm your heart.

The Japanese green tea is almost invariably served unsweetened. You'll have to forgo Tibetan style tea, which contains rancid butter—it has too much saturated fat!

Iced tea is made clear as a bell by adding 1 teaspoon of tea for each cup of cold water; place in a large glass container and refrigerate overnight. In the morning pour off or strain. Half fill glasses with cracked ice or ice cubes then fill glasses with clear tea, sweeten to taste with granulated sugar or liquid sugar substitute, add a squeeze and a slice of lemon and orange, and a sprig of mint. The mint is optional. Pouring hot tea over ice cubes sometimes gives a cloudy looking tea, but it is often done when in a hurry. For really good iced tea try the above method.

TEA WITHOUT ANY ADDITIONS IS PRACTICALLY CALORIE AND SODIUM FREE.

Coffee

Regardless of how you make it, have all utensils clean. Coffee that is made in pots which contain remnants of other coffee is bitter. So clean the pot well with soap or detergent and plenty of hot water. Scouring the inside of the coffee pot with metal abrasives will markedly alter the taste and not for the better.

Use freshly ground coffee. Keep it capped and in the refrigerator, as drying and heating changes the oils present and they become rancid. Start with fresh cold water and never allow the coffee, once made, to boil. Use a coffee pot with a capacity to fit the situation, that is don't make 3 cups in a 12 cup pot. If you desire only a couple of cups, use a small pot. When you finally have brewed the coffee according to directions on the can serve it while fresh, flavorful, and aromatic.

Breakfast Recipe

Use 2 tablespoons coffee for 6 ounces ¾ cup) water whether by percolator, drip, vacuum, or filter. The actual technique of making the brew by a particular method is usually outlined by manufacturers of these various pots.

Every jar of instant coffee has directions for brewing on the label. Learn to drink your coffee black or sweeten it with a little artificial sweetener.

Demitasse Italiano

This is usually made with a pot called a *Macchinetta*. Put in the perforated cup 4 tablespoons Medallia D'Oro or similar French or Italian dark roasted coffee for each ¾ of a cup water. Arrange pot upside down, and heat. When hot, some steam will escape. Remove the pot from the heat and turn right side up. The steamed coffee is extracted by the hot water. This coffee is dark, strong, and an excellent finale to any dinner. Put in some sugar or artificial sweetener to taste and a small twist of lemon peel. This is a good way to learn to do without cream. A few cardamom seeds may also be added instead of lemon peel.

ONE CUP OF BLACK COFFEE MAY HAVE UP TO 5 CALORIES. THE SODIUM CONTENT IS NEGLIGIBLE.

Cappuccino

1 tablespoon non fat dried milk
1 cup skim milk
1 cup strong Italian-style coffee
½ teaspoon sugar
Dash of cinnamon and/or nutmeg

Stir dried milk into skim milk until blended. Heat milk, without boiling, until it is steaming; pour quickly into coffee to make it foam. Serve in tall cups and sprinkle each with sugar and, cinnamon and/or nutmeg. Makes 2 cups.

CALORIES per cup: 65

LOW-SODIUM MODIFICATION: Use low-sodium skim milk ☑.

MG. SODIUM per cup: 7

Café Royal

Put 1 teaspoon of Cognac in each demitasse cup of hot Italian or French coffee. Also, a cube of sugar can be soaked in brandy, heated slightly in a spoon, set aflame, and floated on the top of the demitasse.

CALORIES PER CUP: 36

Iced Coffee

Make coffee double strength because it will be diluted from melting ice. Pour over ice cubes. Add sugar substitute ☑ to taste and skim milk enriched with 2 teaspoons non fat dried milk per 8 ounce glass.

CALORIES 25

LOW-SODIUM MODIFICATION: Use low-sodium skim milk ☑.

MG. SODIUM: 1

Whipped Cream Substitute

This is not exactly a beverage, but it is liquid before it is whipped. This whipped topping is a reasonable substitute for whipped cream. Chill bowl and beater. Whip ½ cup non fat dried milk with ½ cup ice water 3 to 4 minutes or until soft peaks form. Add 2 tablespoons lemon juice; beat until stiff. Fold in ¼ cup sugar or sweeten with an artificial sweetener ☑. Serve at once.

Beware of some packaged whipped cream substitutes as they may contain more fats and sodium than your diet allows. Read the labels. If there is any question, do not use the product.

LOW-SODIUM MODIFICATION: Use low-sodium skim milk powder ☑.

Skim Milk

Skim milk may be made at home by adding 6 tablespoons non fat dried milk to ¾ cup of cold water. This may also be used to make a hot or cold chocolate drink.

CALORIES per cup of chocolate milk: 114

LOW SODIUM MODIFICATION: Use low-sodium skim milk ☑.

MG. SODIUM per cup of chocolate milk: 12

Milk and Cream

Whole milk or homogenized whole milk, whipped cream, and sour cream are not for you, whether you are on a restricted fat diet alone or on a low-sodium, low fat regimen. Whole milk and cream are too high in both sodium and saturated fat. There are many alternate choices now available. For example, for those whose sodium is not restricted, try fresh low fat or skim milk. Low fat milk provides more calories and grams of fat per cup than skim milk, but it may still fit into your daily fat allowance if you are a great milk lover and don't like skim milk. Check the Appendix for fat and sodium values and watch the amount of milk you consume, unless it is skim milk.

Low-sodium whole milk is undesirable even for those on a low-sodium diet as it contains just as much saturated or animal fat as regular whole milk. However, there is a modified low-sodium milk powder ☑ with very little sodium, about 13 milligrams per quarter pound. This is fine tasting when reconstituted and flavored, such as when you would use it in a flavored milk shake. Another low-sodium milk powder, Lanolac, has only 15 milligrams sodium per quarter pound.

Though buttermilks are generally low in fat, most varieties contain a great deal of salt. Check with your local dairy for the availability of low-sodium buttermilk. Be sure that the milligrams of sodium per glass are low enough to be used in your diet.

Both low-fat yogurt ☑ and regular yogurt have a fair amount of sodium per cup. Unfortunately, the low-fat has more sodium than the regular, but in any case yogurt is not particularly recommended for people on a strict low-sodium diet. The low-fat variety is fine for those whose sodium intake is not restricted.

Changes can be expected among commercial manufacturers in the field of milk and cream products. Consult your local dairy if low-sodium, low-fat ☑ products are not available at your grocery store.

Milk Shakes

Pour 1 cup of chilled skim milk into a blender or mixing bowl; add 2 teaspoons non fat dried milk and 1 teaspoon of instant coffee or vanilla, sweeten to taste. Beat until thick and foamy.

VARIATIONS: Crack two ice cubes and add to the blender before mixing the milk shake. Use various fruit juices or pieces of fruit, such as a peeled ripe white peach or a few raspberries. One teaspoon of liqueur, brandy, or rum is equally delicious and makes an excellent substitute for an egg nog. Flavor a vanilla milk shake with nutmeg. Two teaspoons of orange juice or a half ripe banana will give you a real treat. One teaspoon of egg white will also greatly increase the body and creaminess of the shake.

CALORIES per glass: 125

LOW-SODIUM MODIFICATION: Use low-sodium milk ☑ and low-sodium skim milk powder ☑, avoid the egg white.

MG. SODIUM per glass: 14

WINES AND SPIRITS: SEE APPENDIX

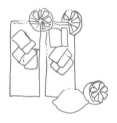

Fruit Wine Punch

½ cup sugar
½ cup water
    Large piece of ice
2 lemons
2 oranges
1 lime
½ cup strawberries
½ cup raspberries
1 bottle dry white wine
1 bottle extra-dry champagne
    Fresh mint
    Small pineapple spears

Heat sugar and water together until sugar is dissolved; chill. Place a piece of ice in a punch bowl and pour the syrup over ice. Squeeze the lemons and oranges, thinly slice the lime, and slice the strawberries. Add the juice and fruit to the punch bowl along with the raspberries. Pour in the wine and champagne; stir gently. Garnish with sprigs of mint. Stand a pineapple spear in each glass before ladling in the punch. Serves 12.

CALORIES per punch cup (½ cup): 148

MG. SODIUM per punch cup: 7

VARIATIONS: Crushed pineapple may be added to the punch. You can step up the flavor by adding some vodka, Cognac, or other brandy. To make a non-alcoholic punch, use plain soda (club soda) in place of the wine and champagne. Ginger ale is another good substitute for the wine, but it will add sodium (see Appendix).

Cocoa

Cocoa contains hard fat, so it must be taken sparingly. A good way to make cocoa is to first make a chocolate syrup. Keep it in a jar in the refrigerator and use as needed. Mix ¼ cup cocoa with ½ cup sugar; blend in ½ cup water and heat together until syrupy. To make a cup of cocoa, stir 2 tablespoons of this syrup into 1 cup of skim milk and heat. Add a few drops of vanilla and melt a small marshmallow on top before serving.

CALORIES per cup: 165

CALORIES per cup with marshmallow: 185

LOW-SODIUM MODIFICATION: Dutch process cocoa contains more sodium than the other dry varieties. Also, many persons add a little salt to cocoa; avoid this.

MG. SODIUM per cup: 15

MG. SODIUM per cup with marshmallow: 18

Vegetable Juices

These juices, as commonly sold, contain sodium, but there are special low-sodium varieties ☑. An additional help in this regard is to use the vegetables themselves. Use a blender or use a homogenizer, and make your own juice. Directions are given in books that come with homogenizers or blenders.

PICNIC SPECIALTIES

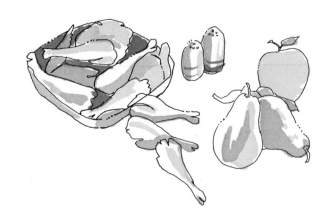

"Tra-la-la", lets picnic on the grass—skip the hamburger stand! Sit down on the grass near a babbling brook, or in a folding chair if the ground is too hard or wet.

Get out the card table, the paper and plastic things, and lets have fun the low fat or low-sodium way, eating to our hearts content!

There are times when snacks or between meal tidbits are not suitable. A trip to the park, zoo, museum, or out in the country can be a memorable occasion when you carry all the tasty wholesome foods you and your family enjoy. You won't need to struggle with the usual small restaurant or snack bar that serves only hot dogs, hamburgers, and sodas.

All sizes and shapes of plastic containers are available for packing food on the go. Carry the food in a basket or insulated bag for short trips, or for a long automobile trip, you can place the food in an inexpensive styrofoam cold chest to keep things fresh and crisp. Plastic and paper plates are convenient to use and simplify the cleanup. The following recipes fit such impromptu feasts, but don't forget to select foods that interest you from the rest of the book, such as cold or hot soups, spreads, desserts, beverages, and salads.

Hot Consommé

    5 pounds chicken necks and backs
    4 quarts water
    1 stalk celery
    1 onion, quartered
    1 envelope (1 tablespoon) unflavored gelatin

    ¼ cup water
      Juice of ½ lemon
    1 tablespoon chopped parsley
    1 teaspoon finely chopped green onion tops
    1 tablespoon dry white table wine
      Salt to taste

Place the chicken necks and backs in a large kettle with the water, celery, and onion. Simmer for 2 hours; strain into a large bowl. Chill overnight. Carefully remove the fat that has solidified on the top. Measure out 4 cups of the chicken broth and freeze the rest to use for another occasion. Soften gelatin in the ¼ cup water. Heat the 4 cups chicken broth, add the softened gelatin, and stir until it is completely dissolved. Add the lemon juice, parsley, green onion tops, wine, and salt. Pour the hot broth into a vacuum bottle and take along a small box of matzoh crackers or melba toast. This will make a great starter for your outing.

CALORIES per cup: 25

VARIATIONS: For each cup of chicken broth, add 2 cups tomato juice, a speck of garlic powder, and a little monosodium glutamate and salt to taste. Serve hot, or chill and serve cold with thin slices of lemon. This will make 31 calories per cup.

LOW-SODIUM MODIFICATION: Cook the chicken without salt. Delete monosodium glutamate and add lemon juice to taste. Be sure there is no sodium in the tomato juice.

MG. SODIUM per cup (plain): 2

MG. SODIUM per cup using tomato juice: 5

Salad Nicoise

1 head romaine lettuce
1 small red Italian onion, thinly sliced
1 small cucumber, peeled and sliced
½ green or sweet red pepper
5 pitted ripe olives, sliced
1 strip anchovy, chopped
1 can (7 oz.) water-pack tuna fish
3 tablespoons French dressing
1 small clove garlic, mashed or minced

Break the romaine into bite size pieces and place in a chilled plastic bowl that has a tight fitting lid. Add the onion, cucumber, green or red pepper, olives, and anchovy. Drain tuna, break into fair size chunks, and place on the lettuce. Cover bowl and keep chilled. Pour the French dressing into a small bottle and add the garlic. When you are ready to serve, pour the dressing over the salad and toss lightly. Serves 4.

CALORIES per serving: 142

LOW-SODIUM MODIFICATION: Delete the anchovy strip and olives. Use low-sodium tuna ☑. Be sure the French dressing contains no salt; add a speck of dry mustard and a little lemon juice to sharpen the dressing.

MG. SODIUM per serving: 25

Tuna Salad Sandwich

1 can water-pack tuna fish
1 stalk celery, finely chopped
1 tablespoon French dressing
½ teaspoon lemon juice
8 thin slices rye or pumpernickel bread
4 leaves Boston lettuce

Drain tuna and break up with a fork. Mix with the celery, French dressing, and lemon juice. (Use unsaturated mayonnaise ☑ if you prefer it to the French dressing.) Spread the tuna mixture on 4 slices of bread, cover with lettuce leaves, and top with the other 4 slices of bread. Wrap sandwiches in waxed paper or slip into small plastic bags for the trip to the museum. Take a cold apple and buy a container of black coffee when you get there. No need then to worry about what's in your lunch—you know. Makes 4 sandwiches.

CALORIES per sandwich: 195

VARIATIONS: If you have a blender, try homogenizing the tuna fish filling into a creamy mixture. Don't blend so long however that it becomes liquid.

LOW-SODIUM MODIFICATION: Be extra certain your fish isn't packed in salted water. Use low-sodium unsaturated mayonnaise ☑ and no salt in the French dressing. Low-sodium bread ☑ or toast is the thing for your sandwich.

MG. SODIUM per sandwich: 42

Stuffed Celery

Combine ¼ cup low-fat cottage cheese ☑ with 1 teaspoon finely chopped onion or chives and salt and Tabasco to taste. Spread filling in 4 large tender white stalks of celery. Wrap the celery in plastic film and carry with you on your outing.

CALORIES per stuffed stalk celery: 18

VARIATIONS: Omit onion and flavor the cottage cheese with a few pineapple bits and a little sugar. Trim with slim slices of black, white, or red radish.

LOW-SODIUM MODIFICATION: Use low-sodium low-fat cottage cheese ☑. Omit salt; instead use a little lemon juice or low-sodium flavoring ☑. Don't add so much lemon that the cheese is too moist. Since celery is high in sodium, limit yourself to one small stalk.

MG. SODIUM per 1 small stalk (plain): 25

Tomatoes Bombay

1 cup cold cooked rice
1 tablespoon French dressing
1 strip pimiento, finely chopped
1 scallion or green onion, finely chopped
⅛ teaspoon salt
   Dash of cayenne
2 medium sized tomatoes

Toss the rice together with the French dressing, pimiento, scallion, salt, and cayenne. Cut out the hard portion at the stem end of each tomato, then cut off a cap. With a small spoon, remove the seeds and pulp, leaving firm shells; turn upside down to drain for a few minutes. Spoon rice mixture into tomatoes, sprinkle a few drips of French dressing and lemon juice over the filling, and replace the caps. Pack the tomatoes in a bowl, cover, and chill. Be sure to take small paper plates and forks along for the picnic. Serve the tomatoes with a piece of cold roast chicken (skin removed). Serves 2.

CALORIES per filled tomato: 126

LOW-SODIUM MODIFICATION Omit salt: sharpen the French dressing with lemon juice and a dash of curry powder. Be sure the rice was cooked without salt.

MG. SODIUM per tomato: 5

Peanut Butter and Jelly Sandwiches

Most peanut butter contains 97 milligrams sodium per tablespoon, but there are now low-sodium types ☑ available. Additionally, common peanut butter is homogenized which really means that the oils have been saturated, making the fats harder. Avoid this product and select natural non-homogenized peanut butter with no sodium added. Toast thin slices of whole wheat bread, then cool. Spread each piece of bread with 1½ teaspoons peanut butter and 1½ teaspoons artificially sweetened raspberry preserves. Cover, of course, with another thin slice of toasted bread, and wrap. During the day when hunger strikes like a ravenous wolf, you're all set, especially if you've included in your bag or basket a few radishes, celery sticks, carrot sticks, and an apple or pear.

CALORIES per sandwich: 230

VARIATIONS: Mix 1 tablespoon chopped raisins and 1 tablespoon chopped dried apricots with 2 tablespoons peanut butter. Thin with a little skim milk and add a dash of lemon juice. This filling will make 4 sandwiches. Or thin peanut butter with chili sauce ☑ for a flavorful filling.

LOW-SODIUM MODIFICATION: Use low-sodium peanut butter ☑ and don't forget the low-sodium bread ☑. Omit celery. Use low-sodium chili sauce ☑ in the variation.

MG. SODIUM per sandwich: 17

Individual Top Crust Chicken Pies

    1 teaspoon unflavored gelatin
    1 cup chicken bouillon
    1 small onion, chopped
    2 tablespoons unsaturated margarine ☑
    2 tablespoons flour
    1 tablespoon dry white table wine
    1 sprig parsley, chopped
      Salt and pepper to taste
    2 cups diced cooked chicken
    8 mushrooms, sliced
    ½ recipe Basic Pie Crust (see Breads, Cookies, Cakes, Pies)
    2 teaspoons brandy or dry white table wine

Soften gelatin in ¼ cup of the chicken bouillon. Sauté onion in margarine until golden; blend in the flour. Add the remaining ¾ cup chicken bouillon slowly, and stirring, cook until smooth and thick. Stir the softened gelatin into sauce until gelatin is dissolved. Add the 1 tablespoon wine, parsley, salt, and pepper. In 4 individual 4-inch tart or pie pans place the chicken and mushrooms, dividing it equally, so each pie has ½ cup chicken and 2 sliced mushrooms. Pour sauce over the chicken. Roll out pastry and cut 4 tops; fit on pans, seal edges, and cut a slash in each top crust. Bake in a very hot oven (450°) for 10 minutes, then reduce heat to 350° and continue cooking 25 minutes or until browned and bubbly. Pour ½ teaspoon brandy or wine into each pie through the slits in the crust. Serve warm or cold. Makes four 4-inch pies.

CALORIES per pie: 404

VARIATIONS: Add a bit of tarragon; increase gelatin to 2 teaspoons if you plan to serve cold and like a thicker filling.

LOW-SODIUM MODIFICATION: Use low-sodium chicken bouillon ☑; avoid salt when cooking the chicken or making the pastry. Use low-sodium unsaturated margarine ☑.

MG. SODIUM per pie: 100

Cold Roast Chicken

3 pound roasting chicken or capon
1 stalk celery
1 onion
1 sliver of garlic
1 tablespoon brandy or dry white table wine
1 tablespoon corn oil
½ teaspoon salt
Paprika

Going on a trip? Going to the park with the kids, or off to the circus? It's easy to fill up with butter and oil soaked popcorn, so arrive armed with your lunch. Roast a chicken the day before, or have roast chicken for supper and save a piece for your next day's lunch. Skin the chicken with a sharp knife, or have your meat man do it for you; remove wing tips. Rinse inside and out and pat dry with paper toweling. Put celery, onion, and garlic in the cavity with a little salt and brandy or white wine. Close the openings; rub corn oil over the outside of the chicken. Sprinkle with the ½ teaspoon salt and a little paprika. Place chicken on a rack in a roasting pan and loosely cover with aluminum foil. Roast in a very hot oven (475°) for 10 minutes, then reduce heat to 350° and cook for 40 minutes. Remove foil and continue cooking 20 minutes or until chicken is browned and tender. Prick near the leg joint with a fork; the juices should run clear with no coloring of pink. Do not baste chicken with the pan drippings. Serve hot or cold.

CALORIES per piece of chicken breast: 104

CALORIES per chicken leg: 112

VARIATIONS: Instead of seasoning the chicken with celery and onion, put several sprigs of fresh tarragon or rosemary in the cavity or rub with a teaspoon of dried tarragon or rosemary. If you serve the hot chicken at the table, warm 2 tablespoons brandy and light, then pour over chicken for a spectacular view and scrumptious taste.

LOW-SODIUM MODIFICATION: Avoid salt and celery; use a little salt substitute ☑. Lemon juice goes well with the tarragon.

MG. SODIUM per piece of chicken breast: 80

MG. SODIUM per chicken leg: 72

Note: Save a piece of chicken for your junket in the country, or if you are going downtown to the library, eat it in the park on a bench.

Vegetable Sandwiches

Spread 12 slices of bread with about 2 teaspoons of *Mustard Butter* on each slice. Top 6 of the slices with *Dilled Cucumber Filling* or just plain radish slices. Cover with remaining bread slices to make sandwiches and wrap.

MUSTARD BUTTER:
½ cup softened unsaturated margarine ☑
½ tablespoon prepared mustard
⅛ teaspoon salt
Dash of cayenne pepper

Thoroughly cream margarine; beat in remaining ingredients.

DILLED CUCUMBER FILLING:
¼ cup vinegar
2 tablespoons water
1 teaspoon sugar
¼ teaspoon dried dillweed
¼ teaspoon salt
Dash of pepper
1 large cucumber, thinly sliced

Combine all ingredients. Cover and marinate in refrigerator 3 hours, stirring once or twice. Drain cucumber slices well and arrange atop each of 6 slices bread spread with Mustard Butter.

CALORIES per sandwich: 265

LOW-SODIUM MODIFICATION: Use low-sodium bread ☑, low-sodium unsaturated margarine ☑, and low-sodium prepared mustard ☑. (You can substitute 1 teaspoon regular dry mustard, if you wish.) Omit salt.

MG. SODIUM per sandwich: 20

Guacamole

1 ripe avocado
½ small onion, finely chopped
1 teaspoon lemon juice
¼ teaspoon salt
⅛ teaspoon monosodium glutamate
Dash of cayenne or ½ green chili pepper, seeded and chopped
1 slice lemon

Peel avocado; cut in half and remove seed. Mash avocado until only a few lumps remain, then mix with the onion, lemon juice, salt, monosodium glutamate, and cayenne or green chili pepper. Pack in a plastic container, place the lemon slice on top, and cap. Carry a plastic bag of carrot sticks and raw cauliflower sections for dipping. Serves 4.

CALORIES per serving: 100

LOW-SODIUM MODIFICATION: Delete salt and monosodium glutamate; depend on lemon juice, cayenne, or low-sodium gourmet seasoning ☑. A tomato, peeled, seeded, and chopped may be mixed in.

MG. SODIUM per serving: 3

Specialty Breads

Look for zweibach, melba toast, matzohs, toasted low-shortening breads, toasted rye rounds, garlic and onion melba toast, low shortening cracked and whole wheat breads, sesame seed breads, Scandinavian flat breads, water crackers, and many others. They will all add variety to any picnic menu.

LOW-SODIUM MODIFICATION: Check all breads for sodium content. Avoid pretzels, saltines, soda crackers, and other salted crackers and chips.

Pickled Watermelon Rind

Choose watermelon with a thick, firm rind. Peel off the green skin and scrape away any pink flesh. Cut the rind in neat squares or slices. (The pieces will shrink somewhat so don't make them too small.) You should have 2 quarts of cut rind. Boil the rind in water to cover for 5 minutes; drain and cool. Put the rind in 2 quarts of water with 2 tablespoons of slaked lime (available at drug store) and allow to steep overnight.

Pour off the liquid and discard; wash the rind thoroughly in cold water. Cover rind with boiling water and simmer until it is tender enough to be pierced with a fork; drain. Make a syrup with 2 cups sugar, 1 cup cider vinegar, and 4 cups water. Add a spice bag made by tying 1 tablespoon each allspice and whole cloves, 2 cinnamon sticks, and a piece of fresh ginger root in a square of cheesecloth. Cook syrup and spices for 5 minutes, then add rind and simmer for 30 minutes. Let stand, covered, for 24 hours. Then add 3 cups of vinegar and sugar substitute ☑ equal to 3 cups sugar, bring to a boil, and simmer until rind is transparent. Remove the spice bag. If the syrup gets too thick while cooking, add ¼ to ½ cup hot water as necessary. Pack the rind in hot sterilized jars. Heat the syrup to boiling, pour it over the rind in the jars, and seal. A few jars of this will last the winter and into the next watermelon season. Makes 4 pints.

CALORIES per ¼ cup serving: 60

LOW-SODIUM MODIFICATION: Follow basic recipe.

MG. SODIUM per ¼ cup serving: 3

Spiced Crab Apples

Wash and dry 5 pounds crab apples. Leave the stems on the apples but cut out the blossom ends. Make a syrup with 4 cups cider vinegar and 5 cups sugar. Add a spice bag made by tying 1 tablespoon whole cloves, 2 cinnamon sticks, and a piece of fresh ginger root in a square or cheesecloth. Cook the syrup and spices 5 minutes, then add the crab apples and cook just until tender. Do not overcook or you'll end up with applesauce. Pack the fruit in hot sterilized jars, pour on the hot syrup (remove spice bag first), and seal. Makes 5 quarts.

CALORIES per apple: 90

LOW-SODIUM MODIFICATION: Follow basic recipe.

MG. SODIUM per apple: ½

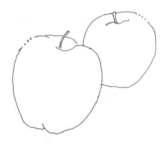

Pickled Cantaloupe Balls

Select a cantaloupe or Persian melon that is firm and slightly under ripe. Cut in half and remove seeds; cut fruit into balls with a French ball cutter. Simmer fruit in water to cover until tender but firm; drain. Make a syrup with ½ cup water, 1½ cups sugar, and a slice of lemon or orange. Add a spice bag which contains 1 cinnamon stick, 1 teaspoon whole cloves, and a small piece of fresh ginger root. Bring the syrup and spices to a boil and cook until sugar is completely dissolved, then pour over the drained fruit. Cover and let stand overnight. The next day pour off the syrup, add 1 cup cider vinegar, and bring to a boil. Again pour over the fruit and let stand overnight. Repeat this process two more times without adding anything more to the syrup. When you are ready to pack the fruit, place in hot sterilized jars. Remove spice bag, heat syrup to boiling, and pour over fruit. Seal. Use as a relish, not a dessert. Makes 2 pints.

CALORIES per ½ cup serving: 162

LOW-SODIUM MODIFICATION: Follow basic recipe.

MG. SODIUM per ½ cup serving: 7

Candied Grapefruit Peel

Save the skins from 4 grapefruits that are clean and free from blemishes; cut skins in quarters and remove any excess white portion or membrane. Place peel in a saucepan and cover with water. Bring to a boil and cook slowly for 15 minutes; drain. Cover with fresh water and boil again until peel is tender. Drain and cut peel into ½-inch wide strips. Make a syrup with ¼ cup sugar, sugar substitute ☑ equal to ¼ cup sugar, ½ cup water, and 1 tablespoon white corn syrup. Combine syrup and peel and bring to a boil. Remove from heat and let stand overnight. The next day pour off the syrup and simmer for 20 minutes; pour it over peel and allow to stand again overnight. Repeat once more cooking the syrup then pouring over the peel and standing overnight. Remove peel from syrup and allow to drain on a rack. Roll peel in granulated sugar and store in a can with a tight fitting cover. Have a piece when you really crave some candy. Most candy contains many things besides sugar and your intake is hard to control. With this confection you know what you are eating.

CALORIES per piece: 35

VARIATIONS: Follow the basic recipe and use thick orange or lemon peel. The last time the peel stands in the syrup, you can add a tablespoon of rum.

LOW-SODIUM MODIFICATION: Follow basic recipe.

MG. SODIUM per piece: 5

Spritzers

Pour a little red or white wine over ice in a tumbler and add club soda to taste.

CALORIES per 4 ounces (½ cup) of wine: 100

MG. SODIUM per 4 ounces (½ cup) of wine: 5

Splits of White or Rosé

Splits of white or rosé wine are small bottles which are suitable for a small piquenique. Cool the bottles at home and take to the picnic in an insulated cooler. Don't forget the bottle opener or cork screw.

Bon Appétit

Finding a low-cost lunch that fits your diet is a real problem. Bringing the daily routine from home doesn't help much either. But why not bring along the kind of lunch box delicacies that will turn your brown bag doldrums into an exciting repast!

Here are some tempting lunch box specials, using many of the recipes from this book.

MONDAY

Chilled Gazpacho (p. 35)
—add the garnishes after pouring the chilled soup into a widemouth vacuum bottle.
A couple of Rye Krisp Wafers
Carrot Curls and Radishes
Baked Apple (p. 114)
—it will just fit into the decorated plastic margarine container you've been saving.

TOTAL CALORIES: 318

MG. SODIUM: 34

TUESDAY

Cold Roast Chicken Breast (p. 131)
Marinated Green Bean Salad (p. 88)
Fruit Kebabs (p. 95)
—pack a couple of them, using a colorful assortment of fruits.
2 Orange Refrigerator Cookies (p. 105)

TOTAL CALORIES: 316

MG. SODIUM: 116

WEDNESDAY

Salad Nicoise (p. 129)
—bring the dressing in a separate container to add just at lunch time.
Whole Wheat Muffin (p. 101)
—split and spread with unsaturated margarine before leaving home.
Oriental Orange (p. 116)

TOTAL CALORIES: 391

MG. SODIUM: 33

THURSDAY

Dilled Cold Veal (p. 60)
—start with a slice of sour dough—or low sodium—bread. Top with a lettuce leaf, the thin sliced veal and a couple tablespoons of the Dill Sauce.

Fluffy Orange Mold (p. 90)
—spoon carefully into a widemouth, shallow vacuum container.

TOTAL CALORIES: 393

MG. SODIUM: 223

FRIDAY

Split Pea Soup (p. 39)
—keep piping hot in your thermos.
Bread Sticks (3 or 4)
Assorted Fresh Fruit Wedges with Aloha Dip (p. 30)
—pack a double portion of the dip in a small baby food jar, or container of similar size.

TOTAL CALORIES: 299

MG. SODIUM: 57

For these special lunches, you may want some special equipment. Attractive thermal lunch bags to keep hot things hot and cold things cold can be found at many variety stores. Snap-top plastic containers are suitable for many of the "wet" lunch items. Wrap meats, sandwiches, vegetables and fruits in plastic or foil.

Make lunch at your desk as attractive to look at as it is good to eat. It helps a lot, particularly when you are on a special diet. Stock a file drawer with colorful paper plates, napkins, hot and cold cups, plastic knives, forks and spoons—and you'll have the best set desk in the office!

HAPPY HOLIDAY RECIPES

Selections from this book are easily arranged to fulfill the requirements of an exacting hostess. Here are a few feast suggestions. Thanksgiving dinner, for instance, could include the following:

Shrimp cocktail, p. 33
Roast turkey, p. 57
Brown sauce, p. 110
Cranberry-Kumquat Relish, p. 113
Broccoli Italienne, p. 72
Sweet Potatoes with Orange, p. 82
No Bake Pumpkin Pie, p. 104
Cappuccino, p. 125

TOTAL CALORIES PER PERSON: 1053

MG. SODIUM PER PERSON: 156

HOW TO USE THE APPENDIX

Foods are listed alphabetically in the Appendix for easier reference. Brand names, calories, milligrams of sodium, grams of saturated fat and grams of unsaturated fat, are listed when known. The words "high", "low", and "medium" have been added to give you a general idea of the amounts of saturated and unsaturated fat in a particular food. In certain cases where this information is not known, the amounts are estimated. "High" means that the saturated or unsaturated fat content is over 30% of the total calories; "medium" between 15% and 30% and "low" less than 15%.

Only truly unsaturated (polyunsaturated) fats are listed. Therefore, oleic acid, which is neither saturated nor significantly unsaturated, is omitted.

Remember that foods should be chosen not only for their relatively low saturated fat content but for their relatively high unsaturated fat content, like some nuts, vegetable oils, and margarines.

Specialty foods will be found under the general headings for these foods. For example, under margarines you will find "regular margarine", "unsaturated margarine", and "low-sodium unsaturated margarine". The names of some companies making these special products are also listed.

A table comparing the saturated and unsaturated fats in some of the commercially available margarines and oils, and a table giving some of the commonly used weights and measures have been included.

Abbreviations

Ckd. = *Cooked*	*Oz.* = *Ounce*
Cnd. = *Canned*	*Pc.* = *Piece*
Drsg. = *Dressing*	*Qt.* = *Quart*
Grd. = *Ground*	*Reg.* = *Regular*
Med. = *Medium*	*Tbsp.* = *Tablespoon*
Neg. = *Negligible*	*Tsp.* = *Teaspoon*

APPENDIX

Approximate Food Values

ITEM	SPECIAL BRANDS	PORTION	CAL.	SODIUM mgms.	Sat. Fat gms.	Unsat. Fat gms.
Ala, dry	Fisher's	1 cup	600	5	neg.	neg.
Ale, mild		8 oz.	98	unkn.	neg.	neg.
All-bran		1/2 cup	73	392	1/2 (low)	neg.
Allspice, grd.		1 tsp.	neg.	2	neg.	neg.
Almond Extract		1 tsp.	neg.	neg.	neg.	neg.
Almonds, raw		1 cup	848	4	6 (low)	15 (med.)
Anise Seed		1 tsp.	neg.	neg.	neg.	neg.
Anchovy Paste		1 tsp.	14	686	3/4 (high)	1/2 (med.)
Apple, raw		1 med.	76	1	neg.	neg.
Cider		1/2 cup	62	1	neg.	neg.
Juice		1/2 cup	60	1	neg.	neg.
Sauce, canned		1/2 cup	92	3	neg.	neg.
Without sugar	Tillie Lewis / Featherweight / Nutradiet / Monarch	1/2 cup	40	3	neg.	neg.
Apricots, raw		3 med.	54	1	neg.	neg.
Canned		4 halves	97	5	neg.	neg.
Without sugar	Tillie Lewis / Featherweight / Nutradiet	4 halves	45	1	neg.	neg.
Dried	Monarch	5 halves	49	2	neg.	neg.
Nectar		1/2 cup	70	1	neg.	none
Arrowroot		1 Tbsp.	29	.4	none	neg.
Artichoke, globe		1 large	51	41	neg.	neg.
Asparagus, raw		6 stalks	21	3	neg.	neg.
Canned		6 stalks	22	394	neg.	neg.
Low-sodium, canned	S & W / Cellu / Monarch	6 stalks	22	4	neg.	neg.
Frozen, uncooked	Tillie Lewis	6 stalks	21	3	neg.	neg.
Avocado		1/2 small	179	3	4 (med.)	2 (low)
Bacon, fried crisp		2 slices	97	160	3 1/2 (high)	1 (low)
Low-sodium, canned	Cellu	2 slices	65	7	2 1/2 (med.)	1 (low)
Baking Powder, Regular		1 tsp.	4	408	neg.	neg.
Low-sodium	Cellu	1 tsp.	4	1	neg.	neg.
Baking Soda		1 tsp.	none	1232	neg.	neg.
Banana		1 small	85	1	neg.	neg.
Barley		1 cup	710	6	neg.	1 (low)
Basil		1 tsp.	neg.	neg.	none	none
Bass, Black Sea, raw		1 oz.	31	20	1/2 (low)	neg.
Bay Leaf		1 leaf	neg.	none	none	neg.
Beans, dry		1/2 cup	321	1	neg.	neg.
Beans, Red Kidney, dry						
Raw		1/2 cup	343	10	neg.	neg.
Canned		1/2 cup	120	4	neg.	neg.
Beans, Garbanzos, dry, raw		1/2 cup	360	26	1/2 (low)	neg.
Beans, Lima, raw		1/2 cup	128	1	neg.	neg.
Canned		1/2 cup	76	248	neg.	neg.
Dry, raw	Monarch	1/2 cup	345	4	neg.	neg.
Low-sodium	S & W	1/2 cup	76	2	neg.	neg.
Frozen, raw	Cellu	4 Tbsp.	109	varies	neg.	neg.

ITEM	SPECIAL BRANDS	PORTION	CAL.	SODIUM mgms.	Sat. Fat gms.	Unsat. Fat gms.
Candy (continued)						
Sweet Chocolate	Douglas Shaw	1 oz.	143	10	8 (high)	neg.
Sugar-Free Hard		1 pc.	9	37	none	none
Sugar-Free Hard	Estee	1 pc.	10	neg.	none	none
Cantaloupe, raw		1/4 melon	30	12	neg.	neg.
(also Casaba, Persian, and Crenshaw melons)		1/4 melon	30	12	neg.	neg.
Caraway Seed		1 tsp.	neg.	none	none	none
Carbonated Beverages						
Black Cherry	Canada Dry	6 oz.	93	80	none	none
Club Soda (no sugar)	Canada Dry	6 oz.	.1	250	none	none
Cola	Canada Dry	6 oz.	77	none	none	none
Collins Mix	Canada Dry	6 oz.	64	80	none	none
Ginger Ale	Canada Dry	6 oz.	64	none	none	none
Grape	Canada Dry	6 oz.	100	80	none	none
Wink	Canada Dry	6 oz.	89	80	none	none
Hi-Spot	Canada Dry	6 oz.	73	85	none	none
Bitter Lemon	Canada Dry	6 oz.	78	80	none	none
Orange	Canada Dry	6 oz.	96	80	none	none
Quinine Water	Canada Dry	6 oz.	71	none	none	none
Root Beer	Canada Dry	6 oz.	78	80	none	none
Strawberry	Canada Dry	6 oz.	85	80	none	none
Tahitian Treat	Canada Dry	6 oz.	93	80	none	none
Coca-cola		8 oz.	78	2	none	none
Club Soda	White Rock	6 oz.	80	1.7	none	none
Ginger Ale		6 oz.	80	18	none	none
Pepsi-cola		8 oz.	106	36	none	none
Carbonated Beverages, Low-calorie						
Ginger Ale	Belfast	6 oz.	1	29	none	none
Orange	Belfast	6 oz.	1	20	none	none
Root Beer	Belfast	6 oz.	1	2	none	none
Lemon-lime		6 oz.	1	23	none	none
Cherry	Canada Dry	6 oz.	1	94	none	none
Coffee	Canada Dry	6 oz.	1.7	93	none	none
Cola	Canada Dry	6 oz.	1	101	none	none
Cream	Canada Dry	6 oz.	1	111	none	none
Ginger	Canada Dry	6 oz.	1	21	none	none
Grape	Canada Dry	6 oz.	1	124	none	none
Lemon	Canada Dry	6 oz.	1	161	none	none
Orange	Canada Dry	6 oz.	1	107	none	none
Root Beer	Canada Dry	6 oz.	1	106	none	none
Diet Rite Cola		8 oz.	1	32	none	none
Like		6 oz.	1	neg.	none	none
Tab		6 oz.	1	unkn.	none	none
Sugar Free Bitter Lemon Calso		8 oz.	trace	none	none	none
Sugar Free Quintonic Calso		8 oz.	trace	none	none	none
Carrots, raw		1 large	23	28	neg.	neg.
Canned	S & W	1/2 cup	22	204	neg.	neg.
Low-sodium, canned	Cellu / Monarch					
Carp, raw	Tillie Lewis	1/2 cup	22	26	neg.	neg.
Cashews, raw, roasted		1 oz.	39	14	1/2 (low)	neg.
Catsup, regular		1 cup	770	20	11 (med.)	5 (low)
Low-sodium	Cellu	1 Tbsp.	17	221	neg.	neg.
		1 Tbsp.	8	1	neg.	neg.

Food	Brand	Amount				
Beans, green, raw		1/2 cup	18	1	neg.	neg.
Canned	S & W	1/2 cup	14	258	neg.	neg.
Low-sodium, canned	Cellu					
	Monarch					
	Tillie Lewis					
Frozen, raw		1/2 cup	14	1	neg.	neg.
Bean Sprouts, raw		1 cup	35	2	neg.	neg.
Beef, raw, lean		1 oz.	49	6	2 (high)	neg.
Corned, raw		1 oz.	65	20	4 (high)	neg.
Dried		1 oz.	83	369	3/4 (low)	neg.
Heart, raw		1 oz.	58	1219	2 (high)	neg.
Kidney, raw		1 oz.	31	24	3 (high)	neg.
Kosher, raw, lean		1 oz.	40	57	3/4 (low)	neg.
Liver, raw		1 oz.	52	454	3/4 (high)	neg.
Thymus, raw, unsmoked		1 oz.	39	37	3 (high)	neg.
Tongue, raw, unsmoked		1 oz.	52	27	2 1/2 (high)	neg.
Hash, corned beef		1/2 cup	56	23	3 (med.)	neg.
Beets, raw		1/2 cup	141	540	neg.	neg.
Canned		1/2 cup	29	40	neg.	neg.
Low-sodium, canned	S & W	1/2 cup	31	196	neg.	neg.
	Cellu					
	Monarch					
	Tillie Lewis					
Greens, fresh cooked		1/2 cup	31	38	neg.	neg.
Beer		8 oz.	112	17	none	none
Blackberries, raw		1/2 cup	41	1	neg.	neg.
Blueberries, raw		1/2 cup	43	1	neg.	neg.
Boysenberries, raw		1/2 cup	45	1	neg.	neg.
Frozen		1/2 cup	113	1	neg.	neg.
Bluefish, raw		1 oz.	35	19	1 (low)	neg.
Brandy		1 oz.	73	1	none	none
Brazil Nuts, raw, shelled		1 oz.	915	neg.	18 (med.)	24 (med.)
Bread, Boston Brown, with raisins		1 slice	105	134	1/4 (low)	neg.
Rye		1 slice	57	138	neg.	neg.
Low-sodium		1 slice	57	7	neg.	neg.
White		1 slice	63	117	neg.	neg.
Low-sodium	Langendorf	1 slice	63	7	neg.	neg.
	Oroweat					
	Specialty Baking Co.					
Whole Wheat		1 slice	55	117	1/2 (low)	neg.
Low-sodium		1 slice	55	7	neg.	neg.
Broccoli, raw		1 stalk	29	15	neg.	neg.
Frozen, raw		1 stalk	23	15	neg.	neg.
Brussel Sprouts		9 med.	47	12	neg.	neg.
Frozen, raw		9 med.	47	12	neg.	neg.
Butter, regular		1 tsp.	33	50	2 (high)	neg.
		1 cup	1604	2240	101 (high)	6 (low)
Unsalted		1 tsp.	33	1	2 (high)	neg.
		1 cup	1604	22	101 (high)	6 (low)
Buttermilk		1 cup	86	317	neg.	neg.
Cultured		1 cup	unkn.	unkn.	neg.	neg.
Low-sodium		1 cup	12	8	neg.	neg.
Cabbage, raw		1/2 cup	7	12	neg.	neg.
Chinese, raw		1 cup			neg.	neg.
Candy						
Bar	Baby Ruth	2 1/2 oz.	290	67	6 (med.)	1 1/2 (low)
Bar	Milky Way	2 1/2 oz.	284	165	3 1/2 (med.)	1 1/2 (low)
Bar	Oh Henry	2 1/2 oz.	290	29	6 (med.)	1 1/2 (low)
Gum Drop		8 small	33	4	none	none
Milk Chocolate		1 oz.	143	21	5 (high)	neg.
Peppermint Patty	Schrafft's	1 patty	125	3	5 (med.)	neg.

Food	Brand	Amount				
Cauliflower, raw		1/2 cup	13	10	neg.	neg.
Frozen, raw		1/2 cup	25	20	neg.	neg.
Caviar, salmon, canned		1 tsp.	30	220	1 1/2 (high)	neg.
Celery		3 sm. stalks	99	50	neg.	neg.
Celery Flakes		1 tsp.	neg.	115	neg.	neg.
Celery Salt		1 tsp.	neg.	840	neg.	neg.
Celery Seed, whole		1 tsp.	15	4	neg.	neg.
Chard, fresh ckd.		1/2 cup		86	neg.	6 (high)
Cheese						
Cheddar		1 oz.	113	198	5 (high)	6 (high)
Cheddar, low-sodium	Neilson's	1 oz.	113	3	5 (high)	neg.
	Cellu	1 Tbsp., grated	27	1		
Cheezola, low cholesterol	Fischer	1 oz.	90	490	1 (high)	neg.
Cheezola, low sodium and low cholesterol	Fischer	1 oz.	90	183	1.5 (low)	neg.
Countdown, low calorie	Fischer	1 oz.	40	475	0.3 (low)	none
Cottage, creamed		1 oz.	108	328	2 1/2 (med.)	neg.
Creamed, low-sodium		1/2 cup	108	23	2 1/2 (med.)	0.7 (low)
Dry, low-sodium		1/2 cup	75	23	neg.	1 (low)
Cream Cheese		2 Tbsp.	112	75	6 (high)	neg.
Lite Line	Borden	1 oz.	44	454	2 (high)	neg.
Parmesan		1 oz.	110	206	4 (high)	neg.
Processed		1 oz.	105	425	5 (high)	neg.
Romano		1 oz.	110	205	4 (high)	neg.
Swiss		1 oz.	105	198	4 (high)	neg.
Velveeta		1 oz.	90	454	neg.	neg.
Cherries, raw		15 large	61	2	neg.	neg.
Canned, sour		1/2 cup	61	2	neg.	neg.
Chervil		1 tsp.	neg.	1	none	neg.
Chestnuts		3 small	28	neg.	neg.	neg.
Chicken, light raw		3 1/2 oz.	104	90	0.5 (low)	neg.
Dark, raw		3 1/2 oz.	112	79	2 (med.)	neg.
Unsalted, canned		3 oz.	128	25	2 (low)	neg.
Liver, raw		1 Tbsp.	40	30	(med.)	neg.
Chili Sauce		1 Tbsp.	20	227	neg.	neg.
Low-sodium	Featherweight	1 tsp.	8	1	neg.	neg.
Chili Powder		1 Tbsp.	neg.	57	neg.	neg.
Chives		1 tsp.	neg.	1	neg.	neg.
Chocolate, bitter		1 oz.	142	3	8 (high)	neg.
Semisweet Bits		1 oz.	150	4	5 (high)	neg.
Chocolate Powder	Featherweight	1 tsp.	neg.	neg.	neg.	neg.
Cinnamon		1 tsp.	neg.	1	neg.	neg.
Citron, candied		1 oz.	89	54	neg.	neg.
Clams, soft, raw		4 large	82	36	1 (med.)	neg.
Canned, solids only		1/2 cup	98	unkn.	1 (med.)	neg.
Cloves		1 tsp.	neg.	1	neg.	neg.
Cocoa, Dutch, process		1 Tbsp.	21	50	9 (high)	neg.
Plain		1 Tbsp.	21	neg.	1/2 (med.)	neg.
Coconut, raw, shredded		1/2 cup	161	10	neg.	1/2 (low)
Milk		1/2 cup	30	30	neg.	none
Codfish, raw		1 oz.	21	22	neg.	none
Salted, dried		1 oz.	106	2296	1	none
Coffee, regular		1 Tbsp.	none	neg.	neg.	neg.
Instant		1 tsp.	none	1	neg.	neg.
Sanka		1 tsp.	neg.	neg.	neg.	neg.
Cognac		1 oz.	73	1	neg.	neg.
Collard Greens, frozen		1/2 cup	37	18	1/4 (low)	neg.
Corn, fresh, kernels		1/2 cup	96	trace	1/4 (low)	neg.
Cob		1 med. ear	75	trace	2 (low)	neg.
Canned, drained		1/2 cup	70	196	1/4 (low)	neg.
Creamed Style, canned		1/2 cup	101	290	1/4 (low)	neg.
Frozen, raw		1/2 cup	86	1	neg.	neg.
Low-sodium, canned	S & W	1/2 cup	65	2	1/4 (low)	neg.
	Cellu					
	Monarch					

Nutritional values table (continued). Columns: ITEM · SPECIAL BRANDS · PORTION · CAL. · SODIUM mgms. · Sat. Fat gms. · Unsat. Fat gms.

ITEM	SPECIAL BRANDS	PORTION	CAL.	SODIUM mgms.	Sat. Fat gms.	Unsat. Fat gms.
Low-sodium Gourmet Seasoning	Amplify	1 tsp.	neg.	1	neg.	neg.
Low-sodium Flavoring	Milani's		neg.	neg.	neg.	neg.
	Diazest	1/2 tsp.	neg.	neg.	neg.	neg.
Low-sodium, Low-calorie Piquant Dressing	Featherweight	1 Tbsp.	7.5	.4	neg.	neg.
Macaroni, cooked		1/2 cup	78	1	1/4 (low)	1/4 (low)
Mace, ground		1 tsp.	neg.	2	neg.	neg.
Mackerel, Atlantic, raw		1 oz.	70	14	1 (med.)	neg.
Mackerel, Pacific, raw		1 oz.	51	25	1/2 (low)	1/4 (low)
Margarine, reg.		1 tsp.	34	55	2 1/2 (high)	1/4 (low)
Low-sodium		1 tsp.	34	55	2 1/2 (high)	1/4 (low)
Unsaturated, reg.		1 tsp.	34	5	1/4 (low)	2 (high)
Unsaturated, low-sodium		1 tsp.	34	1	1/3 (low)	1 (med.)
Marjoram		1 tsp.	neg.	neg.	neg.	neg.
Marmalade, orange		1 Tbsp.	55	3	neg.	neg.
Marshmallow		1 average	25	3	neg.	none
Matzoh Meal, unsalted	Manischewitz	1 cup	400	2.8	1 (low)	neg.
Mayonnaise, unsaturated		1 Tbsp.	92	77	1 (low)	6 (high)
Unsaturated, low-sodium	Hain, Balanaise	1 Tbsp.	92	10	1 (low)	6 (high)
Low-salt whipped dressing	Smithers	1 Tbsp.	24	6	unkn.	unkn.
Milk, fresh, whole		1 cup	166	122	5 (med.)	neg.
Fresh, low fat (2%)		1 cup	148	153	3 (low)	neg.
Fresh, skim		1 cup	87	128	neg.	neg.
Evaporated		1/2 cup	173	126	5 (med.)	1/2 (low)
Condensed, sweetened		1 Tbsp.	61	27	1 (med.)	neg.
Dried Milk Powder, nonfat		1 Tbsp.	28	29	neg.	neg.
Low-sodium skim milk powder	Cellu	1 Tbsp.	28	2	neg.	neg.
Reconstituted	Cellu	1 cup	79	8	neg.	neg.
Low-sodium, fresh, whole milk		1 cup	166	12	5 (med.)	neg.
Mint flakes		1 tsp.	neg.	neg.	neg.	neg.
Mixed Vegetables, frozen		1/2 cup	79	71	neg.	neg.
Molasses, cane		1 Tbsp.	50	8	none	none
Muffins (commercial)		1 average	83	1	1 1/2 (med.)	neg.
Mulberries		1/2 cup	42	1	neg.	neg.
Mushrooms, raw		10 small	16	5	neg.	neg.
Canned		1/2 cup	14	488	neg.	neg.
Low-sodium, canned	Cellu	1/2 cup	17	2	neg.	neg.
Mustard Greens, fresh, cooked		1/2 cup	16	41	neg.	neg.
Mustard, ground		1 tsp.	neg.	neg.	neg.	neg.
Prepared		1 tsp.	neg.	65	neg.	neg.
Low-sodium	Plantation	1 tsp.	neg.	3	neg.	neg.
Seed		1 tsp.	neg.	neg.	neg.	neg.
Nectarines, raw		2 med.	60	2	neg.	neg.
Noodles, egg, cooked		1/2 cup	100	3	1/2 (low)	neg.
Nutmeg, ground		1 tsp.	neg.	1	neg.	neg.
Oatmeal, dry		1 cup	312	2	1 (low)	2 (low)
Cooked		1 cup	148	1	1 (low)	1 (low)
Oil, coconut		1 cup	1945	neg.	60 (high)	125 (high)
Unsaturated (all kinds)		1 cup	1945	neg.	24 (low)	17 (low)
Olive		1 cup	1945	neg.	24 (low)	17 (low)
Okra, raw		8 pods	36	1	neg.	neg.
Frozen		8 pods	39	2	neg.	neg.
Cooked		8 pods	25	2	neg.	neg.
Olives, green		1 large	10	156	neg.	neg.
Ripe		12 large	85	512	1 (low)	1 (low)
Stuffed		2 small	10	182	neg.	neg.

ITEM	SPECIAL BRANDS	PORTION	CAL.	SODIUM mgms.	Sat. Fat gms.	Unsat. Fat gms.
Corn, popped, unsalted		1 cup	54	neg.	1/4 (low)	neg.
Cornflakes		1 cup	96	165	1 (low)	neg.
Low-sodium	VanBrode	1 cup	110	2	neg.	neg.
Cornmeal, raw		1 oz.	400	3	1 (low)	2 (low)
Cornstarch		1 Tbsp.	29	neg.	neg.	neg.
Cowpeas, raw, fresh		1/2 cup	87	2	neg.	neg.
Crab, boiled		5/8 cup	105	370	neg.	neg.
Canned		5/8 cup	105	1000	neg.	neg.
Crackers						
Graham		2	55	99	1 (low)	neg.
Matzoh, salted	Manischewitz	1 piece	78	94	neg.	neg.
Unsalted	Manischewitz	1 piece	78	neg.	neg.	neg.
Rye Krisp	Ryvita	1 wafer	47	93	neg.	neg.
Rye Crispbread	Hol Grain	1 wafer	unkn.	neg.	neg.	neg.
Rye Wafer-ets		1 wafer	9	neg.	neg.	neg.
Soda		2 crackers	30	121	1 (med.)	neg.
Melba		1 slice	16	70	neg.	neg.
Low-sodium	Cellu, Devonsheer	1 slice	16	.4	neg.	neg.
Wheat wafers	Estee, Venus	1 wafer	17	neg.	neg.	neg.
Low-sodium crackers	Featherweight	2 crackers	32	neg.	neg.	unkn.
Cranberries, raw		1 cup	54	1	neg.	neg.
Sauce, canned		1 Tbsp.	34	1	neg.	neg.
Juice, sweetened		1/2 cup	80	1	neg.	neg.
Cream, heavy		1 Tbsp.	49	6	3 (high)	1/4 (low)
Half & Half		1/4 cup	82	28	4 (high)	0.5 (low)
Imitation Sour	Imo	1 oz.	50	60	5 (high)	0.6 (low)
	Matey	1 oz.	60	116	1 (low)	0.7 (med.)
Cream Substitutes	Cereal Blend	1 tsp/dry	24	15	0.7 (low)	neg.
	Coffee Mate	1 oz.	12	3.5	¼ (low)	2½ (high)
	Coffee-rich	1 oz.	44	40	0.5 (low)	0.7 (low)
	Mocha Mix	1 tsp/dry	38	20	1 (high)	neg.
	Pream	1 oz.	15	4	0.7 (med.)	0.7 (med.)
	Quip	1 tsp/dry	24	15	neg.	neg.
Cream of Rice, ckd.		1/2 cup	68	neg.	neg.	neg.
Cream of Wheat, reg. ckd.		1/2 cup	67	neg.	neg.	neg.
Quick-cooking, ckd.		1/2 cup	67	17	neg.	neg.
Cream of Tartar		1 tsp.	neg.	8	neg.	neg.
Cucumber, raw		1/2 med.	13	7	neg.	neg.
Currants, dried		1/2 cup	268	20	neg.	neg.
Curry Powder		1 tsp.	neg.	1	neg.	neg.
Dandelion greens, ckd., fresh		1/2 cup	40	76	neg.	neg.
Dates, pitted		1 cup	505	2	neg.	neg.
Dill Dressing, low-sodium		1 Tbsp.	neg.	2	1/2 (low)	neg.
Dill Seed		1 tsp.	neg.	unkn.	neg.	neg.
Duck, raw (domestic)		3 1/2 oz.	300	82	8 (high)	4 (high)
Egg, whole		1 med.	77	70	2 (med.)	neg.
White only		1 med.	15	47	neg.	neg.
Yolk only		1 med.	61	14	2 (med.)	neg.
	Egg Beaters	1/4 cup	100	109	1.2 (low)	3 (low)
	Egg Replacer	1 tsp.	10	0.3	neg.	neg.
	Eggstra	1/2 pkg.	44	32	1.3 (med.)	neg.
	Second Nature	3 Tbsp.	35	79	0.3	0.8 (med.)
Eggplant, raw		1/2 cup	24	2	neg.	neg.
Endive, fresh		4 long leaves	5	3	neg.	neg.
Farina, ckd.		1/2 cup	67	4	neg.	neg.
Fennel, raw		3 1/2 oz.	28	14	neg.	neg.
Fennel Seed		1 tsp.	neg.	1	neg.	neg.
Figs, raw		3 small	90	2	neg.	neg.
Canned		3	129	2	neg.	neg.
Dried		1 large	57	7	neg.	neg.

Fines Herbes		1 tsp.	neg.	1	neg.	neg.
Flounder, raw		1 oz.	19	17	1/4 (low)	neg.
Flour, enriched		1 cup	401	2	neg.	neg.
Self-rising		1 cup	385	1650	neg.	neg.
French Dressing						
Low-sodium	Bernard	1 Tbsp.	neg.	1	neg.	neg.
	Smithers	1 Tbsp.	4	3	neg.	neg.
Fruit Cocktail, canned		1/2 cup	90	6	neg.	neg.
Without sugar, canned	Tillie Lewis					
	Featherweight					
	Nutradiet					
	Monarch	1/2 cup	35	2.5	neg.	neg.
Garlic		1 clove	2	neg.	neg.	neg.
Garlic Powder		1 tsp.	neg.	1	neg.	neg.
Gelatin, plain		1 Tbsp.	34	3	none	none
Dessert, flavored		1 box	324	281	none	none
Low-calorie, flavored	D-Zerta	1/2 cup	9	57	none	none
Low-calorie, low-sodium, flavored	Cellu	1/2 cup	14	3	neg.	neg.
	Tillie Lewis	1/2 cup	7	1	none	none
	Jellathin	1/3 cup	3	8	none	none
Ginger, ground		1 tsp.	neg.	1	neg.	neg.
Whole		1 tsp.	neg.	1	neg.	neg.
Preserved		1 oz.	97	neg.	neg.	neg.
Gin		1 jigger	105	neg.	none	none
Goose, raw (domestic)		3 1/2 oz.	354	82	12 (high)	4 (low)
Liver, raw		1 oz.	50	40	2.5 (high)	neg.
Gooseberries, raw		1/2 cup	29	1	neg.	neg.
Grapefruit, raw		1/2 med.	55	2	neg.	neg.
Juice, sweetened		1/2 cup	70	3	neg.	neg.
Unsweetened		1/2 cup	50	3	neg.	neg.
Grapes, Concord and						
Tokay, raw		22 grapes	70	2	1/4 (low)	neg.
Thompson, seedless		30 grapes	30	1	1/8 (low)	neg.
Juice, sweetened		1/2 cup	75	3	1/4 (low)	neg.
Grape-Nuts		1/4 cup	110	187	neg.	neg.
Gravy Flavoring		1 tsp.	unkn.	4	unknown	unknown
Gum, chewing		1 stick	unkn.	1	none	none
Halibut, raw		1 oz.	36	15	1/4 (low)	neg.
Haddock, raw		1 oz.	22	17	neg.	neg.
Hazel Nuts		11 med.	95	neg.	1 (low)	2 1/2 (med.)
Herring, lake, raw		3 1/2 oz.	100	47	1 1/4 (low)	neg.
Hominy, canned		1 cup	122	605	neg.	neg.
Honey		1 Tbsp.	62	2	neg.	none
Honeydew Melon, raw		1/4 small melon	33	12	neg.	neg.
Horseradish, fresh		1 tsp.	2	1	neg.	neg.
Ice Cream, vanilla		1/6 qt.	193	55	6 (med.)	neg.
Ice Milk, vanilla		1/6 qt.	136	75	3 (med.)	neg.
Jam, jelly		1 Tbsp.	50	1	neg.	neg.
Low-calorie Jams and Jellies		1 tsp.	1	1	neg.	neg.
Kale, fresh, cooked		1/2 cup	23	40	neg.	neg.
Frozen		1/2 cup	40	32	neg.	neg.
Kumquat		6 med.	65	1	neg.	neg.
Lamb, raw, lean		1 oz.	69	26	3 (med.)	neg.
Leeks		1 (5" long)	12	4	neg.	neg.
Lemon, candied peel		1 large pce.	11	5	neg.	neg.
Pulp and juice		1/2 cup	30	1	neg.	neg.
Lemonade, frozen		1/2 cup dil.	104	1	neg.	neg.
Liquid Smoke	Wrights	½ tsp.	none	none	none	none
Lime, pulp and juice		1/2 cup	29	1	neg.	neg.
Lentils, dry		1/2 cup	338	3	neg.	neg.
Lettuce, head		1 sm. leaf	3	2	neg.	neg.
Lingcod, raw		1 oz.	20	18	neg.	neg.
Lobster, boiled		2/3 cup	92	250	1 (low)	neg.
Onions, raw		1 Tbsp.	4	1	neg.	neg.
		1 med.	49	11	neg.	neg.
Onion Powder		1 tsp.	neg.	2	neg.	neg.
Oranges, raw		1 med.	70	2	neg.	neg.
Juice, canned, sweetened		1/2 cup	68	1	neg.	neg.
Juice, frozen, unsweetened		1/2 cup	40	2	neg.	neg.
Peel, fresh		1 tsp.	unkn.	neg.	neg.	neg.
Oregano		1 tsp.	neg.	1	neg.	neg.
Oysters, raw		1/2 cup	66	73	3/4 (low)	neg.
Papaya, fresh		1/2	43	3	neg.	neg.
Paprika		1 tsp.	neg.	2	neg.	neg.
Parsley, flakes		1 tsp.	neg.	29	neg.	neg.
Raw		1 sprig	1	neg.	neg.	neg.
Parsnips, raw		1/2 large	78	8	neg.	neg.
Peaches, raw		1 med.	46	1	neg.	neg.
Canned, sweetened		2 halves	80	2	neg.	neg.
Canned, without sugar	Tillie Lewis					
	S & W					
	Cellu					
	Monarch	1/2 cup	38	2	neg.	neg.
Dried		½ cup	260	16	neg.	neg.
Nectar		1/2 cup	60	1	neg.	neg.
Peanuts, raw, shelled		1 cup	840	10	16 (med.)	21 (med.)
Peanut butter, reg.		1 Tbsp.	92	19	2 (med.)	2 (med.)
Unsaturated		1 Tbsp.	92	19	1/2 (low)	1 1/2 (med.)
Unsaturated, low-sodium	Cellu					
	Hain					
	Monarch	1 Tbsp.	92	neg.	1/2 (low)	1 1/2 (med.)
Pears, raw		1/2 med.	63	2	neg.	neg.
Canned, sweetened		2 halves	79	1	neg.	neg.
Canned, without sugar	Tillie Lewis					
	S & W					
	Cellu					
	Monarch	1/2 cup	40	1	neg.	neg.
Nectar		1/2 cup	65	1	neg.	neg.
Peas, raw		1/2 cup	65	1	neg.	neg.
Canned		1/2 cup	73	216	neg.	neg.
Low-sodium, canned	S & W, Cellu					
	Monarch					
	Tillie Lewis	1/2 cup	73	2.5	neg.	neg.
Dried, split		1 cup	689	40	neg.	neg.
Frozen, unsalted		1/2 cup	75	2	neg.	neg.
Pecans, raw		1 cup	752	1	5 (low)	15 (med.)
Peppers, green, raw		1 shell	16	1	neg.	neg.
Pepper, black & white		1 tsp.	neg.	neg.	neg.	neg.
Peppercorns		4	neg.	neg.	neg.	neg.
Peppermint extract		1 tsp.	neg.	neg.	neg.	neg.
Perch, yellow, salt water, raw		1 oz.	25	22	neg.	neg.
Persimmon, wild		1	78	1	neg.	neg.
Pettijohns Wheat, ckd.		1/2 cup	75	neg.	neg.	neg.
Pickle, dill		1 large	15	1890	neg.	neg.
Low-sodium pickles	Cellu	3 slices	1	neg.	neg.	neg.
Vegetable Relish	Featherweight	1 Tbsp.	3	6	neg.	neg.
Pickling Spice		1 tsp.	neg.	1	neg.	neg.
Pike, yellow, raw		1 oz.	29	15	neg.	neg.
Pimientos, canned		1 med.	11	unkn.	neg.	neg.
Pineapple, raw		1/2 cup	37	1	neg.	neg.
Canned, sweetened		1 slice	95	1	neg.	neg.
Canned, without sugar	Tillie Lewis					
	S & W					
	Cellu					
	Monarch	2 med. slices	46	2	neg.	neg.
Juice, unsweetened		1/3 cup	45	1	neg.	neg.

ITEM	SPECIAL BRANDS	PORTION	CAL.	SODIUM mgms.	Sat. Fat gms.	Unsat. Fat gms.
Plums, raw		2 medium	58	1	neg.	neg.
Canned, in syrup		2 medium	80	1	neg.	neg.
Canned, without sugar	Tillie Lewis, S & W, Cellu					
Pomegranate	Monarch	2 medium	46	2	neg.	neg.
Poppy Seed		1 med.	63	3	neg.	neg.
Pork, raw, lean		1 tsp.	neg.	neg.	neg.	neg.
Ham, cured, raw		1 oz.	71	16	2 (med.)	1/3 (low)
Low-sodium Ham, canned	Cellu	1 oz.	47	312	1 (med.)	neg.
Liver, raw (all except goose)		1 oz.	50	25	2 (high)	neg.
Pancreas, raw		1 oz.	38	23	1/2 (low)	neg.
Salt Pork		1 oz.	52	16	4 (high)	neg.
Postum, dry, Inst.		1 oz.	222	510	20 (high)	neg.
Potatoes, chips (fried in regular oil)		1 tsp.	4	1	neg.	1 (low)
Sweet, raw		10 pieces	108	68	6 (high)	1/2 (low)
Canned		1 small	123	10	1/2 (low)	neg.
White, raw		1/2 cup	117	48	neg.	neg.
Canned		1 med.	70	3	neg.	neg.
Poultry Seasoning		3 tiny	118	497	neg.	neg.
Pretzels		1 tsp.	neg.	neg.	neg.	neg.
Prunes, raw		5 small	18	85	neg.	neg.
Juice		2 med.	58	1	neg.	neg.
Puffed Rice		1 cup	85	2	neg.	neg.
Puffed Wheat		1 cup	55	neg.	neg.	neg.
Pumpkin, canned		1/2 cup	43	neg.	neg.	neg.
Quail, raw, breast		1/2 cup	38	2	neg.	neg.
Rabbit, raw		1 oz.	48	12	1 (med.)	neg.
Radish		1 small	35	11	1 (med.)	neg.
Raisins		1 Tbsp.	1	3	neg.	neg.
Ralston, instant, ckd.		1/2 cup	26	neg.	neg.	neg.
Raspberries, raw		1/2 cup	71	1	neg.	neg.
Red Snapper, raw		1 oz.	70	20	neg.	neg.
Rennet Tablet		1 tablet	25	38	neg.	neg.
Rhubarb, raw		1 cup	unkn.	1	neg.	neg.
Frozen		1/2 cup	19	2	neg.	neg.
Rice, brown, cooked		1 oz.	138	neg.	neg.	neg.
Minute rice, ckd.		1/2 cup	68	neg.	neg.	neg.
Polished, ckd.		1/2 cup	81	neg.	neg.	neg.
Wild, ckd.		1/2 cup	101	1	neg.	neg.
Rockfish, raw, pink		1 oz.	78	19	neg.	neg.
Rosemary		1 tsp.	20	neg.	neg.	neg.
Rum, bacardi		1 jigger	neg.	5	neg.	none
Rutabaga, fresh, ckd.		1/2 cup	105	neg.	neg.	neg.
Sage		1 tsp.	38	neg.	neg.	none
Salmon, raw, pink		3 1/2 oz.	neg.	64	3.7 (med.)	neg.
Canned, pink		2/5 cup	119	387	3 (med.)	neg.
Low-sodium, cnd.	Featherweight, Monarch	1/2 cup	141	56	3.7 (med.)	neg.
Salt	Morton's	1/2 cup	162	68	3.7 (med.)	neg.
Lite Salt	Dia Mel	1 tsp.	188	2361	none	none
Low-sodium	Adolphs, No Salt, Diasal, Eka Salt, Gustamate, "K"-Salt, Lawry's	1/2 tsp.	neg.	550	none	none
Salt Substitutes	Neocurtasal, Nosalt, Saltee Flavor Makers		none			

ITEM	SPECIAL BRANDS	PORTION	CAL.	SODIUM mgms.	Sat. Fat gms.	Unsat. Fat gms.
Soybeans, dry		1/2 cup	403	5	7 (med.)	7 (med.)
Soy Sauce		1 Tbsp.	8	1038	neg.	neg.
Spaghetti, ckd., such as Vermicelli, Linguini, Tagliarini, Fusilli		1/2 cup	109	1	1/4 (low)	neg.
Spearmint		1 tsp.	neg.	2	neg.	neg.
Spinach, fresh, ckd.		1/2 cup	22	45	neg.	neg.
Canned	S & W, Cellu, Monarch	1/2 cup	23	288	neg.	neg.
Low-sodium, canned	Tillie Lewis					
Frozen, cooked		1/2 cup	23	45	neg.	neg.
Squash, summer, raw		1/2 cup	20	70	neg.	neg.
Summer, frozen, cooked		1/2 cup	16	6	neg.	neg.
Winter, raw		1/2 cup	48	1	neg.	neg.
Strawberries, raw		10 large	37	1	neg.	neg.
Frozen		1/2 cup	90	2	neg.	none
Sugar, brown		1 Tbsp.	51	4	none	none
Powdered		1 Tbsp.	31	neg.	none	none
White		1 Tbsp.	48	neg.	none	none
Sugar Substitutes (Calcium sweeteners)	Sucaryl, Jelsweet, Sweetness & Light, Sweeta		neg.	neg.	none	none
Brown	Sugar Twin	1 tsp.	1.5	neg.	neg.	neg.
Sweetbreads		1 oz.	61	32	4 (high)	neg.
Swordfish, raw		1 oz.	33	22	2/3 (med.)	neg.
Syrup, chocolate		1 Tbsp.	42	12	neg.	neg.
Low-calorie	Dia Mel	1 tsp.	3	1	neg.	none
Karo		1 Tbsp.	57	14	none	none
Maple		1 Tbsp.	50	3	none	none
Low-calorie maple		1 Tbsp.	1	unkn.	none	none
Table blends		1 Tbsp.	57	12	neg.	neg.
Sorghum		1 Tbsp.	52	4	**none**	**none**
Tabasco Sauce	McIlhenny	1/4 tsp.	neg.	6	neg.	neg.
Tangerines, raw		1 med.	35	1	neg.	neg.
Juice, canned		1/2 cup	48	1	neg.	neg.
Tapioca		1 Tbsp.	34	neg.	neg.	none
Tarragon		1 tsp.	neg.	neg.	neg.	neg.
Tea, blended, dry		1 tsp.	none	neg.	neg.	neg.
Thyme		1 tsp.	22	1	neg.	neg.
Tomatoes, raw		1 small	22	3	neg.	neg.
Canned		1/2 cup	23	22	neg.	neg.
Low-sodium, canned	S & W, Cellu, Monarch, Tillie Lewis					
Catsup		1/2 cup	23	4	neg.	neg.
Low-sodium	Featherweight	1 Tbsp.	17	221	neg.	neg.
Juice, canned		1 Tbsp.	8	1	neg.	neg.
Low-sodium		1/2 cup	25	278	neg.	neg.
Toothpastes	Amident	1/2 cup	25	4	neg.	neg.
	Pepsodent	1 gram	unkn.	2		
Tooth Powder	Squibb	1 gram	unkn.	65		
	Colgate	1 gram	unkn.	2		
	Dentrix	1 gram	unkn.	8		
Tripe, pickled		1 oz.	28	13	3/4 (med.)	neg.
Trout, lake, raw		1 oz.	55	15	1 (med.)	neg.
Turmeric		1 tsp.	neg.	1	neg.	neg.
Tuna, Albacore		1 oz.	68	10	1 (low)	neg.
Canned, with oil		3 oz.	170	735	2 (low)	4 (low)

Food	Brand	Amount				
New Stedasalt						
Saltaste						
Salt It		1/2 tsp.	none	none	none	none
Sardines, canned in oil		3 oz.	170	735	2 (low)	4 (low)
Sauerkraut, canned		2/3 cup	22	650	4 (high)	neg.
Sausage, Bologna		1 oz.	82	390	10 (high)	1/3 (low)
Frankfurter, cooked		2 average	248	1100	6 (high)	1 (low)
Pork, raw		1 oz.	130	240	neg.	neg.
Scallops, frozen, raw		2–3	78	250	2 (low)	neg.
Sesame Seed		1 oz.	160	5	1/2 (low)	10 (high)
Sesame Tahini	A Sahadi	1 Tbsp.	57	105	1 (med.)	3 1/2 (high)
Shad, raw		1 oz.	48	15	1 (low)	1/4 (low)
Sherbet, orange		1/6 qt.	177	21	3 1/2 (med.)	neg.
Shortenings, hydrogenated		1 Tbsp.	117	neg.	1/3 (low)	1 1/2 (low)
Shrimp, raw		1 oz.	25	39	1/3 (low)	neg.
Low-sodium, canned	Featherweight	1 oz.	18	22	1/3 (low)	neg.
Sole, raw		1 oz.	29	26	neg.	neg.
Soups						
Bouillon cube		1 cube	2–5	960	neg.	neg.
Low-sodium						
Bouillon cube	Bernard	1 cube	11	10	neg.	neg.
	Cellu (chicken)	1 cube	11	17	neg.	neg.
	Cellu (beef)	1 cube				
Beef, canned	Smithers	1/3 can dil.	82	426	2 (med.)	neg.
Beef Tea		6 oz.	8	unkn.	neg.	neg.
Beef Consomme		1/3 can dil.	29	509	neg.	neg.
Chicken Consomme		1/3 can dil.	18	600	1 (low)	1 (low)
Tomato, canned		1/3 can dil.	73	377	1 (low)	neg.
Vegetable, canned		1 cup	64	39	3/4 (low)	neg.
Low-sodium						
Chicken Broth	Claybourne	1 cup	9	28	1 (low)	neg.
Tomato-rice	Claybourne	1 cup	73	35	1 (low)	neg.
Tomato	Campbells	1 cup	95	25	unkn.	neg.
	Andersen's	1 cup	75	25	unkn.	neg.
	Cellu	1 cup	50	22	unkn.	neg.
Vegetable	Andersen's	1 cup	67	35	1 (low)	neg.
	Claybourne	1 cup	100	46	1 (low)	neg.
	Cellu	1 cup	60	30	1 (low)	neg.
Vegetable Beef						
Soybean flour (defatted)		1 cup	356	1	3 (low)	3 (low)
Soybean Cake (Tofu)		3 1/2 oz.	100	7	1 1/2 (med.)	1 1/2 (med.)

Food	Brand	Amount				
Low-sodium, canned	Featherweight	1/2 cup	121	40	1 1/2 (low)	1 1/2 (low)
Canned in water		1 oz.	36	245	1/2 (low)	neg.
Low-sodium, canned in water	Featherweight					
	Chicken of the Sea					
	White Star	1/2 cup	95	31	1 (low)	neg.
Turkey, raw, light		1 oz.	34	14	1 (med.)	neg.
Dark, raw		1 oz.	75	23	2 (med.)	neg.
Liver, raw		1 oz.	40	17	1 (med.)	neg.
Turnips, leaves, fresh, ckd.		1/2 cup	22	10	neg.	neg.
Frozen		1/2 cup	23	23	neg.	neg.
White, raw		1/2 cup	22	26	neg.	neg.
Vanilla Extract		1 tsp.	neg.	neg.	1 (med.)	neg.
Veal, raw, lean		1 oz.	44	28	neg.	neg.
Vegetable Juice Cocktail		1/2 cup	20	240	2 (med.)	neg.
Venison, cooked		1 oz.	60	24	neg.	neg.
Vinegar, cider		1 Tbsp.	2	neg.	neg.	neg.
Wine		1 Tbsp.	2	4	neg.	neg.
Walnuts, English		1 cup	654	4	4 (low)	40 (high)
Water, distilled		1 cup	none	none	none	none
Water Chestnuts		4	20	5	neg.	neg.
Watercress, raw		10 sprigs	2	5	neg.	neg.
Watermelon, pink part		1/2 cup	28	1	neg.	neg.
Wheat Flakes		3/4 cup	88	341	neg.	neg.
Shredded		1 biscuit	102	1	neg.	neg.
Wheatena, ckd.		1/2 cup	76	neg.	none	none
Whiskey, blended		1 jigger	119	neg.	1 1/2 (med.)	neg.
Whitefish, raw		1 oz.	47	15	none	none
Wine, average		4 oz.	84	10	none	none
Champagne		4 oz.	84	10	neg.	neg.
Port		4 oz.	160	12	neg.	neg.
Sauterne		4 oz.	84	10	neg.	neg.
Sherry		4 oz.	168	12	neg.	neg.
Worcestershire Sauce		1 Tbsp.	12	175	unkn.	unkn.
Yams		1/2 cup	101	unkn.	unkn.	unkn.
Yeast, compressed		1 cake	24	neg.	neg.	neg.
Yogurt, regular		1 cup	207	98	7 (med.)	neg.
Low fat		1 cup	120	150	2 (low)	neg.
Zweiback		1 piece	31	19	1/3 (low)	neg.

FOODS HIGH IN POTASSIUM*

| FOOD | AVERAGE SERVING | | POTASSIUM |
	WEIGHT, GM.	APPROXIMATE MEASURE	PER SERVING, MG.
Milk, whole	240	½ pint	353
Grapefruit Juice, canned	240	8 ounces	360
Orange Juice, fresh	240	8 ounces	415
Tomato Juice	240	8 ounces	552
Almonds	30	1 ounce	229
Apricots, dried	15	4 halves	255
Avocado	100	½	510
Lima Beans, canned and frozen	75	½ cup	473
Beet Greens	75	½ cup	417
Brazil Nuts	30	1 ounce	203
Cashews	30	1 ounce	168
Cereals			
Bran	30	1 ounce	323
Whole grain	15 (dry)	½ cup (cooked)	218
Chard, large leaves	75	½ cup	563
Chocolate, unsweetened, bitter	30	1 ounce	249
Cocoa, plain	7	1 tablespoon	98
Coconut, dry	30	1 ounce (½ cup)	224
Currants, dried	30	1 ounce (3 tablespoons)	189
Dates	30	1 ounce (3–4)	233
Figs, dried	30	1 ounce (2 small)	234
Lentils, dried	100	½ cup	1,200
Molasses, medium	80	¼ cup	850
Parsnips	75	½ cup	387
Peas, dry	30	½ cup, cooked	296
Peaches, dried	30	1 ounce (4 medium halves)	330
Peanuts	30	1 ounce	197
Peanut butter	15	1 tablespoon	123
Pecans	30	1 ounce	154
Potatoes	100	½ cup	532
Potato chips	20	7 large	176
Prunes, dried	30	1 ounce (4 medium)	216
Raisins	30	1 ounce (3 tablespoons)	225
Sardines, canned in oil	90	3 ounces	459
Syrup, sorghum	20	1 tablespoon	120
Spinach, fresh	75	½ cup	440
Tomato catsup	17	1 tablespoon	136
Walnuts	30	1 ounce	158
Yeast, bakers	30	1 ounce	201

*Be sure to choose the high potassium foods that are *lowest* in sodium, sugars and saturated fats.

ALCOHOLIC BEVERAGES CALORIE CHART

WHEN WINING REMEMBER THE CALORIES IN ALCOHOL WHICH THE BODY CONVERTS TO FAT, SO WHEN YOU USE ANY OF THESE KEEP IN MIND "MODERATION"

Beer	8 ounce glass	114 calories
Brandy	1 ounce	73 calories
Benedictine	1 cordial glass	69 calories
Gin, dry	1½ ounces	105 calories
Martini	1 cocktail glass	140 calories
Rum	1½ ounces	105 calories
Whiskey	1½ ounces	119 calories
Scotch	1½ ounces	105 calories
Port	1 wine glass	158 calories
Sherry	1 sherry glass	84 calories
Dry Wine	1 wine glass	80 calories

HAPPY THOUGHT!

Alcohol is burnt off in cooking meats, leaving mostly the flavor. Using wine or spirits in cooking doesn't necessarily mean you should drink them too. Discuss this subject with your doctor before indulging.

TABLE OF TEN MARGARINES WITH HIGH UNSATURATED FAT CONTENT

	GRAMS IN 100 GRAMS MARGARINE	
BRAND	UNSATURATED FATTY (LINOLEIC) ACID (grams)	SATURATED FATTY ACIDS (grams)
Chiffon (salted and unsalted)	50	11
Diet Chiffon	21	6
Diet Fleischmann	16	7.5
Diet Mazola	16.7	6
Empress Soft	48	12
Fleischmann Soft	33	15.5
Kraft Soft Safflower Parkay	46.2	10.4
Nucoa Dream Soft	34.5	15.1
Saffola Regular Cube	32.8	12
Saffola Soft	46.4	10.4
Western Brand Soft	41.9	11.3

TABLE OF OILS SHOWING VALUES OF UNSATURATED & SATURATED FATS

OIL	AMOUNT	SATURATED FAT (grams)	UNSATURATED FAT (grams)
Safflower	1 cup	17	180
Corn	1 cup	24	127
Soybean	1 cup	36	125
Cottonseed	1 cup	60	120
Peanut	1 cup	43	70
Olive	1 cup	26	17

TABLE OF MEASURES

Dash	=	2-4 drops		
1 Tablespoon	=	3 teaspoons	=	1/2 fluid ounce
1/4 cup	=	4 Tablespoons	=	2 fluid ounces
1/2 cup	=	8 Tablespoons	=	4 fluid ounces
1 cup	=	16 Tablespoons	=	8 fluid ounces
1 pint	=	2 cups	=	16 fluid ounces
1 quart	=	2 pints	=	32 fluid ounces
1 gallon	=	4 quarts	=	128 fluid ounces

TABLE OF WEIGHTS

1 teaspoon	=	5 grams		
1 Tablespoon	=	15 grams		
2 Tablespoons	=	30 grams	=	1 ounce
1 pound	=	480 grams	=	16 ounces

SOME COMPANIES MANUFACTURING SPECIAL ITEMS
TO USE ON LOW FAT - LOW SODIUM DIETS

BRAND	COMPANY	ADDRESS
Adolph's	Adolph's, Ltd.	Burbank, California
Amplify	Rabin Winters Corp.	El Segundo, California
Andersen	Tillie Lewis Foods, Inc.	Stockton, California 95201
Balanise	Balanced Foods, Inc.	700 Broadway, New York 3, N.Y.
Bernard	Bernard Food Industries, Inc.	1208 E. San Antonio Street San Jose, California
Campbells	Campbell Soup Company	General Offices, Camden, New Jersey
Cellu (or Featherweight)	Chicago Dietetic Supply, Inc.	P. O. Box 529 La Grange, Illinois 60525
Cheezola	Fisher Cheese Co.	Box 12 Wapakaneta, Ohio 45895
Claybourne	Clayco Foods, Inc.	Johnson City, New York
Coffee-Rich	Rich Products Corp.	1146 Niagra St., Buffalo 13, N.Y.
Co-Salt	U.S.V. Pharmeceutical Corp.	New York, New York
Dia Mel	Dia Mel Diet Control Sales, Inc.	Brooklyn 7, New York
Estee	Estee Candy Co., Inc.	New York, New York
Fleischmann	Standard Brands, Inc.	Betts Avenue Stamford, Connecticut
Hain	Hain Pure Food Company, Inc.	Los Angeles, California
Jellathin	Perkins-Kellogg Food Co.	Perkin's Building Los Angeles 57, California
Jelsweet	Mutual Citrus Products Co.	Anaheim, California
Milani	Milani Foods, Inc.	Los Angeles, Calif., 90064
Nutradiet	S & W Fine Foods, Inc.	333 Schwerin Street San Francisco, California 94134
Plantation	Plantation Foods, Inc.	Newark, New Jersey
Sucaryl	Abbott Laboratories	North Chicago, Illinois
Sweetness and Light	Abbott Laboratories	North Chicago, Illinois
Venus	Venus Wheat Wafers, Inc.	678 Columbus Avenue Boston, Massachusetts

BIBLIOGRAPHY

1. An Invitation to Delicious Dining, Lever Brothers Co., New York.

2. Bagg, Elma W., Cooking Without a Grain of Salt, Doubleday and Co., Inc., New York, 1964.

3. Belinkie, Helen, The Gourmet in the Low Calorie Kitchen, David McKay Co., Inc., New York, 1961.

4. Bowes, Anna, and Church, Charles, Food Values of Portions Commonly Used, J. B. Lippincott Co., Philadelphia, 1963.

5. Calorie-Saving Recipes with Sucaryl, Abbott Laboratories, Chicago, Illinois.

6. Davidson, C. D. and Committee, Sodium Restricted Diets, Publication #325, National Research Council, Washington, D.C., 1954.

7. Field, Florence, Gourmet Cooking for Cardiac Diets, Revised Edition, Collier Books, New York, 1962.

8. Guide to Corn Oil Cooking, Corn Products Co., New York.

9. How to Reduce *Sensibly* and Safely with Yami Yogurt.

10. Kaufman, William I., The Sugar-Free Cookbook, Doubleday and Co., Inc., New York, 1964.

11. Koten, Bernard, The Low Calory Cookbook, Hillman Books, New York, 1960.

12. Low Sodium Diets Can Be Delicious, Standard Brands Inc., New York, 1962.

13. Naomi, Barry, Eating Yourself Slim the French Way, House and Gardens, Conde Nast Publications, Inc., September, 1975.

14. Nichols, N. B., Freezing and Canning Cookbook, Farm Journal, Doubleday and Co., Inc., New York.

15. Payne, Alma Smith, and Callahan, Dorothy, The Low Sodium, Fat-Controlled Cookbook, Little, Brown and Co., Boston, 1960.

16. Quat, Helen, The Wonderful World of Freezer Cooking, Hearthside Press, 1964.

17. Rider, Alan K., Should Hyperlipoproteinemi Be Treated in Patients With Coronary Artery Disease? Journal of the American Medical Association, July 21, 1975, Vol. 233, No. 3, pp. 275–277.

18. Seranne, Ann, Complete Book of Home Preserving, Doubleday and Co., Inc., New York.

19. Sweet*10 Calorie Slim Recipes, Pillsbury Kitchens, Minneapolis.

20. The Meat Maker, Sunkist Growers, Inst. Division, Los Angeles.

21. Waldo, Myra, Cooking for Your Heart and Health, G. P. Putnams Sons, New York, 1961.

22. Watt, B. K., Merrill, A. L., et. al., Composition of Foods, Agriculture Handbook, #8, U. S. Dept. of Agriculture, 1963.

23. Wechsberg, Joseph, La Nature Des Choses (A Profile of Michel Guerard, French Chef), The New Yorker Magazine, July 28, 1975.

24. Woot Tsuen Wu Leun, R. K. Pecot, B. K. Watt, et. al. Composition of Foods Used in Far Eastern Countries, Agricultural Handbook #34, U. S. Dept. of Agriculture, 1952.

25. Yogurt Recipes, Knudsen Creamery Co., Los Angeles.

26. Zubige, Frederick T., Eat, Drink, and Lower Your Cholesterol, McGraw-Hill Book Co., Inc., New York, 1963.

INDEX